OMNIPOTENT GOVERNMENT

OMNIPOTENT GOVERNMENT

The Rise of the Total State and Total War

Ludwig von Mises, 1881-

Libertarian Press, Inc.
Spring Mills, PA 16875

ISBN 0-910884-15-3

MANUFACTURED IN THE UNITED STATES OF AMERICA

61,510

Contents

Contents

Preface

IN dealing with the problems of social and economic policies, the social sciences consider only one question: whether the measures suggested are really suited to bringing about the effects sought by their authors, or whether they result in a state of affairs which—*from the viewpoint of their supporters*—is even more undesirable than the previous state which it was intended to alter. The economist does not substitute his own judgment about the desirability of ultimate ends for that of his fellow citizens. He merely asks whether the ends sought by nations, governments, political parties, and pressure groups can indeed be attained by the methods actually chosen for their realization.

It is, to be sure, a thankless task. Most people are intolerant of any criticism of their social and economic tenets. They do not understand that the objections raised refer only to unsuitable methods and do not dispute the ultimate ends of their efforts. They are not prepared to admit the possibility that they might attain their ends more easily by following the economists' advice than by disregarding it. They call an enemy of their nation, race, or group anyone who ventures to criticize their cherished policies.

This stubborn dogmatism is pernicious and one of the root causes of the present state of world affairs. An economist who asserts that minimum wage rates are not the appropriate means of raising the wage earners' standard of living is neither a "labor baiter" nor an enemy of the workers. On the contrary, in suggesting more suitable methods for the improvement of the wage earners' material well-being, he contributes as much as he can to a genuine promotion of their prosperity.

To point out the advantages which everybody derives from the working of capitalism is not tantamount to defending the vested interests of the capitalists. An economist who forty or fifty years ago advocated the preservation of the system of private property and free enterprise did not fight for the selfish class interests of the *then* rich. He wanted a free hand left to those unknown among his penniless contemporaries who had the ingenuity to develop all those new industries which today render the life of the common man more pleasant. Many pioneers of these industrial changes, it is true, became rich. But they acquired their wealth by supplying the public with motor cars, airplanes, radio sets, refrigerators, moving and talking pictures, and a variety of less spectacular but no less useful innovations. These new products were certainly not an achievement of offices and bureaucrats. Not a single technical improvement can be credited to the Soviets. The best that the Russians have achieved was to copy some of the improvements of the capitalists whom they continue to disparage. Mankind has not reached the stage of ultimate technological perfection. There is ample room for further progress and for further improvement of the standards of living. The creative and inventive spirit subsists notwithstanding all assertions to the contrary. But it flourishes only where there is economic freedom.

Neither is an economist who demonstrates that a nation (let us call it Thule) hurts its own essential interests in its conduct of foreign-trade policies and in its dealing with domestic minority groups, a foe of Thule and its people.

It is futile to call the critics of inappropriate policies names and to cast suspicion upon their motives. That might silence the voice of truth, but it cannot render inappropriate policies appropriate.

The advocates of totalitarian control call the attitudes of their opponents negativism. They pretend that while they themselves are demanding the improvement of unsatisfactory conditions, the others are intent upon letting the evils endure. This is to judge all social questions from the viewpoint of narrow-minded bureaucrats. Only to bureaucrats can the idea occur that establishing new offices, promulgating new decrees, and increasing the number of government employees alone can be described as positive and beneficial measures, whereas everything else is passivity and quietism.

The program of economic freedom is not negativistic. It aims positively at the establishment and preservation of the system of market economy based on private ownership of the means of production and free enterprise. It aims at free competition and at the sovereignty of the consumers. As the logical outcome of these demands the true liberals are opposed to all endeavors to substitute government control for the operation of an unhampered market economy. Laissez faire, laissez passer does not mean: let the evils last. On the contrary, it means: do not interfere with the operation of the market because such interference must necessarily restrict output and make people poorer. It means furthermore: do not abolish or cripple the capitalist system which, in spite of all obstacles put in its way by governments and politicians, has raised the standard of living of the masses in an unprecedented way.

Liberty is not, as the German precursors of Nazism asserted, a negative ideal. Whether a concept is presented in an affirmative or in a negative form is merely a question of idiom. *Freedom from want* is tantamount to the expression *striving after a state of affairs under which people are better supplied with necessities. Freedom of speech is* tantamount to *a state of affairs under which everybody can say what he wants to say.*

At the bottom of all totalitarian doctrines lies the belief that the rulers are wiser and loftier than their subjects and that they therefore know better what benefits those ruled than they themselves. Werner Sombart, for many years a fanatical champion of Marxism and later a no less fanatical advocate of Nazism, was bold enough to assert frankly that the Führer gets his orders from God, ʻhe supreme Führer of the universe, and that Führertum is a permanent revelation.* Whoever admits this, must, of course, stop questioning the expediency of government omnipotence.

Those disagreeing with this theocratical justification of dictatorship claim for themselves the right to discuss freely the problems involved. They do not write *state* with a capital S. They do not shrink from analyzing the metaphysical notions of Hegelianism and Marxism. They reduce all this high-sounding oratory to the simple question: are the means suggested suitable to attain the ends sought? In answering this question, they hope to render a service to the great majority of their fellow men.

Ludwig von Mises

New York, January, 1944

ACKNOWLEDGMENT

I AM grateful to the Rockefeller Foundation and to the National Bureau of Economic Research for grants which enabled me to undertake this study. Mr. Henry Hazlitt has helped me greatly with his criticism and suggestions and by editing the whole manuscript. Mr. Arthur Goodman has advised me in linguistic and stylistic problems. Mr. Eugene Davidson of Yale University Press has assisted me in many ways. The responsibility for all opinions expressed is, of course, exclusively my own.

---

* *Deutscher Sozialismus* (Charlottenburg, 1934), p. 213. American ed., *A New Social Philosophy,* translated and edited by K. F. Geiser (Princeton, 1937), p. 194.

OMNIPOTENT GOVERNMENT

Introduction

I

THE essential point in the plans of the German National Socialist Workers' party is the conquest of *Lebensraum* for the Germans, i.e., a territory so large and rich in natural resources that they could live in economic self-sufficiency at a standard not lower than that of any other nation. It is obvious that this program, which challenges and threatens all other nations, cannot be realized except through the establishment of German world hegemony.

The distinctive mark of Nazism is not socialism or totalitarianism or nationalism. In all nations today the "progressives" are eager to substitute socialism for capitalism. While fighting the German aggressors Great Britain and the United States are, step by step, adopting the German pattern of socialism. Public opinion in both countries is fully convinced that government all-round control of business is inevitable in time of war, and many eminent politicians and millions of voters are firmly resolved to keep socialism after the war as a permanent new social order. Neither are dictatorship and violent oppression of dissenters peculiar features of Nazism. They are the Soviet mode of government, and as such advocated all over the world by the numerous friends of present-day Russia. Nationalism—an outcome of government interference with business, as will be shown in this book—determines in our age the foreign policy of every nation. What characterizes the Nazis as such is their special kind of nationalism, the striving for Lebensraum.

This Nazi goal does not differ in principle from the aims of the earlier German nationalists, whose most radical group called themselves in the thirty years preceding the first World War *Alldeutsche* (Pan-Germans). It was this ambition which pushed the Kaiser's Germany into the first World War and—twenty-five years later—kindled the second World War.

The Lebensraum program cannot be traced back to earlier German ideologies or precedents in German history of the last five hundred years. Germany had its chauvinists as all other nations had. But chauvinism is not nationalism. Chauvinism is the overvaluation of one's own nation's achievements and qualities and the disparagement of other nations; in itself it does not result in any action. Nationalism, on the other hand, is a blueprint for political and military action and the attempt to realize these plans. German history, like the history of other nations, is the record of princes eager for conquest; but these emperors, kings, and dukes wanted to acquire wealth and power for themselves and for their kin, not Lebensraum for their nation. German aggressive nationalism is a phenomenon of the last sixty years. It developed out of modern economic conditions and economic policies.

Neither should nationalism be confused with the striving for popular government, national self-determination and political autonomy. When the German nineteenth-century liberals aimed at a substitution of a democratic government of the whole German nation for the tyrannical rule of thirty-odd princes, they did not harbor any hostile designs against other nations. They wanted to get rid of despotism and to establish parliamentary government. They did not thirst for conquest and territorial expansion. They did not intend to incorporate into the German state of their dreams the Polish and Italian territories which their princes had conquered; on the contrary, they sympathized with the aspirations of the Polish and the Italian liberals to establish independent Polish and Italian democracies. They were eager to promote the welfare of the German nation, but they did not believe that oppression of foreign nations and inflicting harm on foreigners best served their own nation.

Neither is nationalism identical with patriotism. Patriotism is the zeal for one's own nation's welfare, flowering, and freedom. Nationalism is one of the various methods proposed for the attainment of these ends. But the liberals contend that the means recommended by nationalism are inappropriate, and that their application would not only not realize the ends sought but on the contrary must result in disaster for the nation. The liberals too are patriots, but their opinions with regard to the right ways toward national prosperity and greatness radically differ from those of the nationalists. They recommend free trade, international division of labor, good will, and peace among the nations, not for the sake of foreigners but for the promotion of the happiness of their own nation.

It is the aim of nationalism to promote the well-being of the whole nation or of some groups of its citizens by inflicting harm on foreigners. The outstanding method of modern nationalism is discrimination against foreigners in the economic sphere. Foreign goods are excluded from the domestic market or admitted only after the payment of an import duty. Foreign labor is barred from competition in the domestic labor market. Foreign capital is liable to confiscation. This economic nationalism must result in war whenever those injured believe that they are strong enough to brush away by armed violent action the measures detrimental to their own welfare.

A nation's policy forms an integral whole. Foreign policy and domestic policy are closely linked together; they are but one system; they condition each other. Economic nationalism is the corollary of the present-day domestic policies of government interference with business and of national planning, as free trade was the complement of domestic economic freedom. There can be protectionism in a country with domestic free trade, but where there is no domestic free trade protectionism is indispensable. A national government's might is limited to the territory subject to its sovereignty. It does not have the power to interfere directly with conditions abroad. Where there is free trade, foreign competition would even in the short run frustrate the aims sought by the various measures of government intervention with domestic business. When the domestic market is not to some extent insulated from foreign markets, there can be no question of government control. The further a nation goes on the road toward public regulation and regimentation, the more it is pushed toward economic isolation. International division of labor becomes suspect because it hinders the full use of national sovereignty. The trend toward autarky is essentially a trend of domestic economic policies; it is the outcome of the endeavor to make the state paramount in economic matters.

Within a world of free trade and democracy there are no incentives for war and conquest. In such a world it is of no concern whether a nation's sovereignty stretches over a larger or a smaller territory. Its citizens cannot derive any advantage from the annexation of a province. Thus territorial problems can be treated without bias and passion; it is not painful to be fair to other people's claims for self-determination. Free-trade Great Britain freely granted dominion status, i.e., virtual autonomy and political independence, to the British settlements overseas, and ceded the Ionian Islands to Greece. Sweden did not venture military action to prevent the rupture of the bond linking Norway to Sweden; the royal house of Bernadotte lost its Norwegian crown, but for the individual citizen of Sweden it was immaterial whether or not his king was sovereign of Norway too. In the days of liberalism people could believe that plebiscites and the decisions of international tribunals would peacefully settle all disputes among nations. What was needed to safeguard peace was the overthrow of antiliberal governments. Some wars and revolutions were still considered unavoidable in order to eliminate the last tyrants and to destroy some still-existing trade walls. And if this goal were ever attained, no more causes for war would be left. Mankind would be in a position to devote all its efforts to the promotion of the general welfare.

But while the humanitarians indulged in depicting the blessings of this liberal utopia, they did not realize that new ideologies were on the way to supplant liberalism and to shape a new order arousing antagonisms for which no peaceful solution could be found. They did not see it because they viewed these new mentalities and policies as the continuation and fulfillment of the essential tenets of liberalism. Antiliberalism captured the popular mind disguised as true and genuine liberalism. Today those styling themselves liberals are supporting programs entirely opposed to the tenets and doctrines of the old liberalism. They disparage private ownership of the means of production and the market economy, and are enthusiastic friends of totalitarian methods of economic management. They are striving for government omnipotence, and hail every measure giving more power to officialdom and government agencies. They condemn as a reactionary and an economic royalist whoever does not share their predilection for regimentation.

These self-styled liberals and progressives are honestly convinced that they are true democrats. But their notion of democracy is just the opposite of that of the nineteenth century. They confuse democracy with socialism. They not only do not see that socialism and democracy are incompatible but they believe that socialism alone means real democracy. Entangled in this error, they consider the Soviet system a variety of popular government.

European governments and parliaments have been eager for more than sixty years to hamper the operation of the market, to interfere with business, and to cripple capitalism. They have blithely ignored the warnings of economists. They have erected trade barriers, they have fostered credit expansion and an easy money policy, they have taken recourse to price control, to minimum wage rates, and to subsidies. They have transformed taxation into confiscation and expropriation; they have proclaimed heedless spending as the best method to increase wealth and welfare. But when the inevitable consequences of such policies, long before predicted by the economists, became more and more obvious, public opinion did not place the blame on these cherished policies; it indicted capitalism. In the eyes of the public not anticapitalistic policies but capitalism is the root cause of economic depression, of unemployment, of inflation and rising prices, of monopoly and of waste, of social unrest and of war.

The fateful error that frustrated all the endeavors to safeguard peace was precisely that people did not grasp the fact that only within a world of pure, perfect, and unhampered capitalism are there no incentives for aggression and conquest. President Wilson was guided by the idea that only autocratic governments are war-like, while democracies cannot derive any profit from conquest and therefore cling to peace. What President Wilson and the other founders of the League of Nations did not see was that this is valid only within a system of private ownership of the means of production, free enterprise, and unhampered market economy. Where there is no economic freedom, things are entirely different. In our world of etatism,* in which every nation is eager to insulate itself and to strive toward autarky, it is quite wrong to assert that no man can derive any gain from conquest. In this age of trade walls and migration barriers, of foreign exchange control and of ex-propriation of foreign capital, there are ample incentives for war and conquest. Nearly every citizen has a material interest in the nullification of measures by which foreign governments may injure him. Nearly every citizen is therefore eager to see his own country mighty and powerful, because he expects personal advantage from its military might. The enlargement of the territory subject to the sovereignty of its own government means at least relief from the evils which a foreign government has inflicted upon him.

We may for the moment abstain from dealing with the problem of whether democracy can survive under a system of government interference with business or of socialism. At any rate it is beyond doubt that under etatism the plain citizens themselves turn toward aggression, provided the military prospects for success are favorable. Small nations cannot help being victimized by other nations' eco-nomic nationalism. But big nations place confidence in the valor of their armed forces. Present-day bellicosity is not the outcome of the greed of princes and of Junker oligarchies; it is a pressure group policy whose distinctive mark lies in the methods applied but not in the incentives and motives. German, Italian, and Japanese workers strive for a higher standard of living when fighting against other nations' economic nationalism. They are badly mistaken; the means chosen are not appropriate to attain the ends sought. But their errors are consistent with the doctrines of class war and social revolution so widely accepted today. The imperialism of the Axis is not a policy that grew out of the aims of an upper class. If we were to apply the spurious concepts of popular Marxism, we

---

* The term "etatism" (derived from the French *état*—state) seems to me preferable to the newly coined term "statism." It clearly expresses the fact that etatism did not originate in the Anglo-Saxon countries, and has only lately got hold of the Anglo-Saxon mind.

should have to style it labor imperialism. Paraphrasing General Clausewitz' famous dictum, one could say: it is only the continuation of domestic policy by other means, it is domestic class war shifted to the sphere of international relations.

For more than sixty years all European nations have been eager to assign more power to their governments, to expand the sphere of government compulsion and coercion, to subdue to the state all human activities and efforts. And yet pacifists have repeated again and again that it is no concern of the individual citizen whether his country is large or small, powerful or weak. They have praised the blessings of peace while millions of people all over the world were putting all their hopes upon aggression and conquest. They have not seen that the only means to lasting peace is to remove the root causes of war. It is true that these pacifists have made some timid attempts to oppose economic nationalism. But they have never attacked its ultimate cause, etatism—the trend toward government control of business—and thus their endeavors were doomed to fail.

Of course, the pacifists are aiming at a supernational world authority which could peacefully settle all conflicts between various nations and enforce its rulings by a supernational police force. But what is needed for a satisfactory solution of the burning problem of international relations is neither a new office with more committees, secretaries, commissioners, reports, and regulations, nor a new body of armed executioners, but the radical overthrow of mentalities and domestic policies which must result in conflict. The lamentable failure of the Geneva experiment was precisely due to the fact that people, biased by the bureaucratic superstitions of etatism, did not realize that offices and clerks cannot solve any problem. Whether or not there exists a supernational authority with an international parliament is of minor importance. The real need is to abandon policies detrimental to the interests of other nations. No international authority can preserve peace if economic wars continue. In our age of international division of labor, free trade is the prerequisite for any amicable arrangement between nations. And free trade is impossible in a world of etatism.

The dictators offer us another solution. They are planning a "New Order," a system of world hegemony of one nation or of a group of nations, supported and safeguarded by the weapons of victorious armies. The privileged few will dominate the immense majority of "inferior" races. This New Order is a very old concept. All conquerors have aimed at it; Genghis Khan and Napoleon were precursors of the Führer. History has witnessed the failure of many endeavors to impose peace by war, coöperation by coercion, unanimity by slaughtering dissidents. Hitler will not succeed better than they. A lasting order cannot be established by bayonets. A minority cannot rule if it is not supported by the consent of those ruled; the rebellion of the opppressed will overthrow it sooner or later, even if it were to succeed for some time. But the Nazis have not even the chance to succeed for a short time. Their assault is doomed.

II

THE present crisis of human civilization has its focal point in Germany. For more than half a century the Reich has been the disturber of the peace. The main concern of European diplomacy, in the thirty years preceding the first World War, was to keep Germany in check by various schemes and tricks. But for German bellicosity, neither the Czars' craving for power nor the antagonisms and rivalries of the various nationalities of southeastern Europe would have seriously disturbed the world's peace. When the devices of appeasement broke down in 1914, the forces of hell burst forth.

The fruits of the victory of the Allies were lost by the shortcomings of the peace treaties, by the faults of the postwar policies, and by the ascendancy of economic nationalism. In the turmoil of these years between the two wars, when every nation was eager to inflict as much harm on other nations as possible, Germany was free to prepare a more tremendous assault. But for the Nazis, neither Italy nor Japan would be a match for the United Nations. This new war is a German war as was the first World War.

It is impossible to conceive the fundamental issues of this most terrible of all wars ever fought without an understanding of the main facts of German history. A hundred years ago the Germans were quite different from what they are today. At that time it was not their ambition to surpass the Huns and to outdo Attila. Their guiding stars were Schiller and Goethe, Herder and Kant, Mozart and Beethoven. Their leitmotiv was liberty, not conquest and oppression. The stages of the process which transformed the nation once styled by foreign observers that of the poets and thinkers into that of ruthless gangs of the Nazi Storm Troops ought to be known by everybody who wants to mold his own judgment on current world political affairs and problems. To understand the springs and tendencies of Nazi aggressiveness is of the highest importance both for the political and military conduct of the war and for the shaping of a durable postwar order. Many mistakes could have been avoided and many sacrifices spared by a better and clearer insight into the essence and the forces of German nationalism.

It is the task of the present book to trace the outlines of the changes and events which brought about the contemporary state of German and European affairs. It seeks to correct many popular errors which sprang from legends badly distorting historical facts and from doctrines misrepresenting economic developments and policies. It deals both with history and with fundamental issues of sociology and economics. It tries not to neglect any point of view the elucidation of which is necessary for a full description of the world's Nazi problem.

III

In the history of the last two hundred years we can discern two distinctive ideological trends. There was first the trend toward freedom, the rights of man, and self-determination. This individualism resulted in the fall of autocratic government, the establishment of democracy, the evolution of capitalism, technical improvements, and an unprecedented rise in standards of living. It substituted enlightenment for old superstitions, scientific methods of research for inveterate prejudices. It was an epoch of great artistic and literary achievements, the age of immortal musicians, painters, writers, and philosophers. And it brushed away slavery, serfdom, torture, inquisition, and other remnants of the dark ages.

In the second part of this period individualism gave way to another trend, the trend toward state omnipotence. Men now seem eager to vest all powers in governments, i.e., in the apparatus of social compulsion and coercion. They aim at totalitarianism, that is, conditions in which all human affairs are managed by governments. They hail every step toward more government interference as progress toward a more perfect world; they are confident that the governments will transform the earth into a paradise. Characteristically, nowadays in the countries furthest advanced toward totalitarianism even the use of the individual citizen's leisure time is considered as a task of the government. In Italy *dopolavoro* and in Germany *Freizeitgestaltung* are regular legitimate fields of government interference. To such an extent are men entangled in the tenets of state idolatry that they do not see the paradox of a government-regulated leisure.

It is not the task of this book to deal with all the problems of *statolatry* or *etatism*. Its scope is limited to the treatment of the consequences of etatism for international relations. In our age of international division of labor, totalitarianism within several scores of sovereign national governments is self-contradictory. Economic considerations are pushing every totalitarian government toward world domination. The Soviet government is by the deed of its foundation not a national government but a universal government, only by unfortunate conditions temporarily prevented from exercising its power in all countries. Its official name does not contain any reference to Russia. It was the aim of Lenin to make it the nucleus of a world government; there are in every country parties loyal only to the Soviets, in whose eyes the domestic governments are usurpers. It is not the merit of the Bolsheviks that these ambitious plans have not succeeded up to now and that the expected world revolution has not appeared. The Nazis have not changed the official designation of their country, the Deutsches Reich. But their literary champions consider the Reich the only legitimate government, and their political chiefs openly crave world hegemony. The intellectual leaders of Japan have been imbued at European universities with the spirit of etatism, and, back home, have revived the old tenet that their divine Emperor, the son of Heaven, has a fair title to rule all peoples. Even the Duce, in spite of the military impotence of his country, proclaimed his intention to reconstruct the ancient Roman Empire. Spanish Falangists babble about a restoration of the domain of Philip II.

In such an atmosphere there is no room left for the peaceful coöperation of nations. The ordeal through which mankind is going in our day is not the outcome of the operation of uncontrollable natural forces. It is rather the inevitable result of the working of doctrines and policies popular with millions of our contemporaries.

However, it would be a fateful mistake to assume that a return to the policies of liberalism abandoned by the civilized nations some decades ago could cure these evils and open the way toward peaceful coöperation of nations and toward prosperity. If Europeans and the peoples of European descent in other parts of the earth had not yielded to etatism, if they had not embarked upon vast schemes of government interference with business, our recent political, social, and economic disasters could have been avoided. Men would live today under more satisfactory conditions and would not apply all their skill and all their intellectual powers to mutual extermination. But these years of antagonism and conflict have left a deep impression on human mentality, which cannot easily be eradicated. They have marked the souls of men, they have disintegrated the spirit of human coöperation, and have engendered hatreds which can vanish only in centuries. Under present conditions the adoption of a policy of outright laissez faire and laissez passer on the part of the civilized nations of the West would be equivalent to an unconditional surrender to the totalitarian nations. Take, for instance, the case of migration barriers. Unrestrictedly opening the doors of the Americas, of Australia, and of Western Europe to immigrants would today be equivalent to opening the doors to the vanguards of the armies of Germany, Italy, and Japan.

There is no other system which could safeguard the smooth coördination of the peaceful efforts of individuals and nations but the system today commonly scorned as Manchesterism. We may hope—although such hopes are rather feeble—that the peoples of the Western democratic world will be prepared to acknowledge this fact, and to abandon their present-day totalitarian tendencies. But there can be no doubt that to the immense majority of men militarist ideas appeal much more than those of liberalism. The most that can be expected for the immediate future is the separation of the world into two sections: a liberal, democratic, and capitalist West with about one quarter of the total world population, and a militarist and totalitarian East embracing the much greater part of the earth's surface and its population. Such a state of affairs will force upon the West policies of defense which will seriously hamper its efforts to make life more civilized and economic conditions more prosperous.

Even this melancholy image may prove too optimistic. There are no signs that the peoples of the West are prepared to abandon their policies of etatism. But then they will be prevented from giving up their mutual economic warfare, their economic nationalism, and from establishing peaceful relations among their own countries. Then we shall stand where the world stood in the period between the two world wars. The result will be a third war, more dreadful and more disastrous than its precursors.

It is the task of the last part of this book to discuss the conditions which could preserve at least for the Western democracies some amount of political and economic security. It is its aim to find out whether there is any imaginable scheme which could make for durable peace in this age of the omnipotence of the state.

IV

THE main obstacle both to every attempt to study in an unbiased way the social, political, and economic problems of our day, and to all endeavors to substitute more satisfactory policies for those which have resulted in the present crisis of civilization, is to be found in the stubborn, intransigent dogmatism of our age. A new type of superstition has got hold of people's minds, the worship of the state. People demand the exercise of the methods of coercion and compulsion, of violence and threat. Woe to anybody who does not bend his knee to the fashionable idols!

The case is obvious with present-day Russia and Germany. One cannot dispose of this fact by calling the Russians and the Germans barbarians and saying that such things cannot and will not happen with the more civilized nations of the West. There are only a few friends of tolerance left in the West. The parties of the Left and of the Right are everywhere highly suspicious of freedom of thought. It is very characteristic that in these years of the desperate struggle against the Nazi aggression a distinguished British pro-Soviet author has the boldness to champion the cause of inquisition. "Inquisition," says T. G. Crowther, "is beneficial to science when it protects a rising class." * For "the danger or value of an inquisition depends on whether it is used on behalf of a reactionary or a progres-siving governing class." † But who is "progressive" and who is "re-actionary"? There is a remarkable difference with regard to this issue between Harold Laski and Alfred Rosenberg.

It is true that outside of Russia and Germany dissenters do not yet risk the firing squad or slow death in a concentration camp.‡ But few are any longer ready to pay serious attention to dissenting views. If a man tries to question the doctrines of etatism or national-ism, hardly anyone ventures to weigh his arguments. The heretic is ridiculed, called names, ignored. It has come to be regarded as insolent or outrageous to criticize the views of powerful pressure groups or political parties, or to doubt the beneficial effects of state omnipotence. Public opinion has espoused a set of dogmas which there is less and less freedom to attack. In the name of progress and freedom both progress and freedom are being out-lawed.

Every doctrine that has recourse to the police power or to other

* Crowther, *Social Relations of Science* (London, 1941), p. 333.

† *Idem*, p. 331.

‡ Fascism too is a totalitarian system of ruthless oppression. However, there still are some slight differences between Fascism on the one hand and Nazism and Bolshevism on the other hand. The philosopher and historian Benedetto Croce has lived in Naples, carfully shadowed by the police, but free to write and to publish several books imbued with the spirit of democracy and with the love of liberty. Professor Antonio Graziadei, a communist ex-member of the Italian Parliament, has clung unswervingly to his communistic ideas. Nevertheless he has lived in Italy and written and published (with the most eminent Italian publishing houses) books which are orthodox Marxian. There are still more cases of this type. Such exceptional facts do not alter the charac-teristic features of Fascism. But the historian does not have the right to ignore them.

methods of violence or threat for its protection reveals its inner weakness. If we had no other means to judge the Nazi doctrines, the single fact that they seek shelter behind the Gestapo would be sufficient evidence against them. Doctrines which can stand the trial of logic and reason can do without persecuting skeptics.

This war was not caused by Nazism alone. The failure of all other nations to stop the rise of Nazism in time and to erect a barrier against a new German aggression was not less instrumental in bringing about the disaster than were the events of Germany's domestic evolution. There was no secrecy about the ambitions of the Nazis. The Nazis themselves advertised them in innumerable books and pamphlets, and in every issue of their numerous newspapers and periodicals. Nobody can reproach the Nazis with having concocted their plots clandestinely. He who had ears to hear and eyes to see could not help but know all about their aspirations.

The responsibility for the present state of world affairs lies with those doctrines and parties that have dominated the course of politics in the last decades. Indicting Nazism is a queer way to exculpate the culprits. Yes, the Nazis and their allies are bad people. But it should be the primary aim of politics to protect nations against the dangers originating from the hostile attitudes of bad people. If there were no bad people, there would not be any need for a government. If those in a position to direct the activities of governments do not succeed in preventing disaster, they have given proof that they are not equal to their task.

There was in the last twenty-five years but one political problem: to prevent the catastrophe of this war. But the politicians were either struck with blindness or incapable of doing anything to avoid the impending disaster.

The parties of the Left are in the happy position of people who have received a revelation telling them what is good and what is bad. They know that private property is the source of all ills, and that public control of the means of production will transform the earth into a paradise. They wash their hands of any responsibility; this "imperialist" war is simply an outcome of capitalism, as all wars have been. But if we pass in review the political activities of the socialist and communist parties in the Western democracies, we can easily discover that they did all that they could to encourage the Nazi plans for aggression. They have propagated the doctrine that disarmament and neutrality are the best means to stop the Nazis and the other Axis powers. They did not intend to aid the Nazis. But if they had had this intention, they could not have acted differently.

The ideals of the Left are fully realized in Soviet Russia. Here is Marxism supreme; the proletarians alone rule. But Soviet Russia failed even more lamentably than any other nation in preventing this war. The Russians knew very well that the Nazis were eager to conquer the Ukraine. Nevertheless, they behaved as Hitler wanted them to behave. Their policies contributed a good deal to the ascendancy of Nazism in Germany, to the rearmament of Germany, and finally to the outbreak of the war. It is no excuse for them that they were suspicious of the capitalist nations. There is no excuse for a policy harmful to one's own cause. No one can deny that the agreement of August, 1939, brought disaster for Russia. Stalin would have served his country far better by collaborating with Great Britain than by his compromise with the Nazis.

The same holds true for the conduct of all other European countries. One could hardly imagine a more fatuous policy than that of Poland, when in 1938 it annexed a part of Czechoslovakia, or that of Belgium, when in 1936 it severed the ties of the alliance which linked it with France. The fate of the Poles, the Czechs, the Norwegians, the Dutch, the Belgians, the Greeks, and the Yugoslavs deserves profound pity. But one cannot help asserting that they helped to bring their misfortune upon themselves. This second World War would never have broken out if the Nazis had expected to encounter on the first day of hostilities a united and adequately armed front of Great Britain, France, Russia, the United States, and all the small democracies of Europe, led by a unified command.

An investigation of the root causes of the ascendancy of Nazism must show not only how domestic German conditions begot Nazism but also why all other nations failed to protect themselves against the havoc. Seen from the viewpoint of the British, the Poles, or the Austrians, the chief question is not: What is wrong with the Nazis? but: What was wrong with our own policies with regard to the Nazi menace? Faced with the problem of tuberculosis, doctors do not ask: What is wrong with the germs? but: What is wrong with our methods of preventing the spread of the disease?

Life consists in adjusting oneself to actual conditions and in taking account of things as they really are, not as one would wish them to be. It would be more pleasant if there were neither germs nor dangerous barbarians. But he who wants to succeed has to fix his glance upon reality, not to indulge in wishful dreams.

There is no hope left for a return to more satisfactory conditions if people do not understand that they have failed completely in the main task of contemporary politics. All present-day political, social, and economic doctrines, and all parties and pressure groups applying them, are condemned by an unappealable sentence of history. Nothing can be expected from the future if men do not realize that they were on the wrong path.

It is not a mark of hostility to any nation to establish the fact that its policies were entirely wrong and have resulted in a disastrous failure. It is not a sign of hostility to the members of any class, pressure group, or organization to try to point out wherein they were mistaken and how they have contributed to the present unsatisfactory state of affairs. The main task of contemporary social science is to defy the taboo by which the established doctrines seek to protect their fallacies and errors against criticism. He who, in the face of the tremendous catastrophe whose consequences cannot yet be completely seen, still believes that there are some doctrines, institutions, or policies beyond criticism, has not grasped the meaning of the portents.

Let the example of Germany stand as a warning to us. German *Kultur* was doomed on the day in 1870 when one of the most eminent German scientists—Emil du Bois-Reymond—could publicly boast, without meeting contradiction, that the University of Berlin was "the intellectual bodyguard of the house of Hohenzollern." Where the universities become bodyguards and the scholars are eager to range themselves in a "scientific front," the gates are open for the entry of barbarism. It is vain to fight totalitarianism by adopting totalitarian methods. Freedom can only be won by men unconditionally committed to the principles of freedom. The first requisite for a better social order is the return to unrestricted freedom of thought and speech.

V

WHOEVER wishes to understand the present state of political affairs must study history. He must know the forces which gave rise to our problems and conflicts. Historical knowledge is indispensable for those who want to build a better world.

Unfortunately the nationalists approach history in another temper. For them the past is not a source of information and instruction but an arsenal of weapons for the conduct of war. They search for facts which can be used as pretexts and excuses for their drives for aggression and oppression. If the documents available do not provide such facts, they do not shrink from distorting truth and from falsifying documents.

In the early nineteenth century a Czech forged a manuscript in order to prove that his people's medieval ancestors had already reached a high stage of civilization and had produced fine literary works. For many decades Czech scholars fanatically asserted the authenticity of this poem, and for a long time the official curriculum of the Czech state gymnasiums of old Austria made its reading and interpretation the main topic in the teaching of Czech literature. About fifty years later a German forged the Ura Linda Chronicle in order to prove that the "Nordics" created a civilization older and better than that of any other people. There are still Nazi professors who are not ready to admit that this chronicle is the clumsy forgery of an incompetent and stupid backwoodsman. But let us assume for the sake of argument that these two documents are authentic. What could they prove for the nationalists' aspirations? Do they support the claim of the Czechs to deny autonomy to several million Germans and Slovaks, or the claim of the Germans to deny autonomy to all Czechs?

There is, for instance, the spurious dispute as to whether Nicholas Copernicus was a Pole or a German. The documents available do not solve the problem. It is at any rate certain that Copernicus was educated in schools and universities whose only language was Latin, that he knew no other mathematical and astronomical books than those written in Latin or Greek, and that he himself wrote his treatises in Latin only. But let us assume for the sake of argument that he really was the son of parents whose language was German. Could this provide a justification for the methods applied by the Germans in dealing with the Poles? Does it exculpate the German schoolteachers who—in the first decade of our century—flogged small children whose parents objected to the substitution of the German catechism for the Polish catechism in the schools of Prussia's Polish provinces? Does it today entitle the Nazis to slaughter Polish women and children?

It is futile to advance historical or geographical reasons in support of political ambitions which cannot stand the criticism of democratic principles. Democratic government can safeguard peace and international coöperation because it does not aim at the oppression of other peoples. If some peoples pretend that history or geography gives them the right to subjugate other races, nations, or peoples, there can be no peace.

It is unbelievable how deep-rooted these vicious ideas of hegemony, domination, and oppression are even among the most distinguished contemporaries. Señor Salvador de Madariaga is one of the most internationally minded of men. He is a scholar, a statesman, and a writer, and is perfectly familiar with the English and French languages and literatures. He is a democrat, a progressive, and an enthusiastic supporter of the League of Nations and of all endeavors to make peace durable. Yet his opinions on the political problems of his own country and nation are animated by the spirit of intransigent nationalism. He condemns the demands of the Catalans and the Basques for independence, and advocates Castilian hegemony for racial, historical, geographical, linguistic, religious, and economic considerations. It would be justifiable if Sr. Madariaga were to refute the claims of these linguistic groups on the ground that it is impossible to draw undisputed border lines and that their independence would therefore not eliminate but perpetuate the causes of conflict; or if he were in favor of a transformation of the Spanish state of Castilian hegemony into a state in which every linguistic group enjoyed the freedom to use its own idiom. But this is not at all the plan of Sr. Madariaga. He does not advocate the substitution of a supernational government of the three linguistic groups, Castilians, Catalans, and Basques, for the Castile-dominated state of Spain. His ideal for Spain is Castilian supremacy. He does not want "Spain to let go the work of centuries in one generation." * However, this work was not an achievement of the peoples concerned; it was the result of dynastic intermarriage. Is it right to object to the claims of the Catalans that in the twelfth century the Count of Barcelona married the King of Aragon's daughter and that in the fifteenth century the King of Aragon married the Queen of Castile?

Sr. Madariaga goes even further and denies to the Portuguese the right of autonomy and statehood. For "the Portuguese is a Spaniard with his back to Castile and his eyes on the Atlantic Sea." † Why, then, did not Spain absorb Portugal too? To this Sr. Madariaga gives a strange answer: "Castile could not marry both east and west at one time"; perhaps Isabel, "being a woman after all, . . . preferred Ferdinand's looks to Alfonso's, for of such things, also, history is made." ‡

Sr. Madariaga is right in quoting an eminent Spanish author, Angel Ganivet, to the effect that a union of Spain and Portugal must be the outcome "of their own free will." § But the trouble is that the Portuguese do not long for Castilian or Spanish overlordship.

Still more amazing are Sr. Madariaga's views on Spain's colonial and foreign affairs. Speaking of the American colonies, he observes that the Spanish monarchy organized them "faithful to its guiding principle—the fraternity of all men." ‖ However, Bolivar, San

* Madariaga, *Spain* (London, 1942), p. 176.
† *Idem*, p. 185.
‡ *Idem*, p. 187.
§ *Idem*, p. 197.
‖ *Idem*, p. 49.

Martin, and Morelos did not like this peculiar brand of fraternity. Then Sr. Madariaga tries to justify Spanish aspirations in Morocco by alluding to Spain's "position which history, geography and inherent destiny seemed obviously to suggest." * For an unbiased reader there is hardly any difference between such an "inherent destiny" and the mystical forces to which Messrs. Hitler, Mussolini, and Stalin refer in annexing small countries. If "inherent destiny" justifies Spanish ambitions in Morocco, does it not in the same way support Russian appetites for the Baltic countries and Caucasian Georgia, German claims with regard to Bohemia and the Netherlands, Italy's title to Mediterranean supremacy?

We cannot eradicate the past from our memories. But it is not the task of history to kindle new conflicts by reviving hatreds long since dead and by searching the archives for pretexts for new conflicts. We do not have to revenge crimes committed centuries ago by kings and conquerors; we have to build a new and better world order. It is without any relevance to the problems of our time whether the age-old antagonisms between the Russians and the Poles were initiated by Russian or by Polish aggression, or whether the atrocities committed in the Palatinate by the mercenaries of Louis XIV were more nefarious than those committed by the Nazis today. We have to prevent once and for all the repetition of such outrages. This aim alone can elevate the present war to the dignity of mankind's most noble undertaking. The pitiless annihilation of Nazism is the first step toward freedom and peace.

Neither destiny nor history nor geography nor anthropology must hinder us from choosing those methods of political organization which can make for durable peace, international coöperation, and economic prosperity.

* Madariaga, *op. cit.,* p. 200.

PART I

THE COLLAPSE OF
GERMAN LIBERALISM

I. GERMAN LIBERALISM

1. The Ancien Régime and Liberalism

IT is a fundamental mistake to believe that Nazism is a revival or a continuation of the policies and mentalities of the *ancien régime* or a display of the "Prussian spirit." Nothing in Nazism takes up the thread of the ideas and institutions of older German history. Neither Nazism nor Pan-Germanism, from which Nazism stems and whose consequent evolution it represents, is derived from the Prussianism of Frederick William I or Frederick II, called the Great. Pan-Germanism and Nazism never intended to restore the policy of the electors of Brandenburg and of the first four kings of Prussia. They have sometimes depicted as the goal of their endeavors the return of the lost paradise of old Prussia; but this was mere propaganda talk for the consumption of a public which worshiped the heroes of days gone by. Nazism's program does not aim at the restoration of something past but at the establishment of something new and unheard of.

The old Prussian state of the house of Hohenzollern was completely destroyed by the French on the battlefields of Jena and Auerstädt (1806). The Prussian Army surrendered at Prenzlau and Ratkau, the garrisons of the more important fortresses and citadels capitulated without firing a shot. The King took refuge with the Czar, whose mediation alone brought about the preservation of his realm. But the old Prussian state was internally broken down long before this military defeat; it had long been decomposed and rotten, when Napoleon gave it the finishing stroke. For the ideology on which it was based had lost all its power; it had been disintegrated by the assault of the new ideas of liberalism.

Like all the other princes and dukes who have established their sovereign rule on the debris of the Holy Roman Empire of the Teutonic Nation, the Hohenzollerns too regarded their territory as a family estate, whose boundaries they tried to expand through violence, ruse, and family compacts. The people living within their possessions were subjects who had to obey orders. They were appurtenances of the soil, the property of the ruler who had the right to deal with them *ad libitum*. Their happiness and welfare were of no concern.

Of course, the king took an interest in the material well-being of his subjects. But this interest was not founded on the belief that it is the purpose of civil government to make the people prosperous. Such ideas were deemed absurd in eighteenth-century Germany. The king was eager to increase the wealth of the peasantry and the townsfolk because their income was the source from which his revenue was derived. He was not interested in the subject but in the taxpayer. He wanted to derive from his administration of the country the means to increase his power and splendor. The German princes envied the riches of Western Europe, which provided the kings of France and of Great Britain with funds for the maintenance of mighty armies and navies. They encouraged commerce, trade, mining, and agriculture in order to raise the public revenue. The subjects, however, were simply pawns in the game of the rulers.

But the attitude of these subjects changed considerably at the end of the eighteenth century. From Western Europe new ideas began to penetrate into Germany. The people, accustomed to obey blindly the God-given authority of the princes, heard for the first time the words liberty, self-determination, rights of man, parliament, constitution. The Germans learned to grasp the meaning of dangerous watchwords.

No German has contributed anything to the elaboration of the great system of liberal thought, which has transformed the structure of society and replaced the rule of kings and royal mistresses by the government of the people. The philosophers, economists, and sociologists who developed it thought and wrote English or French. In the eighteenth century the Germans did not even succeed in achieving readable translations of these English, Scotch, and French authors. What German idealistic philosophy produced in this field is poor indeed when compared with contemporary English and French thought. But German intellectuals welcomed Western ideas of freedom and the rights of man with enthusiasm. German classical literature is imbued with them, and the great German composers set to music verses singing the praises of liberty. The poems, plays, and other writings of Frederick Schiller are from beginning to end a hymn to liberty. Every word written by Schiller was a blow to the old political system of Germany; his works were fervently greeted by nearly all Germans who read books or frequented the theater. These intellectuals, of course, were a minority only. To the masses books and theaters were unknown. They were the poor serfs in the eastern provinces, they were the inhabitants of the Catholic countries, who only slowly succeeded in freeing themselves from the tight grasp of the Counter-Reformation. Even in the more advanced western parts and in the cities there were still many illiterates and semiliterates. These masses were not concerned with any political issue; they obeyed blindly, because they lived in fear of punishment in hell, with which the church threatened them, and in a still greater fear of the police. They were outside the pale of German civilization and German cultural life; they knew only their regional dialects, and could hardly converse with a man who spoke only the German literary language or another dialect. But the number of these backward people was steadily decreasing. Economic prosperity and education spread from year to year. More and more people reached a standard of living which allowed them to care for other things besides food and shelter, and to employ their leisure in something more than drinking. Whoever rose from misery and joined the community of civilized men became a liberal. Except for the small group of princes and their aristocratic retainers practically everyone interested in political issues was liberal. There were in Germany in those days only liberal men and indifferent men; but the ranks of the indifferent continually shrank, while the ranks of the liberals swelled.

All intellectuals sympathized with the French Revolution. They scorned the terrorism of the Jacobins but unswervingly approved the great reform. They saw in Napoleon the man who would safeguard and complete these reforms and—like Beethoven—took a dislike to him as soon as he betrayed freedom and made himself emperor.

Never before had any spiritual movement taken hold of the whole German people, and never before had they been united in their feelings and ideas. In fact the people, who spoke German and were the subjects of the Empire's princes, prelates, counts, and urban patricians, became a nation, the German nation, by their reception of the new ideas coming from the West. Only then there came into being what had never existed before: a German public opinion, a German public, a German literature, a German Fatherland. The Germans now began to understand the meaning of the ancient authors which they had read in school. They now conceived the history of their nation as something more than the struggle of princes for land and revenues. The subjects of many hundreds of petty lords became Germans through the acceptance of Western ideas.

This new spirit shook the foundations on which the princes had built their thrones—the traditional loyalty and subservience of the subjects who were prepared to acquiesce in the despotic rule of a group of privileged families. The Germans dreamed now of a German state with parliamentary government and the rights of man. They did not care for the existing German states. Those Germans who styled themselves "patriots," the new-fangled term imported from France, despised these seats of despotic misrule and abuse. They hated the tyrants. And they hated Prussia most because it appeared to be the most powerful and therefore most dangerous menace to German freedom.

The Prussian myth, which the Prussian historians of the nineteenth century fashioned with a bold disregard of facts, would have us believe that Frederick II was viewed by his contemporaries as they themselves represent him—as the champion of Germany's greatness, protagonist in Germany's rise to unity and power, the nation's hero. Nothing could be further from the truth. The military campaigns of the warrior king were to his contemporaries struggles to increase the possessions of the house of Brandenburg, which concerned the dynasty only. They admired his strategical talents but they detested the brutalities of the Prussian system. Whoever praised Frederick within the borders of his realm did so from necessity, to evade the indignation of a prince who wreaked stern vengeance upon every foe. When people outside of Prussia praised him, they were disguising criticism of their own rulers. The subjects of petty princes found this irony the least dangerous way to disparage their pocket-size Neros and Borgias. They glorified his military achievements but called themselves happy because they were not at the mercy of his whims and cruelties. They approved of Frederick only in so far as he fought their domestic tyrants.

At the end of the eighteenth century German public opinion was as unanimously opposed to the ancien régime as in France on the eve of the Revolution. The German people witnessed with indifference the French annexation of the left bank of the Rhine, the defeats of Austria and of Prussia, the breaking-up of the Holy Empire, and the establishment of the Rhine Confederacy. They hailed the reforms forced upon the governments of all their states by the ascendancy of the French ideas. They admired Napoleon as a great general and ruler just as they had previously admired Frederick of Prussia. The Germans began to hate the French only when—like the French subjects of the Emperor—they finally became tired of the endless burdensome wars. When the Great Army had been wrecked in Russia, the people took an interest in the campaigns which finished Napoleon, but only because they hoped that his downfall would result in the establishment of parliamentary government. Later events dispelled this illusion, and there slowly grew the revolutionary spirit which led to the upheaval of 1848.

It has been asserted that the roots of present-day nationalism and Nazism are to be found in the writings of the Romantics, in the plays of Heinrich von Kleist, and in the political songs which accompanied the final struggle against Napoleon. This, too, is an error. The sophisticated works of the Romantics, the perverted feelings of Kleist's plays, and the patriotic poetry of the wars of liberation did not appreciably move the public; and the philosophical and sociological essays of those authors who recommended a return to medieval institutions were considered abstruse. People were not interested in the Middle Ages but in the parliamentary activities of the West. They read the books of Goethe and Schiller, not of the Romantics; went to the plays of Schiller, not of Kleist. Schiller became the preferred poet of the nation; in his enthusiastic devotion to liberty the Germans found their political ideal. The celebration of Schiller's hundredth anniversary (in 1859) was the most impressive political demonstration that ever took place in Germany. The German nation was united in its adherence to the ideas of Schiller, to the liberal ideas.

All endeavors to make the German people desert the cause of freedom failed. The teachings of its adversaries had no effect. In vain Metternich's police fought the rising tide of liberalism.

Only in the later decades of the nineteenth century was the hold of liberal ideas shaken. This was effected by the doctrines of etatism. Etatism—we will have to deal with it later—is a system of socio-political ideas which has no counterpart in older history and is not linked up with older ways of thinking, although—with regard to the technical character of the policies which it recommends—it may with some justification be called neo-Mercantilism.

2. The Weakness of German Liberalism

At about the middle of the nineteenth century those Germans interested in political issues were united in their adherence to liberalism. Yet the German nation did not succeed in shaking off the yoke of absolutism and in establishing democracy and parliamentary government. What was the reason for this?

Let us first compare German conditions with those of Italy, which was in a similar situation. Italy, too, was liberal minded, but the Italian liberals were impotent. The Austrian Army was strong enough to defeat every revolutionary upheaval. A foreign army kept Italian liberalism in check; other foreign armies freed Italy from this control. At Solferino, at Königgrätz, and at the banks of the Marne the French, the Prussians, and the English fought the battles which rendered Italy independent of the Habsburgs.

Just as Italian liberalism was no match for the Austrian Army, so German liberalism was unable to cope with the armies of Austria and Prussia. The Austrian Army consisted mainly of non-German soldiers. The Prussian Army, of course, had mostly German-speaking men in its ranks; the Poles, the other Slavs, and the Lithuanians were a minority only. But a great number of these men speaking one of the German dialects were recruited from those strata of society which were not yet awakened to political interests. They came from the eastern provinces, from the eastern banks of the Elbe River. They were mostly illiterate, and unfamiliar with the mentality of the intellectuals and of the townsfolk. They had never heard anything about the new ideas; they had grown up in the habit of obeying the Junker, who exercised executive and judicial power in their village, to whom they owed imposts and corvée (unpaid statute labor), and whom the law considered as their legitimate overlord. These virtual serfs were not capable of disobeying an order to fire upon the people. The Supreme War Lord of the Prussian Army could trust them. These men, and the Poles, formed the detachments which defeated the Prussian Revolution in 1848.

Such were the conditions which prevented the German liberals from suiting their actions to their word. They were forced to wait until the progress of prosperity and education could bring these backward people into the ranks of liberalism. Then, they were convinced, the victory of liberalism was bound to come. Time worked for it. But, alas, events belied these expectations. It was the fate of Germany that before this triumph of liberalism could be achieved liberalism and liberal ideas were overthrown—not only in Germany but everywhere—by other ideas, which again penetrated into Germany from the West. German liberalism had not yet fulfilled its task when it was defeated by etatism, nationalism, and socialism.

3. The Prussian Army

The Prussian Army which fought in the battles of Leipzig and Waterloo was very different from the army which Frederick William I had organized and which Frederick II had commanded in three great wars. That old army of Prussia had been smashed and destroyed in the campaign of 1806 and never revived.

The Prussian Army of the eighteenth century was composed of men pressed into service, brutally drilled by flogging, and held together by a barbaric discipline. They were mainly foreigners.

The kings preferred foreigners to their own subjects. They believed that their subjects could be more useful to the country when working and paying taxes than when serving in the armed forces. In 1742 Frederick II set as his goal that the infantry should consist of two thirds foreigners and one third natives. Deserters from foreign armies, prisoners of war, criminals, vagabonds, tramps, and people whom the crimps had entrapped by fraud and violence were the bulk of the regiments. These soldiers were prepared to profit by every opportunity for escape. Prevention of desertion was therefore the main concern of the conduct of military affairs. Frederick II begins his main treatise of strategy, his *General Principles of Warfare,* with the exposition of fourteen rules on how to hinder desertion. Tactical and even strategical considerations had to be subordinated to the prevention of desertion. The troops could only be employed when tightly assembled together. Patrols could not be sent out. Strategical pursuit of a defeated enemy force was impossible. Marching or attacking at night and camping near forests were strictly avoided. The soldiers were ordered to watch each other constantly, both in war and in peace. Civilians were obliged by the threat of the heaviest penalties to bar the way to deserters, to catch them, and deliver them to the army.

The commissioned officers of this army were as a rule noblemen. Among them, too, were many foreigners; but the greater number belonged to the Prussian Junker class. Frederick II repeats again and again in his writings that commoners are not fit for commmissions because their minds are directed toward profit, not honor. Although a military career was very profitable, as the commander of a company drew a comparatively high income, a great part of the landed aristocracy objected to the military profession for their sons. The kings used to send out policemen to kidnap the sons of noble landowners and put them into their military schools. The education provided by these schools was hardly more than that of an elementary school. Men with higher education were very rare in the ranks of Prussian commissioned officers.*

Such an army could fight and—under an able commander—conquer, only as long as it encountered armies of a similar structure. It scattered like chaff when it had to fight the forces of Napoleon.

The armies of the French Revolution and of the first Empire were recruited from the people. They were armies of free men, not of crimped scum. Their commanders did not fear desertion. They could therefore abandon the traditional tactics of moving forward in deployed lines and of firing volleys without taking aim.

---

* Delbrück, *Geschichte der Kriegskunst* (Berlin, 1920), Part IV, pp. 273 ff., 348 ff.

They could adopt a new method of combat, that is, fighting in columns and skirmishing. The new structure of the army brought first a new tactic and then a new strategy. Against these the old Prussian Army proved impotent.

The French pattern served as a model for the organization of the Prussian Army in the years 1808–13. It was built upon the principle of compulsory service of all men physically fit. The new army stood the test in the wars of 1813–15. Consequently its organization was not changed for about half a century. How this army would have fought in another war against a foreign aggressor will never be known; it was spared this trial. But one thing is beyond doubt, and was attested by events in the Revolution. of 1848: only a part of it could be relied on in a fight against the people, the "domestic foe" of the government, and an unpopular war of aggression could not be waged with these soldiers.

In suppressing the Revolution of 1848 only the regiments of the Royal Guards, whose men were selected for their allegiance to the King, the cavalry, and the regiments recruited from the eastern provinces could be considered absolutely reliable. The army corps recruited from the west, the militia (*Landwehr*), and the reservists of many eastern regiments were more or less infected by liberal ideas.

The men of the guards and of the cavalry had to give three years of active service, as against two years for the other parts of the forces. Hence the generals concluded that two years was too short a time to transform a civilian into a soldier unconditionally loyal to the King. What was needed in order to safeguard the political system of Prussia with its royal absolutism exercised by the Junkers was an army of men ready to fight—without asking questions—against everybody whom their commanders ordered them to attack. This army—His Majesty's army, not an army of the Parliament or of the people—would have the task of defeating any revolutionary movement within Prussia or within the smaller states of the German Confederation, and of repelling possible invasions from the West which could force the German princes to grant constitutions and other concessions to their subjects. In Europe of the 1850's, where the French Emperor and the British Prime Minister, Lord Palmerston, openly professed their sympathies with the popular movements menacing the vested interests of kings and aristocrats, the army of the house of Hohenzollern was the *rocher de bronze* amid the rising tide of liberalism. To make this army reliable and invincible meant not only preserving the Hohenzollerns and their aristocratic retainers; it meant much more: the salvation of civilization from the threat of revolution and anarchy. Such was the philosophy of Frederick Julius Stahl and of the Right-wing Hegelians, such were the ideas of the Prussian historians of the *Kleindeutsche* school of history, such was the mentality of the military party at the court of King Frederick William IV. This King, of course, was a sickly neurotic, whom every day brought nearer to complete mental disability. But the generals, led by General von Roon and backed by Prince William, the King's brother and heir apparent to the throne, were clearheaded and steadily pursued their aim.

The partial success of the revolution had resulted in the establishment of a Prussian Parliament. But its prerogatives were so restricted that the Supreme War Lord was not prevented from adopting those measures which he deemed indispensable for rendering the army a more reliable instrument in the hands of its commanders.

The experts were fully convinced that two years of active service was sufficient for the military training of the infantry. Not for reasons of a technical military character but for purely political considerations the King prolonged active service for the infantry regiments of the line from two years to two and a half in 1852 and to three in 1856. Through this measure the chances of success against a repetition of the revolutionary movement were greatly improved. The military party was now confident that for *the immediate future* they were strong enough, with the Royal Guards and with the men doing active service in the regiments of the line, to conquer poorly armed rebels. Relying on this, they decided to go further and thoroughly reform the organization of the armed forces.

The goal of this reform was to make the army both stronger and more loyal to the King. The number of infantry battalions would be almost doubled, the artillery increased 25 per cent, and many new regiments of cavalry formed. The number of yearly recruits would be raised from under 40,000 to 63,000, and the ranks of commissioned officers increased correspondingly. On the other hand the militia would be transformed into a reserve of the active army. The older men were discharged from service in the militia as not fully reliable. The higher ranks of the militia would be entrusted to commissioned officers of the professional corps.*

Conscious of the strength which the prolongation of active service had already given them, and confident that they would for the time being suppress a revolutionary attempt, the court carried out this reform without consulting Parliament. The King's lunacy had

* Ziekursch, *Politische Geschichte des neuen deutschen Kaiserreichs* (Frankfurt, 1925–30), I, 29 ff.

in the meanwhile become so manifest that Prince William had to be installed as prince regent; the royal power was now in the hands of a tractable adherent of the aristocratic clique and of the military hotspurs. In 1859, during the war between Austria and France, the Prussian Army had been mobilized as a measure of precaution and to safeguard neutrality. The demobilization was effected in such a manner that the main objectives of the reform were attained. In the spring of 1860 all the newly planned regiments had already been established. Only then the cabinet brought the reform bill to Parliament and asked it to vote the expenditure involved.*

The struggle against this army bill was the last political act of German liberalism.

4. The Constitutional Conflict in Prussia

The Progressives, as the liberals in the Prussian lower chamber (chamber of deputies) called their party, bitterly opposed the reform. The chamber voted repeatedly against the bill and against the budget. The King—Frederick William IV had now died and William I had succeeded him—dissolved Parliament, but the electors returned a majority of Progressives. The King and his ministers could not break the opposition of the legislative body. But they clung to their plan and carried on without constitutional approval and parliamentary assent. They led the new army into two campaigns, and defeated Denmark in 1864 and Austria in 1866. Only then, after the annexation of the kingdom of Hanover, the possessions of the Elector of Hessen, the duchies of Nassau, Schleswig, and Holstein, and the Free City of Frankfort, after the establishment of Prussian hegemony over all states of Northern Germany and the conclusion of military conventions with the states of Southern Germany by which these too surrendered to the Hohenzollern, did the Prussian Parliament give in. The Progressive party split, and some of its former members supported the government. Thus the King got a majority. The chamber voted indemnification for the unconstitutional conduct of affairs by the government and belatedly sanctioned all measures and expenditures which they had opposed for six years. The great Constitutional Conflict resulted in full success for the King and in a complete defeat for liberalism.

When a delegation of the chamber of deputies brought the King the Parliament's accommodating answer to his royal speech at the opening of the new session, he haughtily declared that it was his

* Sybel, *Die Begründung des deutschen Reiches unter Wilhelm I* (2d ed. Munich, 1889), II, 375; Ziekursch, *op. cit.*, I, 42.

duty to act as he had in the last years and that he would act the same way in the future too should similar conditions occur again. But in the course of the conflict he had more than once despaired. In 1862 he had lost all hope of defeating the resistance of the people, and was ready to abdicate. General von Roon urged him to make a last attempt by appointing Bismarck prime minister. Bismarck rushed from Paris, where he represented Prussia at the court of Napoleon III. He found the King "worn out, depressed, and discouraged." When Bismarck tried to explain his own view of the political situation, William interrupted him, saying: "I see exactly how all this will turn out. Right here, in this Opera square on which these windows look, they will behead first you and a little later me too." It was hard work for Bismarck to infuse courage into the trembling Hohenzollern. But finally, Bismarck reports, "My words appealed to his military honor and he saw himself in the position of an officer who has the duty of defending his post unto death." *

Still more frightened than the King were the Queen, the royal princes, and many generals. In England Queen Victoria spent sleepless nights thinking of the position of her eldest daughter married to the Prussian Crown Prince. The royal palace of Berlin was haunted by the ghosts of Louis XVI and Marie Antoinette.

All these fears, however, were unfounded. The Progressives did not venture a new revolution, and they would have been defeated if they had.

These much-abused German liberals of the 1860's, these men of studious habits, these readers of philosophical treatises, these lovers of music and poetry, understood very well why the upheaval of 1848 had failed. They knew that they could not establish popular government within a nation where many millions were still caught in the bonds of superstition, boorishness, and illiteracy. The political problem was essentially a problem of education. The final success of liberalism and democracy was beyond doubt. The trend toward parliamentary rule was irresistible. But the victory of liberalism could be achieved only when those strata of the population from which the King drew his reliable soldiers should have become enlightened and thereby transformed into supporters of liberal ideas. Then the King would be forced to surrender, and the Parliament would obtain supremacy without bloodshed.

The liberals were resolved to spare the German people, whenever possible, the horrors of revolution and civil war. They were confident that in a not-too-distant future they themselves would get full control of Prussia. They had only to wait.

* Bismarck, *Gedanken und Erinnerungen* (new ed. Stuttgart, 1922), I, 325 ff.

5. The "Little German" Program

The Prussian Progressives did not fight in the Constitutional Conflict for the destruction or weakening of the Prussian Army. They realized that under the circumstances Germany was in need of a strong army for the defense of its independence. They wanted to wrest the army from the King and to transform it into an instrument for the protection of German liberty. The issue of the conflict was whether the King or Parliament should control the army.

The aim of German liberalism was the replacement of the scandalous administration of the thirty-odd German states by a unitary liberal government. Most of the liberals believed that this future German state must not include Austria. Austria was very different from the other German-speaking countries; it had problems of its own which were foreign to the rest of the nation. The liberals could not help seeing Austria as the most dangerous obstacle to German freedom. The Austrian court was dominated by the Jesuits, its government had concluded a concordat with Pius IX, the pope who ardently combated all modern ideas. But the Austrian Emperor was not prepared to renounce voluntarily the position which his house had occupied for more than four hundred years in Germany. The liberals wanted the Prussian Army strong because they were afraid of Austrian hegemony, a new Counter-Reformation, and the reëstablishment of the reactionary system of the late Prince Metternich. They aimed at a unitary government for all Germans outside of Austria (and Switzerland). They therefore called themselves Little Germans (*Kleindeutsche*) as contrasted to the Great Germans (*Grossdeutsche*) who wanted to include those parts of Austria which had previously belonged to the Holy Empire.

But there were, besides, other considerations of foreign policy to recommend an increase in the Prussian Army. France was in those years ruled by an adventurer who was convinced that he could preserve his emperorship only by fresh military victories. In the first decade of his reign he had already waged two bloody wars. Now it seemed to be Germany's turn. There was little doubt that Napoleon III toyed with the idea of annexing the left bank of the Rhine. Who else could protect Germany but the Prussian Army?

Then there was one problem more, Schleswig-Holstein. The citizens of Holstein, of Lauenburg, and of southern Schleswig bitterly opposed the rule of Denmark. The German liberals cared little for the sophisticated arguments of lawyers and diplomats concerning the claims of various pretenders to the succession in the Elbe duchies. They did not believe in the doctrine that the question of who should rule a country must be decided according to the provisions of feudal law and of century-old family compacts. They supported the Western principle of self-determination. The people of these duchies were reluctant to acquiesce in the sovereignty of a man whose only title was that he had married a princess with a disputed claim to the succession in Schleswig and no right at all to the succession in Holstein; they aimed at autonomy within the German Confederation. This fact alone seemed important in the eyes of the liberals. Why should these Germans be denied what the British, the French, the Belgians, and the Italians had got? But as the King of Denmark was not ready to renounce his claims, this question could not be solved without a recourse to arms.

It would be a mistake to judge all these problems from the point of view of later events. Bismarck freed Schleswig-Holstein from the yoke of its Danish oppressors only in order to annex it to Prussia; and he annexed not only southern Schleswig but northern Schleswig as well, whose population desired to remain in the Danish kingdom. Napoleon III did not attack Germany; it was Bismarck who kindled the war against France. Nobody foresaw this outcome in the early 'sixties. At that time everybody in Europe, and in America too, deemed the Emperor of France the foremost peacebreaker and aggressor. The sympathies which the German longing for unity encountered abroad were to a great extent due to the conviction that a united Germany would counterbalance France and thus make Europe safe for peace.

The Little Germans were also misled by their religious prejudices. Like most of the liberals they thought of Protestantism as the first step on the way from medieval darkness to enlightenment. They feared Austria because it was Catholic; they preferred Prussia because the majority of its population was Protestant. In spite of all experience they hoped that Prussia was more open to liberal ideas than Austria. Political conditions in Austria, to be sure, were in those critical years unsatisfactory. But later events have proved that Protestantism is no more a safeguard of freedom than Catholicism. The ideal of liberalism is the complete separation of church and state, and tolerance—without any regard to differences among the churches.

But this error also was not limited to Germany. The French liberals were so deluded that they at first hailed the Prussian victory at Königgrätz (Sadova). Only on second thought did they realize that Austria's defeat spelled the doom of France too, and they raised —too late—the battle cry *Revanche pour Sadova*.

Königgrätz was at any rate a crushing defeat for German liberalism. The liberals were aware of the fact that they had lost a campaign. They were nevertheless full of hope. They were firmly resolved to proceed with their fight in the new Parliament of Northern Germany. This fight, they felt, must end with the victory of liberalism and the defeat of absolutism. The moment when the King would no longer be able to use "his" army against the people seemed to come closer every day.

6. The Lassalle Episode

It would be possible to deal with the Prussian Constitutional Conflict without even mentioning the name of Ferdinand Lassalle. Lassalle's intervention did not influence the course of events. But it foreboded something new; it was the dawn of the forces which were destined to mold the fate of Germany and of Western civilization.

While the Prussian Progressives were involved in their struggle for freedom, Lassalle attacked them bitterly and passionately. He tried to incite the workers to withdraw their sympathies from the Progressives. He proclaimed the gospel of class war. The Progressives, as representatives of the bourgeoisie, he held, were the mortal foes of labor. You should not fight the state but the exploiting classes. The state is your friend; of course, not the state governed by Herr von Bismarck but the state controlled by me, Lassalle.

Lassalle was not on the pay roll of Bismarck, as some people suspected. Nobody could bribe Lassalle. Only after his death did some of his former friends take government money. But as both Bismarck and Lassalle assailed the Progressives, they became virtual allies. Lassalle very soon approached Bismarck. The two used to meet clandestinely. Only many years later was the secret of these relations revealed. It is vain to discuss whether an open and lasting coöperation between these two ambitious men would have resulted if Lassalle had not died very shortly after these meetings from a wound received in a duel (August 31, 1864). They both aimed at supreme power in Germany. Neither Bismarck nor Lassalle was ready to renounce his claim to the first place.

Bismarck and his military and aristocratic friends hated the liberals so thoroughly that they would have been ready to help the socialists get control of the country if they themselves had proved too weak to preserve their own rule. But they were—for the time being—strong enough to keep a tight rein on the Progressives. They did not need Lassalle's support.

It is not true that Lassalle gave Bismarck the idea that revolutionary socialism was a powerful ally in the fight against liberalism.

Bismarck had long believed that the lower classes were better royalists than the middle classes.* Besides, as Prussian minister in Paris he had had opportunity to observe the working of Caesarism. Perhaps his predilection toward universal and equal suffrage was strengthened by his conversations with Lassalle. But for the moment he had no use for Lassalle's coöperation. The latter's party was still too small to be considered important. At the death of Lassalle the Allgemeine Deutsche Arbeiterverein had not much more than 4,000 members.†

Lassalle's agitation did not hinder the activities of the Progressives. It was a nuisance to them, not an obstacle. Neither had they anything to learn from his doctrines. That Prussia's Parliament was only a sham and that the army was the main stronghold of Prussia's absolutism was not new to them. It was exactly because they knew it that they fought in the great conflict.

Lassalle's brief demagogical career is noteworthy because for the first time in Germany the ideas of socialism and etatism appeared on the political scene as opposed to liberalism and freedom. Lassalle was not himself a Nazi; but he was the most eminent forerunner of Nazism, and the first German who aimed at the Führer position. He rejected all the values of the Enlightenment and of liberal philosophy, but not as the romantic eulogists of the Middle Ages and of royal legitimism did. He negated them; but he promised at the same time to realize them in a fuller and broader sense. Liberalism, he asserted, aims at spurious freedom, but I will bring you true freedom. And true freedom means the omnipotence of government. It is not the police who are the foes of liberty but the bourgeoisie.

And it was Lassalle who spoke the words which characterize best the spirit of the age to come: "The state is God." ‡

* Ziekursch, *op. cit.*, I, 107 ff.
† Oncken, *Lassalle* (Stuttgart, 1904), p. 393.
‡ Gustav Mayer, "Lassalleana," *Archiv für Geschichte des Sozialismus*, I, 196.

II. THE TRIUMPH OF MILITARISM

1. The Prussian Army in the New German Empire

IN the late afternoon of September 1, 1870, King William I, surrounded by a pompous staff of princes and generals, was looking down from a hill south of the Meuse at the battle in progress, when an officer brought the news that the capitulation of Napoleon III and his whole army was imminent. Then Moltke turned to Count Falkenberg, who like himself was a member of the Parliament of Northern Germany, and remarked: "Well, dear colleague, what happened today settles our military problem for a long time." And Bismarck shook hands with the highest of the German princes, the heir to the throne of Württemberg, and said: "This day safeguards and strengthens the German princes and the principles of conservatism." * In the hour of overwhelming victory these were the first reactions of Prussia's two foremost statesmen. They triumphed because they had defeated liberalism. They did not care a whit for the catchwords of the official propaganda: conquest of the hereditary foe, safeguarding the nation's frontiers, historical mission of the house of Hohenzollern and of Prussia, unification of Germany, Germany foremost in the world. The princes had overthrown their own people; this alone seemed important to them.

In the new German Reich the Emperor—not in his position as Emperor but in his position as King of Prussia—had full control of the Prussian Army. Special agreements which Prussia—not the Reich—had concluded with 23 of the other 24 member states of the Reich incorporated the armed forces of these states into the Prussian Army. Only the royal Bavarian Army retained some limited peacetime independence, but in the event of war it too was subject to full control by the Emperor. The provisions concerning recruiting and the length of active military service had to be fixed by the Reichstag; parliamentary consent was required, moreover, for the budgetary allowance for the army. But the Parliament had no influence over the management of military affairs. The army was the army of the King of Prussia, not of the people or the Parliament. The Emperor and King was Supreme War Lord and commander in chief. The chief of the Great General Staff was the Kaiser's first assistant in the conduct of operations. The army was an institution not within but above the apparatus of civil administration. Every military commander had the right and the duty to

* Ziekursch, *Politische Geschichte des neuen deutschen Kaiserreichs*, I, 298.

interfere whenever he felt that the working of the nonmilitary administration was unsatisfactory. He had to account for his interference to the Emperor only. Once, in 1913, a case of such military interference, which had occurred in Zabern, led to a violent debate in Parliament; but Parliament had no jurisdiction over the matter, and the army triumphed.

The reliability of this army was unquestionable. No one could doubt that all parts of the forces could be used to quell rebellions and revolutions. The mere suggestion that a detachment could refuse to obey an order, or that men of the reserve when called to active duty might stay out, would have been considered an absurdity. The German nation had changed in a very remarkable way. We shall consider later the essence and cause of this great transformation. The main political problem of the 'fifties and early 'sixties, the problem of the reliability of the soldiers, had vanished. All German soldiers were now unconditionally loyal to the Supreme War Lord. The army was an instrument which the Kaiser could trust. Tactful persons were judicious enough not to point out explicitly that this army was ready to be used against a potential domestic foe. But to William II such inhibitions were strange. He openly told his recruits that it was their duty to fire upon their fathers, mothers, brothers, or sisters if he ordered them to do so. Such speeches were criticized in the liberal press; but the liberals were powerless. The allegiance of the soldiers was absolute; it no longer depended on the length of active service. The army itself proposed in 1892 that the infantry return to two years of active duty only. In the discussion of this bill in Parliament and in the press there was no longer any question of the political reliability of the soldiers. Everybody knew that the army was now, without any regard to the length of active service, "nonpolitical and nonpartisan," i.e., a docile and manageable tool in the hands of the Emperor.

The government and the Reichstag quarreled continuously about military affairs. But considerations of the usefulness of the forces for the preservation of the hardly disguised imperial despotism did not play any role at all. The army was so strong and reliable that a revolutionary attempt could be crushed within a few hours. Nobody in the Reich wanted to start a revolution; the spirit of resistance and rebellion had faded. The Reichstag would have been prepared to consent to any expenditure for the army proposed by the government if the problem of raising the necessary funds had not been difficult to solve. In the end the army and navy always got the money that the General Staff asked for. To the increase of the armed forces financial considerations were a smaller obstacle than the shortage of the supply of men whom the generals considered eligible for commissions on active duty. With the expansion of the armed forces it had long become impossible to give commissions to noblemen only. The number of nonaristocratic officers steadily grew. But the generals were not ready to admit into the ranks of commissioned officers on active duty any but those commoners of "good and wealthy families." Applicants of this type were available only in limited numbers. Most of the sons of the upper middle class preferred other careers. They were not eager to become professional officers and to be treated with disdain by their aristocratic colleagues.

Both the Reichstag and the liberal press time and again criticized the government's military policy also from the technical point of view. The General Staff were strongly opposed to such civilian interference. They denied to everybody but the army any comprehension of military problems. Even Hans Delbrück, the eminent historian of warfare and author of excellent strategical dissertations, was for them only a layman. Officers in retirement, who contributed to the opposition press, were called biased partisans. Public opinion at last acknowledged the General Staff's claim to infallibility, and all critics were silenced. Events of World War I proved, of course, that these critics had a better grasp of military methods than the specialists of the General Staff.

2. German Militarism

The political system of the new German Empire has been called militarism. The characteristic feature of militarism is not the fact that a nation has a powerful army or navy. It is the paramount role assigned to the army within the political structure. Even in peacetime the army is supreme; it is the predominant factor in political life. The subjects must obey the government as soldiers must obey their superiors. Within a militarist community there is no freedom; there are only obedience and discipline.*

The size of the armed forces is not in itself the determining factor. Some Latin-American countries are militarist although their armies are small, poorly equipped, and unable to defend the country against a foreign invasion. On the other hand, France and Great Britain were at the end of the nineteenth century nonmilitarist, although their military and naval armaments were very strong.

Militarism should not be confused with despotism enforced by a foreign army. Austria's rule in Italy, backed by Austrian regi-

* Herbert Spencer, *The Principles of Sociology* (New York, 1897), III, 588.

ments composed of non-Italians, and the Czar's rule in Poland, safe-guarded by Russian soldiers, were such systems of despotism. It has already been mentioned that in the 'fifties and early 'sixties of the past century conditions in Prussia were analogous. But it was different with the German Empire founded on the battlefields of Königgrätz and of Sedan. This Empire did not employ foreign soldiers. It was not preserved by bayonets but by the almost unanimous consent of its subjects. The nation approved of the system, and therefore the soldiers were loyal too. The people acquiesced in the leadership of the "state" because they deemed such a system fair, expedient, and useful for them. There were, of course, some objectors, but they were few and powerless.*

The deficiency in this system was its monarchical leadership. The successors of Frederick II were not fit for the task assigned to them. William I had found in Bismarck an ingenious chancellor. Bismarck was a high-spirited and well-educated man, a brilliant speaker, and an excellent stylist. He was a skillful diplomat and in every respect surpassed most of the German nobility. But his vision was limited. He was familiar with country life, with the primitive agricultural methods of Prussian Junkers, with the patriarchal conditions of the eastern provinces of Prussia, and the life at the courts of Berlin and St. Petersburg. In Paris he met the society of Napoleon's court; he had no idea of French intellectual trends. He knew little about German trade and industry and the mentality of businessmen and professional people. He kept out of the way of scientists, scholars, and artists. His political credo was the old-fashioned loyalty of a king's vassal. In September, 1849, he told his wife: "Don't disparage the King; we are both guilty of this fault. Even if he errs and blunders, we should not speak of him otherwise than as of our parents, since we have sworn fidelity and allegiance to him and his house." Such an opinion is appropriate for a royal chamberlain but it does not suit the omnipotent Prime Minister of a great empire. Bismarck foresaw the evils with which the personality of William II threatened the nation; he was in a good position to become acquainted with the character of the young prince. But, entangled in his notions of loyalty and allegiance, he was unable to do anything to prevent disaster.

People are now unfair to William II. He was not equal to his task. But he was not worse than the average of his contemporaries. It was not his fault that the monarchical principle of succession

---

* Whoever wants to acquaint himself with the political mentality of the subjects of William II may read the novels of Baron Ompteda, Rudolf Herzog, Walter Bloem, and similar authors. These were the stuff the people liked to read. Some of them sold many hundred thousand copies.

made him Emperor and King and that as German Emperor and King of Prussia he had to be an autocrat. It was not the man that failed but the system. If William II had been King of Great Britain, it would not have been possible for him to commit the serious blunders that he could not avoid as King of Prussia. It was due to the frailty of the system that the toadies whom he appointed generals and ministers were incompetent. You may say it was bad luck. For Bismarck and the elder Moltke too were courtiers. Though the victorious field marshal had served with the army as a young officer, a good deal of his career was spent in attendance at court; he was among other things for many years the attendant of a royal prince who lived in sickness and seclusion in Rome and died there. William II had many human weaknesses; but it was precisely the qualities that discredited him with prudent people which rendered him popular with the majority of his nation. His crude ignorance of political issues made him congenial to his subjects, who were as ignorant as he was, and shared his prejudices and illusions.

Within a modern state hereditary monarchy can work satisfactorily only where there is parliamentary democracy. Absolutism —and, still more, disguised absolutism with a phantom constitution and a powerless parliament—requires qualities in the ruler that no mortal man can ever meet. William II failed like Nicholas II and, even earlier, the Bourbons. Absolutism was not abolished; it simply collapsed.

The breakdown of autocracy was due not only to the fact that the monarchs lacked intellectual ability. Autocratic government of a modern great nation burdens the ruler with a quantity of work beyond the capacity of any man. In the eighteenth century Frederick William I and Frederick II could still perform all the administrative business with a few hours of daily work. They had enough leisure left for their hobbies and for pleasure. Their successors were not only less gifted, they were less diligent too. From the days of Frederick William II it was no longer the king who ruled but his favorites. The king was surrounded by a host of intriguing gentlemen and ladies. Whoever succeeded best in these rivalries and plots got control of the government until another sycophant supplanted him.

The camarilla was supreme in the army too. Frederick William I had himself organized the forces. His son had commanded them personally in great campaigns. Herein too their successors proved inadequate. They were poor organizers and incompetent generals. The chief of the Great General Staff, who nominally was merely the King's assistant, became virtually commander in chief. The change remained for a long time unnoticed. As late as the War of 1866 many high-ranking generals were still not aware of the fact that the orders they had to obey did not emanate from the King but from General von Moltke.

Frederick II owed his military successes to a great extent to the fact that the Austrian, French, and Russian armies that he fought were not commanded by their sovereigns but by generals. Frederick concentrated in his hands the whole military, political, and economic strength of his—of course, comparatively small—realm. He alone gave orders. The commanders of the armies of his adversaries had only limited powers. Their position was rendered difficult by the fact that their duties kept them at a distance from the courts of their sovereigns. While they stayed with their armies in the field their rivals continued to intrigue at the court. Frederick could venture daring operations of which the outcome was uncertain. He did not have to account for his actions to anybody but himself. The enemy generals were always in fear of their monarch's disfavor. They aimed at sharing the responsibility with others in order to exculpate themselves in case of failure. They would call their subordinate generals for a council of war, and look for justification to its resolutions. When they got definite orders from the sovereign, which were suggested to him either by a council of war deliberating far away from the field of operations, or by one or several of the host of lazy intrigants, they felt comfortable. They executed the order even when they were convinced that it was inexpedient. Frederick was fully aware of the advantage that the concentration of undivided responsibility in one commander offered. He never called a council of war. He again and again forbade his generals—even under penalty of death—to call one. In a council of war, he said, the more timid party always predominates. A council of war is full of anxiety, because it is too matter of fact.* This doctrine became, like all opinions of King Frederick, a dogma for the Prussian Army. It roused the elder Moltke's anger when somebody said that King William had called a council of war in his campaigns. The King, he declared, would listen to the proposals of his chief of staff and then decide; it had always happened that way.

In practice this principle resulted in the absolute command of the chief of the Great General Staff, whom, of course, the King appointed. Not William I but Helmuth von Moltke led the armies in the campaigns of 1866 and 1870–71. William II used to declare that in case of war he would personally command his armies, and that he needed a chief of staff only in peacetime. But when the first

* Delbrück, *Geschichte der Kriegskunst,* Part IV, pp. 434 ff.

World War broke out this boasting was forgotten. Helmuth von Moltke's nephew, a courtier without any military knowledge or ability, timid and irresolute, sick and nervous, an adept of the doubtful theosophy of Rudolph Steiner, led the German Army into the debacle at the Marne; then he collapsed. The Minister of War, Eric von Falkenhayn, filled the gap spontaneously; and the Kaiser in apathy gave his consent. Very soon Ludendorff began to plot against Falkenhayn. Cleverly organized machinations forced the Emperor in 1916 to replace Falkenhayn by Hindenburg. But the real commander in chief was now Ludendorff, who nominally was only Hindenburg's first assistant.

The German nation, biased by the doctrines of militarism, did not realize that it was the system that had failed. They used to say: We lacked "only" the right man. If Schlieffen had not died too soon! A legend was composed about the personality of this late chief of staff. His sound plan had been ineptly put into execution by his incompetent successor. If only the two army corps which Moltke had uselessly dispatched to the Russian border had been available at the Marne! Naturally, the Reichstag too was considered guilty. There was no mention of the fact that the Parliament had never earnestly resisted the government's proposals concerning allocations for the army. Lieutenant Colonel Hentsch in particular was made the scapegoat. This officer, it was asserted, had transgressed his powers, perhaps he was a traitor. But if Hentsch was really responsible for the order to retreat, then he would have to be deemed the man who saved the German Army from annihilation through encirclement of its right wing. The fable that but for the interference of Hentsch the Germans would have been victorious at the Marne can easily be disposed of.

There is no doubt that the commanders of the German Army and Navy were not equal to their task. But the shortcomings of the generals and admirals—and likewise those of the ministers and diplomats—must be charged to the system. A system that puts incapable men at the top is a bad system. There is no telling whether Schlieffen would have been more successful; he never had the opportunity to command troops in action; he died before the war. But one thing is sure: the "parliamentary armies" of France and Great Britain got at that time commanders who led them to victory. The army of the King of Prussia was not so fortunate.

In accordance with the doctrines of militarism the chief of the Great General Staff considered himself the first servant of the Emperor and King and demanded the chancellor's subordination. These claims had already led to conflicts between Bismarck and Moltke. Bismarck asked that the supreme commander should adjust his conduct to considerations of foreign policy; Moltke bluntly rejected such pretensions. The conflict remained unresolved. In the first World War the supreme commander became omnipotent. The chancellor was in effect degraded to a lower rank. The Kaiser had retained ceremonial and social functions only; Hindenburg, his chief of staff, was a man of straw. Ludendorff, the first quartermaster general, became virtually omnipotent dictator. He might have remained in this position all his life if Foch had not defeated him.

This evolution demonstrates clearly the impracticability of hereditary absolutism. Monarchical absolutism results in the rule of a major-domo, of a shogun, or of a duce.

3. The Liberals and Militarism

The lower chamber of the Prussian Parliament, the *Abgeordnetenhaus,* was based on universal franchise. The citizens of every constituency were divided into three classes, each of which chose the same number of electors for the final poll by which the parliamentary representative of the constituency was elected. The first class was formed of those adult male residents who paid the highest taxes and together contributed one third of the total amount of taxes collected in the district; the second class of those who together contributed the second third, and the third class of those who together contributed the third third. Thus the wealthier citizens had a better franchise than the poorer ones of their constituency. The middle classes predominated in the ballot. For the Reichstag of the North German Federation, and later for that of the Reich, no such discrimination was applied. Every adult male cast his vote directly on the ballot which returned the representative of the constituency; franchise was not only universal but equal and direct. Thus the poorer strata of the nation got more political influence. It was the aim of both Bismarck and Lassalle to weaken by this electoral system the power of the liberal party. The liberals were fully aware that the new method of voting would for some time sap their parliamentary strength. But they were not concerned about that. They realized that the victory of liberalism could be achieved only by an effort of the whole nation. What was important was not to have a majority of liberals within the chamber but to have a liberal majority among the people and thereby in the army. In the Prussian Abgeordnetenhaus the Progressives outnumbered the friends of the government. Nevertheless liberalism was powerless, since the King could still trust in the allegiance of the greater part of the army. What was needed was to bring into the ranks of liberalism those backward ignorant masses whose political indifference was the safeguard of absolutism. Only then would the day of popular government and democracy dawn.

The liberals therefore did not fear that the new electoral system would postpone or seriously imperil their inexorable final victory. The outlook for the immediate future was not very comforting but the ultimate prospects were excellent. One had only to look at France. In that country too an autocrat had founded his despotism upon the loyalty of the army and upon universal and equal franchise. But now the Caesar was crushed and democracy had triumphed.

The liberals did not greatly fear socialism. The socialists had achieved some success. But it could be expected that reasonable workers would soon discover the impracticability of socialist utopias. Why should the wage earners whose standard of living was daily improving be deluded by demagogues who—as rumors whispered—were on the pay roll of Bismarck?

Only later did the liberals become aware of the change taking place in the nation's mentality. For many years they believed that it was only a temporary setback, a short reactionary incident which was doomed to disappear very soon. For them every supporter of the new ideologies was either misguided or a renegade. But the numbers of these apostates increased. The youth no longer joined the liberal party. The old fighters for liberalism grew tired. With every new election campaign their ranks became thinner; with every year the reactionary system which they hated became more powerful. Some faithful men still clung to the ideas of liberty and democracy, gallantly fighting against the united assaults on liberalism from the Right and from the Left. But they were a forlorn squad. Among those born after the battle of Königgrätz almost nobody joined the party of liberalism. The liberals died out. The new generation did not even know the meaning of the word.

4. The Current Explanation of the Success of Militarism

All over the world the overwhelming victory of German militarism is interpreted in accordance with the legends developed by the propaganda of the German Social Democrats. The socialists assert that the German bourgeoisie seceded from the principles of freedom and thus betrayed the "people." Based on Marxian historical materialism absurd theories concerning the essence and the development of imperialism were invented. Capitalism, they say, must result in militarism, imperialism, bloody wars, Fascism, and Nazism. Finance and big business have brought civilization to the verge of destruction; Marxism has the task of saving humanity.

Such interpretations fail to solve the problem. Indeed, they try purposely to put it out of sight. In the early 1860's there were in Germany among the politically minded a few supporters of dynastic absolutism, of militarism and of authoritarian government, who strongly opposed the transition to liberalism, democracy, and popular government. This minority consisted mainly of the princes and their courtiers, the nobility, the commissioned officers of higher ranks, and some civil servants. But the great majority of the bourgeoisie, of the intellectuals, and of the politically minded members of the poorer strata of the population were decidedly liberal and aimed at parliamentary government according to the British pattern. The liberals believed that political education would progress quickly; they were convinced that every citizen who gave up political indifference and became familiar with political issues would support their stand on constitutional questions. They were fully aware that some of these newly politicized men would not join their ranks. It was to be expected that Catholics, Poles, Danes, and Alsatians would form their own parties. But these parties would not support the King's pretensions. Catholics and non-Germans were bound to favor parliamentarism in a predominantly Protestant and German Reich.

The politicization of the whole country went on faster than the liberals had foreseen. At the end of the 'seventies the whole people was inspired by political interests, even passions, and ardently took part in political activities. But the consequences differed radically from those expected by the liberals. The Reichstag did not earnestly challenge the hardly disguised absolutism; it did not raise the constitutional issue; it indulged only in idle talk. And, much more important: the soldiers who now were recruited from a completely politicized nation became so unconditionally reliable that every doubt concerning their readiness to fight for absolutism against a domestic foe was considered an absurdity.

The questions to be answered are not: Why did the bankers and the rich entrepreneurs and capitalists desert liberalism? Why did the professors, the doctors, and the lawyers not erect barricades? We must rather ask: Why did the German nation return to the Reichstag members who did not abolish absolutism? Why was the army, formed for a great part of men who voted the socialist or the Catholic ticket, unconditionally loyal to its commanders? Why could the antiliberal parties, foremost among them the Social Democrats, collect many millions of votes while the groups which remained faithful to the principles of liberalism lost more and more popular support? Why did the millions of socialist voters who indulged in revolutionary babble acquiesce in the rule of princes and courts?

To say that big business had some reasons to support the Hohenzollern absolutism or that the Hanseatic merchants and shipowners sympathized with the increase of the navy is no satisfactory answer to these questions. The great majority of the German nation consisted of wage earners and salaried people, of artisans and shopkeepers, and of small farmers. These men determined the outcome of elections; their representatives sat in Parliament, and they filled the ranks of the army. Attempts to explain the change in the German people's mentality by demonstrating that the class interests of the wealthy bourgeoisie caused them to become reactionary are nonsensical, whether they are as childish as the "steel plate" * legend or as sophisticated as the Marxian theories concerning imperialism.

* The *"Panzerplatten*-doctrine" maintained that German militarism and the trend to increase Germany's armed forces were due to machinations of the heavy industries eager to enlarge their profits. Cf. pp. 132–133.

PART II

NATIONALISM

III. ETATISM

1. The New Mentality

THE most important event in the history of the last hundred years is the displacement of liberalism by etatism. Etatism appears in two forms: socialism and interventionism. Both have in common the goal of subordinating the individual unconditionally to the state, the social apparatus of compulsion and coercion.

Etatism too, like liberalism in earlier days, originated in Western Europe and only later came into Germany. It has been asserted that autochthonous German roots of etatism could be found in Fichte's socialist utopia and in the sociological teachings of Schelling and Hegel. However, the dissertations of these philosophers were so foreign to the problems and tasks of social and economic policies that they could not directly influence political matters. What use could practical politics derive from Hegel's assertion: "The state is the actuality of the ethical idea. It is ethical mind *qua* the substantial will manifest and revealed to itself, knowing and thinking itself, accomplishing what it knows and in so far as it knows it." Or from his dictum: "The state is absolutely rational inasmuch as it is the actuality of the substantial will which it possesses in the particular self-consciousness once that consciousness has been raised to consciousness of its universality." *

Etatism assigns to the state the task of guiding the citizens and of holding them in tutelage. It aims at restricting the individual's freedom to act. It seeks to mold his destiny and to vest all initiative in the government alone. It came into Germany from the West.†

Saint Simon, Owen, Fourier, Pecqueur, Sismondi, Auguste Comte laid its foundations. Lorenz von Stein was the first author to bring the Germans comprehensive information concerning these new

---

* Hegel, *Philosophy of Right*, translated by T. M. Knox (Oxford, 1942), pp. 155–156.
† Hayek, "The Counter-Revolution of Science," *Economica*, VIII, 9–36, 119–150, 281–320.

doctrines. The appearance in 1842 of the first edition of his book, *Socialism and Communism in Present-Day France,* was the most important event in pre-Marxian German socialism. The elements of government interference with business, labor legislation, and trade-unionism * also reached Germany from the West. In America Frederick List became familiar with the protectionist theories of Alexander Hamilton.

Liberalism had taught the German intellectuals to absorb Western political ideas with reverential awe. Now, they thought, liberalism was already outstripped; government interference with business had replaced old-fashioned liberal orthodoxy and would inexorably result in socialism. He who did not want to appear backward had to become "social," i.e., either interventionist or socialist. New ideas succeed only after some lapse of time; years have to pass before they reach the broader strata of intellectuals. List's *National System of Political Economy* was published in 1841, a few months before Stein's book. In 1847 Marx and Engels produced the Communist Manifesto. In the middle 'sixties the prestige of liberalism began to melt away. Very soon the economic, philosophical, historical, and juridical university lectures were representing liberalism in caricature. The social scientists outdid each other in emotional criticism of British free trade and laissez faire; the philosophers disparaged the "stock-jobber" ethics of utilitarianism, the superficiality of enlightenment, and the negativity of the notion of liberty; the lawyers demonstrated the paradox of democratic and parliamentary institutions; and the historians dealt with the moral and political decay of France and of Great Britain. On the other hand, the students were taught to admire the "social kingdom of the Hohenzollerns" from Frederick William I, the "noble socialist," to William I, the great Kaiser of social security and labor legislation. The Social Democrats despised Western "plutodemocracy" and "pseudo-liberty" and ridiculed the teachings of "bourgeois economics."

The boring pedantry of the professors and the boastful oratory of the Social Democrats failed to impress critical people. The élite were conquered for etatism by other men. From England penetrated the ideas of Carlyle, Ruskin, and the Fabians, from France Solidarism. The churches of all creeds joined the choir. Novels and plays propagated the new doctrine of the state. Shaw and Wells, Spielhagen and Gerhart Hauptmann, and hosts of other writers, less gifted, contributed to the popularity of etatism.

* Adolf Weber (*Der Kampf zwischen Kapital and Arbeit,* 3d and 4th eds. Tübingen, 1921, p. 68) says quite correctly in dealing with German trade-unionism: "Form and spirit . . . came from abroad."

2. The State

The state is essentially an apparatus of compulsion and coercion. The characteristic feature of its activities is to compel people through the application or the threat of force to behave otherwise than they would like to behave.

But not every apparatus of compulsion and coercion is called a state. Only one which is powerful enough to maintain its existence, for some time at least, by its own force is commonly called a state. A gang of robbers, which because of the comparative weakness of its forces has no prospect of successfully resisting for any length of time the forces of another organization, is not entitled to be called a state. The state will either smash or tolerate a gang. In the first case the gang is not a state because its independence lasts for a short time only; in the second case it is not a state because it does not stand on its own might. The pogrom gangs in imperial Russia were not a state because they could kill and plunder only thanks to the connivance of the government.

This restriction of the notion of the state leads directly to the concepts of state territory and sovereignty. Standing on its own power implies that there is a space on the earth's surface where the operation of the apparatus is not restricted by the intervention of another organization; this space is the state's territory. Sovereignty (*suprema potestas,* supreme power) signifies that the organization stands on its own legs. A state without territory is an empty concept. A state without sovereignty is a contradiction in terms.

The total complex of the rules according to which those at the helm employ compulsion and coercion is called law. Yet the characteristic feature of the state is not these rules, as such, but the application or threat of violence. A state whose chiefs recognize but one rule, to do whatever seems at the moment to be expedient in their eyes, is a state without law. It does not make any difference whether or not these tyrants are "benevolent."

The term law is used in a second meaning too. We call international law the complex of agreements which sovereign states have concluded expressly or tacitly in regard to their mutual relations. It is not, however, essential to the statehood of an organization that other states should recognize its existence through the conclusion of such agreements. It is the fact of sovereignty within a territory that is essential, not the formalities.

The people handling the state machinery may take over other functions, duties, and activities. The government may own and operate schools, railroads, hospitals, and orphan asylums. Such activities are only incidental to the conception of a state. Whatever other functions it may assume, the state is always characterized by the compulsion and coercion exercised.

With human nature as it is, the state is a necessary and indispensable institution. The state is, if properly administered, the foundation of society, of human coöperation and civilization. It is the most beneficial and most useful instrument in the endeavors of man to promote human happiness and welfare. But it is a tool and a means only, not the ultimate goal. It is not God. It is simply compulsion and coercion; it is the police power.

It has been necessary to dwell upon these truisms because the mythologies and metaphysics of etatism have succeeded in wrapping them in mystery. The state is a human institution, not a superhuman being. He who says "state" means coercion and compulsion. He who says: There should be a law concerning this matter, means: The armed men of the government should force people to do what they do not want to do, or not to do what they like. He who says: This law should be better enforced, means: The police should force people to obey this law. He who says: The state is God, deifies arms and prisons. The worship of the state is the worship of force. There is no more dangerous menace to civilization than a government of incompetent, corrupt, or vile men. The worst evils which mankind ever had to endure were inflicted by bad governments. The state can be and has often been in the course of history the main source of mischief and disaster.

The apparatus of compulsion and coercion is always operated by mortal men. It has happened time and again that rulers have excelled their contemporaries and fellow citizens both in competence and in fairness. But there is ample historical evidence to the contrary too. The thesis of etatism that the members of the government and its assistants are more intelligent than the people, and that they know better what is good for the individual than he himself knows, is pure nonsense. The Führers and the Duces are neither God nor God's vicars.

The essential characteristic features of state and government do not depend on their particular structure and constitution. They are present both in despotic and in democratic governments. Democracy too is not divine. We shall later deal with the benefits that society derives from democratic government. But great as these advantages are, it should never be forgotten that majorities are no less exposed to error and frustration than kings and dictators. That a fact is deemed true by the majority does not prove its truth. That a policy is deemed expedient by the majority does not prove its expediency. The individuals who form the majority are not gods, and their joint conclusions are not necessarily godlike.

3. *The Political and Social Doctrines of Liberalism*

There is a school of thought which teaches that social coöperation of men could be achieved without compulsion or coercion. Anarchism believes that a social order could be established in which all men would recognize the advantages to be derived from coöperation and be prepared to do voluntarily everything which the maintenance of society requires and to renounce voluntarily all actions detrimental to society. But the anarchists overlook two facts. There are people whose mental abilities are so limited that they cannot grasp the full benefits that society brings to them. And there are people whose flesh is so weak that they cannot resist the temptation of striving for selfish advantage through actions detrimental to society. An anarchistic society would be exposed to the mercy of every individual. We may grant that every sane adult is endowed with the faculty of realizing the good of social coöperation and of acting accordingly. However, it is beyond doubt that there are infants, the aged, and the insane. We may agree that he who acts antisocially should be considered mentally sick and in need of cure. But as long as not all are cured, and as long as there are infants and the senile, some provision must be taken lest they destroy society.

Liberalism differs radically from anarchism. It has nothing in common with the absurd illusions of the anarchists. We must emphasize this point because etatists sometimes try to discover a similarity. Liberalism is not so foolish as to aim at the abolition of the state. Liberals fully recognize that no social coöperation and no civilization could exist without some amount of compulsion and coercion. It is the task of government to protect the social system against the attacks of those who plan actions detrimental to its maintenance and operation.

The essential teaching of liberalism is that social coöperation and the division of labor can be achieved only in a system of private ownership of the means of production, i.e., within a market society, or capitalism. All the other principles of liberalism—democracy, personal freedom of the individual, freedom of speech and of the press, religious tolerance, peace among the nations—are consequences of this basic postulate. They can be realized only within a society based on private property.

From this point of view liberalism assigns to the state the task of protecting the lives, health, freedom, and property of its subjects against violent or fraudulent aggression.

That liberalism aims at private ownership of the means of production implies that it rejects public ownership of the means of production, i.e., socialism. Liberalism therefore objects to the socialization of the means of production. It is illogical to say, as many etatists do, that liberalism is hostile to or hates the state, because it is opposed to the transfer of the ownership of railroads or cotton mills to the state. If a man says that sulphuric acid does not make a good hand lotion, he is not expressing hostility to sulphuric acid as such; he is simply giving his opinion concerning the limitations of its use.

It is not the task of this study to determine whether the program of liberalism or that of socialism is more adequate for the realization of those aims which are common to all political and social endeavors, i.e., the achievement of human happiness and welfare. We are only tracing the role played by liberalism and by antiliberalism —whether socialist or interventionist—in the evolution which resulted in the establishment of totalitarianism. We can therefore content ourselves with briefly sketching the outlines of the social and political program of liberalism and its working.

In an economic order based on private ownership of the means of production the market is the focal point of the system. The working of the market mechanism forces capitalists and entrepreneurs to produce so as to satisfy the consumers' needs as well and cheaply as the quantity and quality of material resources and of man power available and the state of technological knowledge allow. If they are not equal to this task, if they produce poor goods, or at too great cost, or not the commodities that the consumers demand most urgently, they suffer losses. Unless they change their methods to satisfy the consumers' needs better, they will finally be thrown out of their positions as capitalists and entrepreneurs. Other people who know better how to serve the consumer will replace them. Within the market society the working of the price mechanism makes the consumers supreme. They determine through the prices they pay and through the amount of their purchases both the quantity and quality of production. They determine directly the prices of consumers' goods, and thereby indirectly the prices of all material factors of production and the wages of all hands employed.

Within the market society each serves all his fellow citizens and each is served by them. It is a system of mutual exchange of services and commodities, a mutual giving and receiving. In that endless rotating mechanism the entrepreneurs and capitalists are the servants of the consumers. The consumers are the masters, to whose whims the entrepreneurs and the capitalists must adjust their investments and methods of production. The market chooses the entrepreneurs and the capitalists, and removes them as soon as they prove failures. The market is a democracy in which every penny gives a right to vote and where voting is repeated every day.

Outside of the market stands the social apparatus of compulsion and coercion, and its steersmen, the government. To state and government the duty is assigned of maintaining peace both at home and abroad. For only in peace can the economic system achieve its ends, the fullest satisfaction of human needs and wants.

But who should command the apparatus of compulsion and coercion? In other words, who should rule? It is one of the fundamental insights of liberal thought that government is based on opinion, and that therefore in the long run it cannot subsist if the men who form it and the methods they apply are not accepted by the majority of those ruled. If the conduct of political affairs does not suit them, the citizens will finally succeed in overthrowing the government by violent action and in replacing the rulers by men deemed more competent. The rulers are always a minority. They cannot stay in office if the majority is determined to turn them out. Revolution and civil war are the ultimate remedy for unpopular rule. For the sake of domestic peace, liberalism aims at democratic government. Democracy is therefore not a revolutionary institution. On the contrary, it is the very means of preventing revolutions. Democracy is a system providing for the peaceful adjustment of government to the will of the majority. When the men in office and their methods no longer please the majority of the nation, they will—in the next election—be eliminated, and replaced by other men and another system. Democracy aims at safeguarding peace within the country and among the citizens.

The goal of liberalism is the peaceful coöperation of all men. It aims at peace among nations too. When there is private ownership of the means of production everywhere and when the laws, the tribunals, and the administration treat foreigners and citizens on equal terms, it is of little importance where a country's frontiers are drawn. Nobody can derive any profit from conquest, but many can suffer losses from fighting. War no longer pays; there is no motive for aggression. The population of every territory is free to determine to which state it wishes to belong, or whether it prefers to establish a state of its own. All nations can coexist peacefully, because no nation is concerned about the size of its state.

This is, of course, a very cool and dispassionate plea for peace and democracy. It is the outcome of a utilitarian philosophy. It is as far from the mystical mythology of the divine right of kings as it is from the metaphysics of natural law or the natural and imprescriptible rights of man. It is founded upon considerations of common utility. Freedom, democracy, peace, and private property are deemed good because they are the best means for promoting human happiness and welfare. Liberalism wants to secure to man a life free from fear and want. That is all.

About the middle of the nineteenth century liberals were convinced that they were on the eve of the realization of their plans. It was an illusion.

4. Socialism

Socialism aims at a social system based on public ownership of the means of production. In a socialist community all material resources are owned and operated by the government. This implies that the government is the only employer, and that no one can consume more than the government allots to him. The term "state socialism" is pleonastic; socialism is necessarily always state socialism. Planning is nowadays a popular synonym for socialism. Until 1917 communism and socialism were usually used as synonyms. The fundamental document of Marxian socialism, which all socialist parties united in the different International Working Men's Associations considered and still consider the eternal and unalterable gospel of socialism is entitled the *Communist Manifesto*. Since the ascendancy of Russian Bolshevism most people differentiate between communism and socialism. But this differentiation refers only to political tactics. Present-day communists and socialists disagree only in respect to the methods to be applied for the achievement of ends which are common to both.

The German Marxian socialists called their party the Social Democrats. It was believed that socialism was compatible with democratic government—indeed that the program of democracy could be fully realized only within a socialist community. In Western Europe and in America this opinion is still current. In spite of all the experience which events since 1917 have provided, many cling stubbornly to the belief that true democracy and true socialism are identical. Russia, the classical country of dictatorial oppression, is considered democratic because it is socialist.

However, the Marxians' love of democratic institutions was a stratagem only, a pious fraud for the deception of the masses.* Within a socialist community there is no room left for freedom. There can be no freedom of the press where the government owns every printing office. There can be no free choice of profession or trade where the government is the only employer and assigns everyone the task he must fulfill. There can be no freedom to settle where one chooses when the government has the power to fix one's place

* Bukharin, *Program of the Communists (Bolshevists)*, p. 29.

of work. There can be no real freedom of scientific research where the government owns all the libraries, archives, and laboratories and has the right to send anyone to a place where he cannot continue his investigations. There can be no freedom in art and literature where the government determines who shall create them. There can be neither freedom of conscience nor of speech where the government has the power to remove any opponent to a climate which is detrimental to his health, or to assign him duties which surpass his strength and ruin him both physically and intellectually. In a socialist community the individual citizen can have no more freedom than a soldier in the army or an inmate in an orphanage.

But, object the socialists, the socialist commonwealth differs in this essential respect from such organizations: the inhabitants have the right to choose the government. They forget, however, that the right to vote becomes a sham in a socialist state. The citizens have no sources of information but those provided by the government. The press, the radio, and the meeting halls are in the hands of the administration. No party of opposition can be organized or can propagate its ideas. We have only to look to Russia or Germany to discover the true meaning of elections and plebiscites under socialism.

The conduct of economic affairs by a socialist government cannot be checked by the vote of parliamentary bodies or by the control of the citizens. Economic enterprises and investments are designed for long periods. They require many years for preparation and realization; their fruits ripen late. If a penal law has been promulgated in May, it can be repealed without harm or loss in October. If a minister of foreign affairs has been appointed, he can be discharged a few months later. But if industrial investments have been once started, it is necessary to cling to the undertaking until it is achieved and to exploit the plant erected as long as it seems profitable. To change the original plan would be wasteful. This necessarily implies that the personnel of the government cannot be easily disposed of. Those who made the plan must execute it. They must later operate the plants erected, because others cannot take over the responsibility for their proper management. People who once agree to the famous four- and five-year plans virtually abandon their right to change the system and the personnel of government not only for the duration of four or five years but for the following years too, in which the planned investments have to be utilized. Consequently a socialist government must stay in office for an indefinite period. It is no longer the executor of the nation's will; it cannot be discharged without sensible detriment if its actions no longer suit the people. It has irrevocable powers. It becomes an authority above the people; it thinks and acts for the community in its own right and does not tolerate interference with "its own business" by outsiders.*

The entrepreneur in a capitalist society depends upon the market and upon the consumers. He has to obey the orders which the consumers transmit to him by their buying or failure to buy, and the mandate with which they have charged him can be revoked at any hour. Every entrepreneur and every owner of means of production must daily justify his social function through subservience to the wants of the consumers.

The management of a socialist economy is not under the necessity of adjusting itself to the operation of a market. It has an absolute monopoly. It does not depend on the wants of the consumers. It itself decides what must be done. It does not serve the consumers as the businessman does. It provides for them as the father provides for his children or the headmaster of a school for the students. It is the authority bestowing favors, not a businessman eager to attract customers. The salesman thanks the customer for patronizing his shop and asks him to come again. But the socialists say: Be grateful to Hitler, render thanks to Stalin; be nice and submissive, then the great man will be kind to you later too.

The prime means of democratic control of the administration is the budget. Not a clerk may be appointed, not a pencil bought, if Parliament has not made an allotment. The government must account for every penny spent. It is unlawful to exceed the allotment or to spend it for other purposes than those fixed by Parliament. Such restrictions are impracticable for the management of plants, mines, farms, and transportation systems. Their expenditure must be adjusted to the changing conditions of the moment. You cannot fix in advance how much is to be spent to clear fields of weeds or to remove snow from railroad tracks. This must be decided on the spot according to circumstances. Budget control by the people's representatives, the most effective weapon of democratic government, disappears in a socialist state.

Thus socialism must lead to the dissolution of democracy. The sovereignty of the consumers and the democracy of the market are the characteristic features of the capitalist system. Their corollary in the realm of politics is the people's sovereignty and democratic control of government. Pareto, Georges Sorel, Lenin, Hitler, and Mussolini were right in denouncing democracy as a capitalist method. Every step which leads from capitalism toward planning is necessarily a step nearer to absolutism and dictatorship.

* Hayek, *Freedom and the Economic System* (Chicago, 1939), pp. 10 ff.

The advocates of socialism who are keen enough to realize this tell us that liberty and democracy are worthless for the masses. People, they say, want food and shelter; they are ready to renounce freedom and self-determination to obtain more and better bread by submitting to a competent paternal authority. To this the old liberals used to reply that socialism will not improve but on the contrary will impair the standard of living of the masses. For socialism is a less efficient system of production than capitalism. But this rejoinder also failed to silence the champions of socialism. Granted, many of them replied, that socialism may not result in riches for all but rather in a smaller production of wealth; nevertheless the masses will be happier under socialism, because they will share their worries with all their fellow citizens, and there will not be wealthier classes to be envied by poorer ones. The starving and ragged workers of Soviet Russia, they tell us, are a thousand times more joyful than the workers of the West who live under conditions which are luxurious compared to Russian standards; equality in poverty is a more satisfactory state than well-being where there are people who can flaunt more luxuries than the average man.

Such debates are vain because they miss the central point. It is useless to discuss the alleged advantages of socialist management. Complete socialism is simply impracticable; it is not at all a system of production; it results in chaos and frustration.

The fundamental problem of socialism is the problem of economic calculation. Production within a system of division of labor, and thereby social coöperation, requires methods for the computation of expenditures asked for by different thinkable and possible ways of achieving ends. In capitalist society market prices are the units of this calculation. But within a system where all factors of production are owned by the state there is no market, and consequently there are no prices for these factors. Thus it becomes impossible for the managers of a socialist community to calculate. They cannot know whether what they are planning and achieving is reasonable or not. They have no means of finding out which of the various methods of production under consideration is the most advantageous. They cannot find a genuine basis of comparison between quantities of different material factors of production and of different services; so they cannot compare the outlays necessary with the anticipated outputs. Such comparisons need a common unit; and there is no such unit available but that provided by the price system of the market. The socialist managers cannot know whether the construction of a new railroad line is more advantageous than the construction of a new motor road. And if they have once decided on the construction of a railroad, they cannot know which of many possible routes it should cover. Under a system of private ownership money calculations are used to solve such problems. But no such calculation is possible by comparing various classes of expenditures and incomes in kind. It is out of the question to reduce to a common unit the quantities of various kinds of skilled and unskilled labor, iron, coal, building materials of different types, machinery, and everything else that the building, the upkeep, and the operation of railroads necessitates. But without such a common unit it is impossible to make these plans the subject of economic calculations. Planning requires that all the commodities and services which we have to take into account can be reduced to money. The management of a socialist community would be in a position like that of a ship captain who had to cross the ocean with the stars shrouded by a fog and without the aid of a compass or other equipment of nautical orientation.

Socialism as a universal mode of production is impracticable because it is impossible to make economic calculations within a socialist system. The choice for mankind is not between two economic systems. It is between capitalism and chaos.

5. Socialism in Russia and in Germany

The attempts of the Russian Bolsheviks and of the German Nazis to transform socialism from a program into reality have not had to meet the problem of economic calculation under socialism. These two socialist systems have been working within a world the greater part of which still clings to a market economy. The rulers of these socialist states base the calculations on which they make their decisions on the prices established abroad. Without the help of these prices their actions would be aimless and planless. Only in so far as they refer to this price system are they able to calculate, keep books, and prepare their plans. With this fact in mind we may agree with the statement of various socialist authors and politicians that socialism in only one or a few countries is not yet true socialism. Of course these men attach a quite different meaning to their assertions. They are trying to say that the full blessings of socialism can be reaped only in a world-embracing socialist community. The rest of us, on the contrary, must recognize that socialism will result in complete chaos precisely if it is applied in the greater part of the world.

The German and the Russian systems of socialism have in common the fact that the government has full control of the means of production. It decides what shall be produced and how. It allots to each individual a share of consumer's goods for his consumption.

These systems would not have to be called socialist if it were otherwise.

But there is a difference between the two systems—though it does not concern the essential features of socialism.

The Russian pattern of socialism is purely bureaucratic. All economic enterprises are departments of the government, like the administration of the army or the postal system. Every plant, shop, or farm stands in the same relation to the superior central organization as does a post office to the office of the postmaster general.

The German pattern differs from the Russian one in that it (seemingly and nominally) maintains private ownership of the means of production and keeps the appearance of ordinary prices, wages, and markets. There are, however, no longer entrepreneurs but only shop managers (*Betriebsführer*). These shop managers do the buying and selling, pay the workers, contract debts, and pay interest and amortization. There is no labor market; wages and salaries are fixed by the government. The government tells the shop managers what and how to produce, at what prices and from whom to buy, at what prices and to whom to sell. The government decrees to whom and under what terms the capitalists must entrust their funds and where and at what wages laborers must work. Market exchange is only a sham. All the prices, wages, and interest rates are fixed by the central authority. They are prices, wages, and interest rates in appearance only; in reality they are merely determinations of quantity relations in the government's orders. The government, not the consumers, directs production. This is socialism in the outward guise of capitalism. Some labels of capitalistic market economy are retained but they mean something entirely different from what they mean in a genuine market economy.

The execution of the pattern in each country is not so rigid as not to allow for some concessions to the other pattern. There are, in Germany too, plants and shops directly managed by government clerks; there is especially the national railroad system; there are the government's coal mines and the national telegraph and telephone lines. Most of these institutions are remnants of the nationalization carried out by the previous governments under the regime of German militarism. In Russia, on the other hand, there are some seemingly independent shops and farms left. But these exceptions do not alter the general characteristics of the two systems.

It is not an accident that Russia adopted the bureaucratic pattern and Germany the *Zwangswirtschaft* pattern. Russia is the largest country in the world and is thinly inhabited. Within its borders it has the richest resources. It is much better endowed by nature than any other country. It can without too great harm to the well-being of its population renounce foreign trade and live in economic self-sufficiency. But for the obstacles which Czarism first put in the way of capitalist production, and for the later shortcomings of the Bolshevik system, the Russians even without foreign trade could have long enjoyed the highest standard of living in the world. In such a country the application of the bureaucratic system of production is not impossible, provided the management is in a position to use for economic calculation the prices fixed on the markets of foreign capitalist countries, and to apply the techniques developed by the enterprise of foreign capitalism. Under these circumstances socialism results not in complete chaos but only in extreme poverty. A few years ago in the Ukraine, the most fertile land of Europe, many millions literally died of starvation.

In a predominantly industrial country conditions are different. The characteristic feature of a predominantly industrial country is that its population must live to a great extent on imported food and imported raw materials.* It must pay for these imports by the export of manufactured goods, which it produces mainly from imported raw materials. Its vital strength lies in its factories and in its foreign trade. Jeopardizing the efficiency of industrial production is equivalent to imperiling the basis of sustenance. If the plants produce worse or at higher cost they cannot compete in the world market, where they must outdo commodities of foreign origin. If exports drop, imports of food and other necessities drop correspondingly; the nation loses its main source of living.

Now Germany is a predominantly industrial country. It did very well when, in the years preceding the first World War, its entrepreneurs steadily expanded their exports. There was no other country in Europe in which the standard of living of the masses improved faster than in imperial Germany. For German socialism there could be no question of imitating the Russian model. To have attempted this would have immediately destroyed the apparatus of German export trade. It would have suddenly plunged into misery a nation pampered by the achievements of capitalism. Bureaucrats cannot meet the competition of foreign markets; they flourish only where they are sheltered by the state, with its compulsion and coercion. Thus the German socialists were forced to take recourse to the methods which they called German socialism. These methods, it is true, are much less efficient than that of private initiative. But they

* The United States, although the country with the most efficient and greatest industry, is not a *predominantly* industrial country, as it enjoys an equilibrium between its processing industries and its production of food and raw materials. On the other hand Austria, whose industry is small compared with that of America, is predominantly industrial because it depends to a great extent on the import of food and raw materials and must export almost half of its industrial output.

are much more efficient than the bureaucratic system of the Soviets.

This German system has an additional advantage. The German capitalists and the Betriebsführer, the former entrepreneurs, do not believe in the eternity of the Nazi regime. They are, on the contrary, convinced that the rule of Hitler will collapse one day and that then they will be restored to the ownership of the plants which in pre-Nazi days were their property. They remember that in the first World War too the Hindenburg program had virtually dispossessed them, and that with the breakdown of the imperial government they were *de facto* reinstated. They believe that it will happen again. They are therefore very careful in the operation of the plants whose nominal owners and shop managers they are. They do their best to prevent waste and to maintain the capital invested. It is only thanks to these selfish interests of the Betriebsführer that German socialism secured an adequate production of armaments, planes, and ships.

Socialism would be impracticable altogether if established as a world-wide system of production, and thus deprived of the possibility of making economic calculations. When confined to one or a few countries in the midst of a world capitalist economy it is only an inefficient system. And of the two patterns for its realization the German is less inefficient than the Russian one.

6. Interventionism

All civilizations have up to now been based on private ownership of the means of production. In the past civilization and private ownership have been linked together. If history could teach us anything, it would be that private property is inextricably linked with civilization.

Governments have always looked askance at private property. Governments are never liberal from inclination. It is in the nature of the men handling the apparatus of compulsion and coercion to overrate its power to work, and to strive at subduing all spheres of human life to its immediate influence. Etatism is the occupational disease of rulers, warriors, and civil servants. Governments become liberal only when forced to by the citizens.

From time immemorial governments have been eager to interfere with the working of the market mechanism. Their endeavors have never attained the ends sought. People used to attribute these failures to the inefficacy of the measures applied and to the leniency of their enforcement. What was wanted, they thought, was more energy and more brutality; then success would be assured. Not until the eighteenth century did men begin to understand that interventionism is necessarily doomed to fail. The classical economists demonstrated that each constellation of the market has a corresponding price structure. Prices, wages, and interest rates are the result of the interplay of demand and supply. There are forces operating in the market which tend to restore this—natural—state if it is disturbed. Government decrees, instead of achieving the particular ends they seek, tend only to derange the working of the market and imperil the satisfaction of the needs of the consumers.

In defiance of economic science the very popular doctrine of modern interventionism asserts that there is a system of economic coöperation, feasible as a permanent form of economic organization, which is neither capitalism nor socialism. This third system is conceived as an order based on private ownership of the means of production in which, however, the government intervenes, by orders and prohibitions, in the exercise of ownership rights. It is claimed that this system of interventionism is as far from socialism as it is from capitalism; that it offers a third solution of the problem of social organization; that it stands midway between socialism and capitalism; and that while retaining the advantages of both it escapes the disadvantages inherent in each of them. Such are the pretensions of interventionism as advocated by the older German school of etatism, by the American Institutionalists, and by many groups in other countries. Interventionism is practiced—except for socialist countries like Russia and Nazi Germany—by every contemporary government. The outstanding examples of interventionist policies are the *Sozialpolitik* of imperial Germany and the New Deal policy of present-day America.

Marxians do not support interventionism. They recognize the correctness of the teachings of economics concerning the frustration of interventionist measures. In so far as some Marxian doctrinaires have recommended interventionism they have done so because they consider it an instrument for paralyzing and destroying the capitalist economy, and hope thereby to accelerate the coming of socialism. But the consistent orthodox Marxians scorn interventionism as idle reformism detrimental to the interests of the proletarians. They do not expect to bring about the socialist utopia by hampering the evolution of capitalism; on the contrary, they believe that only a full development of the productive forces of capitalism can result in socialism. Consistent Marxians abstain from doing anything to interfere with what they deem to be the *natural* evolution of capitalism. But consistency is a very rare quality among Marxians. So most Marxian parties and the trade-unions operated by Marxians are enthusiastic in their support of interventionism.

A mixture of capitalist and socialist principles is not feasible. If, within a society based on private ownership of the means of production, some of these means are publicly owned and operated, this does not make for a mixed system which combines socialism and capitalism. The enterprises owned and operated by the state or by municipalities do not alter the characteristic features of a market economy. They must fit themselves, as buyers of raw materials, of equipment and of labor, and as sellers of goods and services, into the scheme of the market economy. They are subject to the laws determining production for the needs of consumers. They must strive for profits or, at least, to avoid losses. When the government tries to eliminate or to mitigate this dependence by covering the losses of its plants and shops by drawing on the public funds, the only result is that this dependence is shifted to another field. The means for covering the losses must be raised by the imposition of taxes. But this taxation has its effect on the market. It is the working of the market mechanism, and not the government collecting the taxes, that decides upon whom the incidence of the taxes falls and how it affects production and consumption. The market, not the government, determines the working of those publicly operated enterprises.

Nor should interventionism be confused with the German pattern of socialism. It is the essential feature of interventionism that it does not aim at a total abolition of the market; it does not want to reduce private ownership to a sham and the entrepreneurs to the status of shop managers. The interventionist government does not want to do away with private enterprise; it wants only to regulate its working through isolated measures of interference. Such measures are not designed as cogs in an all-round system of orders and prohibitions destined to control the whole apparatus of production and distribution; they do not aim at replacing private ownership and a market economy by socialist planning.

In order to grasp the meaning and the effects of interventionism it is sufficient to study the working of the two most important types of intervention: interference by restriction and interference by price control.

Interference by restriction aims directly at a diversion of production from the channels prescribed by the market and the consumers. The government either forbids the manufacture of certain goods or the application of certain methods of production, or makes such methods more difficult by the imposition of taxes or penalties. It thus eliminates some of the means available for the satisfaction of human needs. The best-known examples are import duties and other trade barriers. It is obvious that all such measures make the people as a whole poorer, not richer. They prevent men from using their knowledge and ability, their labor and material resources as efficiently as they can. In the unhampered market forces are at work tending to utilize every means of production in a way that provides for the highest satisfaction of human wants. The interference of the government brings about a different employment of resources and thereby impairs the supply.

We do not need to ask here whether some restrictive measures could not be justified, in spite of the diminution of supply they cause, by advantages in other fields. We do not need to discuss the problem of whether the disadvantage of raising the price of bread by an import duty on wheat is outweighed by the increase in income of domestic farmers. It is enough for our purpose to realize that restrictive measures cannot be considered as measures of increasing wealth and welfare, but are instead expenditures. They are, like subsidies which the government pays out of the revenue collected by taxing the citizens, not measures of production policy but measures of spending. They are not parts of a system of creating wealth but a method of consuming it.

The aim of price control is to decree prices, wages, and interest rates different from those fixed by the market. Let us first consider the case of maximum prices, where the government tries to enforce prices lower than the market prices.

The prices set on the unhampered market correspond to an equilibrium of demand and supply. Everybody who is ready to pay the market price can buy as much as he wants to buy. Everybody who is ready to sell at the market price can sell as much as he wants to sell. If the government, without a corresponding increase in the quantity of goods available for sale, decrees that buying and selling must be done at a lower price, and thus makes it illegal either to ask or to pay the potential market price, then this equilibrium can no longer prevail. With unchanged supply there are now more potential buyers on the market, namely, those who could not afford the higher market price but are prepared to buy at the lower official rate. There are now potential buyers who cannot buy, although they are ready to pay the price fixed by the government or even a higher price. The price is no longer the means of segregating those potential buyers who may buy from those who may not. A different principle of selection has come into operation. Those who come first can buy; others are too late in the field. The visible outcome of this state of things is the sight of housewives and children standing in long lines before the groceries, a spectacle familiar to everybody who has visited Europe in this age of price control. If the government does not want only those to buy who come first (or who are personal friends of the salesman), while others go home empty handed, it must regulate the distribution of the stocks available. It has to introduce some kind of rationing.

But price ceilings not only fail to increase the supply, they reduce it. Thus they do not attain the ends which the authorities wish. On the contrary, they result in a state of things which from the point of view of the government and of public opinion is even less desirable than the previous state which they had intended to alter. If the government wants to make it possible for the poor to give their children more milk, it has to buy the milk at the market price and sell it to these poor parents with a loss, at a cheaper rate. The loss may be covered by taxation. But if the government simply fixes the price of milk at a lower rate than the market, the result will be the contrary of what it wants. The marginal producers, those with the highest costs, will, in order to avoid losses, go out of the business of producing and selling milk. They will use their cows and their skill for other, more profitable purposes. They will, for example, produce cheese, butter, or meat. There will be less milk available for the consumers, not more. Then the government has to choose between two alternatives: either to refrain from any endeavors to control the price of milk and to abrogate its decree, or to add to its first measure a second one. In the latter case it must fix the prices of the factors of production necessary for the production of milk at such a rate that the marginal producers will no longer suffer losses and will abstain from restricting the output. But then the same problem repeats itself on a remoter plane. The supply of the factors of production necessary for the production of milk drops, and again the government is back where it started, facing failure in its interference. If it keeps stubbornly on pushing forward its schemes, it has to go still further. It has to fix the prices of the factors of production necessary for the production of those factors of production which are needed for the production of milk. Thus the government is forced to go further and further, fixing the prices of all consumer goods and of all factors of production—both human (i.e., labor) and material—and to force every entrepreneur and every worker to continue work at these prices and wages. No branch of industry can be omitted from this all-round fixing of prices and wages and from this general order to produce those quantities which the government wants to see produced. If some branches were to be left free, the result would be a shifting of capital and labor to them and a corresponding fall of the supply of goods whose prices the government has fixed. However, it is precisely these goods which the government considers especially important for the satisfaction of the needs of the masses.*

But when this state of all-round control of business is achieved, the market economy has been replaced by the German pattern of socialist planning. The government's board of production management now exclusively controls all business activities and decides how the means of production—men and material resources—must be used.

The isolated measures of price fixing fail to attain the ends sought. In fact, they produce effects contrary to those aimed at by the government. If the government, in order to eliminate these inexorable and unwelcome consequences, pursues its course further and further, it finally transforms the system of capitalism and free enterprise into socialism.

Many American and British supporters of price control are fascinated by the alleged success of Nazi price control. They believe that the German experience has proved the practicability of price control within the framework of a system of market economy. You have only to be as energetic, impetuous, and brutal as the Nazis are, they think, and you will succeed. These men who want to fight Nazism by adopting its methods do not see that what the Nazis have achieved has been the building up of a system of socialism, not a reform of conditions within a system of market economy.

There is no third system between a market economy and socialism. Mankind has to choose between those two systems—unless chaos is considered an alternative.†

It is the same when the government takes recourse to minimum prices. Practically the most important case of fixing prices at a higher level than that established on the unhampered market is the case of minimum wages. In some countries minimum wage rates are decreed directly by the government. The governments of other countries interfere only indirectly with wages. They give a free hand to the labor unions by acquiescing in the use of compulsion and coercion by unions against reluctant employers and employees. If it were otherwise strikes would not attain the ends which the trade-unions want to attain. The strike would fail to force the employer to grant higher wages than those fixed by the unhampered market, if he were free to employ men to take the place of the strikers. The essence of labor-union policy today is the application or threat of violence under the benevolent protection of the gov-

---

* For the two situations in which price-control measures can be used effectively within a narrowly confined sphere, the reader is referred to Mises' *Nationalökonomie*, pp. 674–675.

† We pass over the fact that, because of the impossibility of economic calculation under it, socialism too must result in chaos.

ernment. The unions represent, therefore, a vital part of the state apparatus of compulsion and coercion. Their fixing of minimum wage rates is equivalent to a government intervention establishing minimum wages.

The labor unions succeed in forcing the entrepreneurs to grant higher wages. But the result of their endeavors is not what people usually ascribe to them. The artificially elevated wage rates cause permanent unemployment of a considerable part of the potential labor force. At these higher rates the marginal employments for labor are no longer profitable. The entrepreneurs are forced to restrict output, and the demand on the labor market drops. The unions seldom bother about this inevitable result of their activities; they are not concerned with the fate of those who are not members of their brotherhood. But it is different for the government, which aims at the increase of the welfare of the whole people and wants to benefit not only union members but all those who have lost their jobs. The government wants to raise the income of all workers; that a great many of them cannot find employment is contrary to its intentions.

These dismal effects of minimum wages have become more and more apparent the more trade-unionism has prevailed. As long as only one part of labor, mostly skilled workers was unionized, the wage rise achieved by the unions did not lead to unemployment but to an increased supply of labor in those branches of business where there were no efficient unions or no unions at all. The workers who lost their jobs as a consequence of union policy entered the market of the free branches and caused wages to drop in those branches. The corollary of the rise in wages for organized workers was a drop in wages for unorganized workers. But with the spread of unionism conditions have changed. Workers now losing their jobs in one branch of industry find it harder to get employment in other lines. They are victimized.

There is unemployment even in the absence of any government or union interference. But in an unhampered labor market there prevails a tendency to make unemployment disappear. The fact that the unemployed are looking for jobs must result in fixing wage rates at a height which makes it possible for the entrepreneurs to employ all those eager to work and to earn wages. But if minimum wage rates prevent an adjustment of wage rates to the conditions of demand and supply, unemployment tends to become a permanent mass phenomenon.

There is but one means to make market wage rates rise for all those eager to work: an increase in the amount of capital goods available which makes it possible to improve technological methods of production and thereby to raise the marginal productivity of labor. It is a sad fact that a great war, in destroying a part of the stock of capital goods, must result in a temporary fall in real wage rates, when the shortage of man power brought about by the enlistment of millions of men is once overcome. It is precisely because they are fully aware of this undesirable consequence that liberals consider war not only a political but also an economic disaster.

Government spending is not an appropriate means to brush away unemployment. If the government finances its spending by collecting taxes or by borrowing from the public, it curtails the private citizens' power to invest and to spend to the same extent that it increases its own spending capacity. If the government finances its spending by inflationary methods (issue of additional paper money or borrowing from the commercial banks) it brings about a general rise of commodity prices. If then *money wage rates* do not rise at all or not to the same extent as commodity prices, mass unemployment may disappear. But it disappears precisely because *real wage rates* have dropped.

Technological progress increases the productivity of human effort. The same amount of capital and labor can now produce more than before. A surplus of capital and labor becomes available for the expansion of already existing industries and for the development of new ones. "Technological unemployment" may occur as a transitory phenomenon. But very soon the unemployed will find new jobs either in the new industries or in the expanding old ones. Many millions of workers are today employed in industries which were created in the last decades. And the wage earners themselves are the main buyers of the products of these new industries.

There is but one remedy for lasting unemployment of great masses: the abandonment of the policy of raising wage rates by government decree or by the application or the threat of violence.

Those who advocate interventionism because they want to sabotage capitalism and thereby finally to achieve socialism are at least consistent. They know what they are aiming at. But those who do not wish to replace private property by German Zwangswirtschaft or Russian Bolshevism are sadly mistaken in recommending price control and labor-union compulsion.

The more cautious and sophisticated supporters of interventionism are keen enough to recognize that government interference with business fails in the long run to attain the ends sought. But, they assert, what is needed is immediate action, a short-run policy. Interventionism is good because its immediate effects are beneficial, even if its remoter consequences may be disastrous. Do not bother about tomorrow; only today counts. With regard to this attitude two points must be emphasized: (1) today, after years and decades of interventionist policies, we are already confronted with the long-run consequences of interventionism; (2) wage interventionism is bound to fail even in the short run, if not accompanied by corresponding measures of protectionism.

7. Etatism and Protectionism

Etatism—whether interventionism or socialism—is a national policy. The national governments of various countries adopt it. Their concern is whatever they consider favors the interests of their own nations. They are not troubled about the fate or the happiness of foreigners. They are free from any inhibitions which would prevent them from inflicting harm on aliens.

We have dealt already with how the policies of etatism hurt the well-being of the whole nation and even of the groups or classes which they are intended to benefit. For the purpose of this book it is still more important to emphasize that no national system of etatism can work within a world of free trade. Etatism and free trade in international relations are incompatible, not only in the long run but even in the short run. Etatism must be accompanied by measures severing the connections of the domestic market with foreign markets. Modern protectionism, with its tendency to make every country economically self-sufficient as far as possible, is inextricably linked with interventionism and its inherent tendency to turn into socialism. Economic nationalism is the unavoidable outcome of etatism.

In the past various doctrines and considerations induced governments to embark upon a policy of protectionism. Economics has exposed all these arguments as fallacious. Nobody tolerably familiar with economic theory dares today to defend these long since unmasked errors. They still play an important role in popular discussion; they are the preferred theme of demagogic fulminations; but they have nothing to do with present-day protectionism. Present-day protectionism is a necessary corollary of the domestic policy of government interference with business. Interventionism begets economic nationalism. It thus kindles the antagonisms resulting in war. An abandonment of economic nationalism is not feasible if nations cling to interference with business. Free trade in international relations requires domestic free trade. This is fundamental to any understanding of contemporary international relations.

It is obvious that all interventionist measures aiming at a rise in domestic prices for the benefit of domestic producers, and all measures whose immediate effect consists in a rise in domestic costs of production, would be frustrated if foreign products were not either barred altogether from competition on the domestic market or penalized when imported. When, other things being unchanged, labor legislation succeeds in shortening the hours of work or in imposing on the employer in another way additional burdens to the advantage of the employees, the immediate effect is a rise in production costs. Foreign producers can compete under more favorable conditions, both on the home market and abroad, than they could before.

The acknowledgment of this fact has long since given impetus to the idea of equalizing labor legislation in different countries. These plans have taken on more definite form since the international conference called by the German Government in 1890. They led finally in 1919 to the establishment of the International Labor Office in Geneva. The results obtained were rather meager. The only efficient way to equalize labor conditions all over the world would be freedom of migration. But it is precisely this which unionized labor of the better-endowed and comparatively underpopulated countries fights with every means available.

The workers of those countries where natural conditions of production are more favorable and the population is comparatively thin enjoy the advantages of a higher marginal productivity of labor. They get higher wages and have a higher standard of living. They are eager to protect their advantageous position by barring or restricting immigration.* On the other hand, they denounce as "dumping" the competition of goods produced abroad by foreign labor remunerated at a lower scale; and they ask for protection against the importation of such goods.

The countries which are comparatively overpopulated—i.e., in which the marginal productivity of labor is lower than in other countries—have but one means to compete with the more favored countries: lower wages and a lower standard of living. Wage rates are lower in Hungary and in Poland than in Sweden or in Canada because the natural resources are poorer and the population is greater in respect to them. This fact cannot be disposed of by an international agreement, or by the interference of an international labor office. The average standard of living is lower in Japan than

* Many Americans are not familiar with the fact that, in the years between the two world wars, almost all European nations had recourse to very strict anti-immigration laws. These laws were more rigid than the American laws, since most of them did not provide for any immigration quotas. Every nation was eager to protect its wage level —a low one when compared with American conditions—against the immigration of men from other countries in which wage rates were still lower. The result was mutual hatred and—in face of a threatening common danger—disunion.

in the United States because the same amount of labor produces less in Japan than in the United States.

Such being the conditions, the goal of international agreements concerning labor legislation and trade-union policies cannot be the equalization of wage rates, hours of work, or other such "pro-labor" measures. Their only aim could be to coördinate these things so that no changes in the previously prevailing conditions of competition resulted. If, for example, American laws or trade-union policies resulted in a 5 per cent rise in construction costs, it would be necessary to find out how much this increased the cost of production in the various branches of industry in which America and Japan are competing or could compete if the relation of production costs changed. Then it would be necessary to investigate what kind of measures could burden Japanese production to such an extent that no change in the competitive power of both nations would take place. It is obvious that such calculations would be extremely difficult. Experts would disagree with regard both to the methods to be used and the probable results. But even if this were not the case an agreement could not be reached. For it is contrary to the interests of Japanese workers to adopt such measures of compensation. It would be more advantageous for them to expand their export sales to the disadvantage of American exports; thus the demand for their labor would rise and the condition of Japanese workers improve effectively. Guided by this idea, Japan would be ready to minimize the rise in production costs effected by the American measures and would be reluctant to adopt compensatory measures. It is chimerical to expect that international agreements concerning socio-economic policies could be substituted for protectionism.

We must realize that practically every new pro-labor measure forced on employers results in higher costs of production and thereby in a change in the conditions of competition. If it were not for protectionism such measures would immediately fail to attain the ends sought. They would result only in a restriction of domestic production and consequently in an increase of unemployment. The unemployed could find jobs only at lower wage rates; if they were not prepared to acquiesce in this solution they would remain unemployed. Even narrow-minded people would realize that economic laws are inexorable, and that government interference with business cannot attain its ends but must result in a state of affairs which—from the point of view of the government and the supporters of its policy—is even less desirable than the conditions which it was designed to alter.

Protectionism, of course, cannot brush away the unavoidable

consequences of interventionism. It can only improve conditions in appearance; it can only conceal the true state of affairs. Its aim is to raise domestic prices. The higher prices provide a compensation for the rise in costs of production. The worker does not suffer a cut in money wages but he has to pay more for the goods he wants to buy. As far as the home market is concerned the problem is seemingly settled.

But this brings us to a new problem: monopoly.

8. Economic Nationalism and Domestic Monopoly Prices

The aim of the protective tariff is to undo the undesired consequences of the rise in domestic costs of production caused by government interference. The purpose is to preserve the competitive power of domestic industries in spite of the rise in costs of production.

However, the mere imposition of an import duty can attain this end only in the case of those commodities whose domestic production falls short of domestic demand. With industries producing more than is needed for domestic consumption a tariff alone would be futile unless supplemented by monopoly.

In an industrial European country, for example Germany, an import duty on wheat raises the domestic price to the level of the world market price plus the import duty. Although the rise in the domestic wheat price results in an expansion of domestic production on the one hand and a restriction of domestic consumption on the other hand, imports are still necessary for the satisfaction of domestic demand. As the costs of the marginal wheat dealer include both the world market price and the import duty, the domestic price goes up to this height.

It is different with those commodities that Germany produces in such quantities that a part can be exported. A German import duty on manufactures which Germany produces not only for the domestic market but for export too would be, as far as export trade is concerned, a futile measure to compensate for a rise in domestic costs of production. It is true that it would prevent foreign manufacturers from selling on the German market. But export trade must continue to be hampered by the rise in domestic production costs. On the other hand the competition between the domestic producers on the home market would eliminate those German plants in which production no longer paid with the rise in costs due to government interference. At the new equilibrium the domestic price would reach the level of the world market price plus a part of the import duty. Domestic consumption would now be lower than it was before the rise in domestic production costs and the imposition of the import duty. The restriction of domestic consumption and the falling off of exports mean a shrinking of production with consequent unemployment and an increased pressure on the labor market resulting in a drop in wage rates. The failure of the Sozialpolitik becomes manifest.*

But there is still another way out. The fact that the import duty has insulated the domestic market provides domestic producers with the opportunity to build up a monopolistic scheme. They can form a cartel and charge the domestic consumers monopoly prices which can go up to a level only slightly lower than the world market price plus the import duty. With their domestic monopoly profits they can afford to sell at lower prices abroad. Production goes on. The failure of the Sozialpolitik is skillfully concealed from the eyes of an ignorant public. But the domestic consumers must pay higher prices. What the worker gains by the rise in wage rates and by pro-labor legislation burdens him in his capacity as consumer.

But the government and the trade-union leaders have attained their goal. They can then boast that the entrepreneurs were wrong in predicting that higher wages and more labor legislation would make their plants unprofitable and hamper production.

Marxian myths have succeeded in surrounding the problem of monopoly with empty babble. According to the Marxian doctrines of imperialism, there prevails within an unhampered market society a tendency toward the establishment of monopolies. Monopoly, according to these doctrines, is an evil originating from the operation of the forces working in an unhampered capitalism. It is, in the eyes of the reformers, the worst of all drawbacks of the laissez-faire system; its existence is the best justification of interventionism; it must be the foremost aim of government interference with business to fight it. One of the most serious consequences of monopoly is that it begets imperialism and war.

There are, it is true, instances in which a monopoly—a world monopoly—of some products could possibly be established without the support of governmental compulsion and coercion. The fact that the natural resources for the production of mercury are very few, for example, might engender a monopoly even in the absence of governmental encouragement. There are instances, again, in

---

* We need not consider the case of import duties so low that only a few or none of the domestic plants can continue production for the home market. In this case foreign competitors could penetrate the domestic market, and prices would reach the level of the world market price plus the whole import duty. The failure of the tariff would be even more manifest.

which the high cost of transportation makes it possible to establish local monopolies for bulky goods, e.g., for some building materials in places unfavorably located. But this is not the problem with which most people are concerned when discussing monopoly. Almost all the monopolies that are assailed by public opinion and against which governments pretend to fight are government made. They are national monopolies created under the shelter of import duties. They would collapse with a regime of free trade.

The common treatment of the monopoly question is thoroughly mendacious and dishonest. No milder expression can be used to characterize it. It is the aim of the government to raise the domestic price of the commodities concerned above the world market level, in order to safeguard in the short run the operation of its pro-labor policies. The highly developed manufactures of Great Britain, the United States, and Germany would not need any protection against foreign competition were it not for the policies of their own governments in raising costs of domestic production. But these tariff policies, as shown in the case described above, can work only when there is a cartel charging monopoly prices on the domestic market. In the absence of such a cartel domestic production would drop, as foreign producers would have the advantage of producing at lower costs than those due to the new pro-labor measure. A highly developed trade-unionism, supported by what is commonly called "progressive labor legislation," would be frustrated even in the short run if domestic prices were not maintained at a higher level than that of the world market, and if the exporters (if exports are to be continued) were not in a position to compensate the lower export prices out of the monopolistic profits drawn on the home market. Where the domestic cost of production is raised by government interference, or by the coercion and compulsion exercised by trade-unions, export trade will need to be subsidized. The subsidies may be openly granted as such by the government, or they may be disguised by monopoly. In this second case the domestic consumers pay the subsidies in the form of higher prices for the commodities which the monopoly sells at a lower price abroad. If the government were sincere in its antimonopolistic gestures, it could find a very simple remedy. The repeal of the import duty would brush away at one stroke the danger of monopoly. But governments and their friends are eager to raise domestic prices. Their struggle against monopoly is only a sham.

The correctness of the statement that it is the aim of the governments to raise prices can easily be demonstrated by referring to conditions in which the imposition of an import duty does not result in the establishment of a cartel monopoly. The American farmers producing wheat, cotton, and other agricultural products cannot, for technical reasons, form a cartel. Therefore the administration developed a scheme to raise prices through restriction of output and through withholding huge stocks from the market by means of government buying and government loans. The ends arrived at by this policy are a substitute for an infeasible farming cartel and farming monopoly.

No less conspicuous are the endeavors of various governments to create international cartels. If the protective tariff results in the formation of a national cartel, international cartelization could in many cases be attained by agreements between the national cartels. Such agreements are often very well served by another pro-monopoly activity of governments, the patents and other privileges granted to new inventions. However, where technical obstacles prevent the construction of national cartels—as is almost always the case with agricultural production—no such international agreements can be built up. Then the governments interfere again. History between the two world wars is an open record of state intervention to foster monopoly and restriction by international agreements. There were schemes for wheat pools, rubber and tin restrictions, and so on.* Of course, most of them collapsed very quickly.

Such is the true story of modern monopoly. It is not an outcome of unhampered capitalism and of an inherent trend of capitalist evolution, as the Marxians would have us believe. It is, on the contrary, the result of government policies aiming at a reform of market economy.

9. Autarky

Interventionism aims at state control of market conditions. As the sovereignty of the national state is limited to the territory subject to its supremacy and has no jurisdiction outside its boundaries, it considers all kinds of international economic relations as serious obstacles to its policy. The ultimate goal of its foreign trade policy is economic self-sufficiency. The avowed tendency of this policy is, of course, only to reduce imports as far as possible; but as exports have no purpose but to pay for imports, they drop concomitantly.

The striving after economic self-sufficiency is even more violent in the case of socialist governments. In a socialist community production for domestic consumption is no longer directed by the tastes and wishes of the consumers. The central board of production management provides for the domestic consumer according

* G. L. Schwartz, "Back to Free Enterprise," *Nineteenth Century and After,* CXXXI (1942), 130.

to its own ideas of what serves him best; it *takes care of the people* but it no longer *serves* the consumer. But it is different with production for export. Foreign buyers are not subject to the authorities of the socialist state; they have to be served; their whims and fancies have to be taken into account. The socialist government is sovereign in purveying to the domestic consumers, but in its foreign-trade relations it encounters the sovereignty of the foreign consumer. On foreign markets it has to compete with other producers producing better commodities at lower cost. We have mentioned earlier how the dependence on foreign imports and consequently on exports influences the whole structure of German socialism.*

The essential goal of socialist production, according to Marx, is the elimination of the market. As long as a socialist community is still forced to sell a part of its production abroad—whether to foreign socialist governments or to foreign business—it still produces for a market and is subject to the laws of the market economy. A socialist system is defective as such as long as it is not economically self-sufficient.

The international division of labor is a more efficient system of production than is the economic autarky of every nation. The same amount of labor and of material factors of production yields a higher output. This surplus production benefits everyone concerned. Protectionism and autarky always result in shifting production from the centers where conditions are more favorable—i.e., from where the output for the same amount of physical input is higher—to centers where they are less favorable. The more productive resources remain unused while the less productive are utilized. The effect is a general drop in the productivity of human effort, and thereby a lowering of the standard of living all over the world.

The economic consequences of protectionist policies and of the trend toward autarky are the same for all countries. But there are qualitative and quantitative differences. The social and political results are different for comparatively overpopulated industrial countries and for comparatively underpopulated agricultural countries. In the predominantly industrial countries the prices of the most urgently needed foodstuffs are going up. This interferes more and sooner with the well-being of the masses than the corresponding rise in the prices of manufactured goods in the predominantly agricultural countries. Besides, the workers in the industrial countries are in a better position to make their complaints heard than the farmers and farm hands in the agricultural countries. The statesmen and economists of the predominantly industrial coun-

* See above, p. 57.

tries become frightened. They realize that natural conditions are putting a check on their country's endeavors to replace imports of food and raw materials by domestic production. They clearly understand that the industrial countries of Europe can neither feed nor clothe their population out of domestic products alone. They foresee that the trend toward more protection, more insulation of every country, and finally self-sufficiency will bring about a tremendous fall in the standard of living, if not actual starvation. Thus they look around for remedies.

German aggressive nationalism is animated by these considerations. For more than sixty years German nationalists have been depicting the consequences which the protectionist policies of other nations must eventually have for Germany. Germany, they pointed out, cannot live without importing food and raw materials. How will it pay for these imports when one day the nations producing these materials have succeeded in the development of their domestic manufactures and bar access to German exports? There is, they told themselves, only one redress: We must conquer more dwelling space, more Lebensraum.

The German nationalists are fully aware that many other nations—for example, Belgium—are in the same unfavorable position. But, they say, there is a very important difference. These are small nations. They are therefore helpless. Germany is strong enough to conquer more space. And, happily for Germany, they say today, there are two other powerful nations, which are in the same position as Germany, namely, Italy and Japan. They are the natural allies of Germany in these wars of the have-nots against the haves.

Germany does not aim at autarky because it is eager to wage war. It aims at war because it wants autarky—because it wants to live in economic self-sufficiency.

10. German Protectionism

The second German Empire, founded at Versailles in 1871, was not only a powerful nation; it was—in spite of the depression which started in 1873—economically very prosperous. Its industrial plants were extremely successful in competing—abroad and at home—with foreign products. Some grumblers found fault with German manufactures; German goods, they said, were cheap but inferior. But the great foreign demand was precisely for such cheap goods. The masses put more stress upon cheapness than upon fine quality. Whoever wanted to increase sales had to cut prices.

In those optimistic 1870's everybody was fully convinced that

Europe was on the eve of a period of peace and prosperity. There were to be no more wars; trade barriers were doomed to disappear; men would be more eager to build up and to produce than to destroy and to kill each other. Of course, farsighted men could not overlook the fact that Europe's cultural preëminence would slowly vanish. Natural conditions for production were more favorable in overseas countries. Capitalism was on the point of developing the resources of backward nations. Some branches of production would not be able to stand the competition of the newly opened areas. Agricultural production and mining would drop in Europe; Europeans would buy such goods by exporting manufactures. But people did not worry. Intensification of the international division of labor was in their eyes not a disaster but on the contrary a source of richer supply. Free trade was bound to make all nations more flourishing.

The German liberals advocated free trade, the gold standard, and freedom of domestic business. German manufacturing did not need any protection. It triumphantly swept the world market. It would have been nonsensical to bring forward the infant-industry argument. German industry had reached its maturity.

Of course, there were still many countries eager to penalize imports. However, the inference from Ricardo's free-trade argument was irrefutable. Even if all other countries cling to protection, every nation serves its own interest best by free trade. Not for the sake of foreigners but for the sake of their own nation, the liberals advocated free trade. There was the great example set by Great Britain, and by some smaller nations, like Switzerland. These countries did very well with free trade. Should Germany adopt their policies? Or should it imitate half-barbarian nations like Russia?

But Germany chose the second path. This decision was a turning point in modern history.

There are many errors current concerning modern German protectionism.

It is important to recognize first of all that the teachings of Frederick List have nothing to do with modern German protectionism. List did not advocate tariffs for agricultural products. He asked for protection of infant industries. In doing this he underrated the competitive power of contemporary German manufacturing. Even in those days, in the early 1840's, German industrial production was already much stronger than List believed. Thirty to forty years later it was paramount on the European continent and could very successfully compete on the world market. List's doctrines played an important role in the evolution of protectionism in Eastern Europe and in Latin America. But the German supporters of protectionism were not justified in referring to List. He did not unconditionally reject free trade; he advocated protection of manufacturing only for a period of transition, and he nowhere suggested protection for agriculture. List would have violently opposed the trend of German foreign-trade policy of the last sixty-five years.

The representative literary champion of modern German protectionism was Adolf Wagner. The essence of his teachings is this: All countries with an excess production of foodstuffs and raw materials are eager to develop domestic manufacturing and to bar access to foreign manufactures; the world is on the way to economic self-sufficiency for each nation. In such a world what will be the fate of those nations which can neither feed nor clothe their citizens out of domestic foodstuffs and raw materials? They are doomed to starvation.

Adolf Wagner was not a keen mind. He was a poor economist. The same is true of his partisans. But they were not so dull as to fail to recognize that protection is not a panacea against the dangers which they depicted. The remedy they recommended was conquest of more space—war. They asked for protection of German agriculture in order to encourage production on the poor soil of the country, because they wanted to make Germany independent of foreign supplies of food for the impending war. Import duties for food were in their eyes a short-run remedy only, a measure for a period of transition. The ultimate remedy was war and conquest.

It would be wrong, however, to assume that the incentive to Germany's embarking upon protectionism was a propensity to wage war. Wagner, Schmoller, and the other socialists of the chair, in their lectures and seminars, long preached the gospel of conquest. But before the end of the 'nineties they did not dare to propagate such views in print. Considerations of war economy, moreover, could justify protection only for agriculture; they were not applicable in the case of protection for the processing industries. The military argument of war preparedness did not play an important role in the protection of Germany's industrial production.

The main motive for the tariff on manufactures was the Sozialpolitik. The pro-labor policy raised the domestic costs of production and made it necessary to safeguard the policy's short-run effects. Domestic prices had to be raised above the world market level in order to escape the dilemma of either lower money wages or a restriction of exports and increase of unemployment. Every new progress of the Sozialpolitik, and every successful strike, disarranged conditions to the disadvantage of the German enterprises and made it harder for them to outdo foreign competitors both on the domestic and on the foreign markets. The much glorified Sozial-politik was only possible within an economic body sheltered by tariffs.

Thus Germany developed its characteristic system of cartels. The cartels charged the domestic consumers high prices and sold cheaper abroad. What the worker gained from labor legislation and union wages was absorbed by higher prices. The government and the trade-union leaders boasted of the apparent success of their policies: the workers received higher *money* wages. But *real* wages did not rise more than the marginal productivity of labor.

Only a few observers saw through all this, however. Some economists tried to justify industrial protectionism as a measure for safeguarding the fruits of Sozialpolitik and of unionism; they advocated *social protectionism (den sozialen Schutzzoll)*. They failed to recognize that the whole process demonstrated the futility of coercive government and union interference with the conditions of labor. The greater part of public opinion did not suspect at all that Sozialpolitik and protection were closely linked together. The trend toward cartels and monopoly was in their opinion one of the many disastrous consequences of capitalism. They bitterly indicted the greediness of capitalists. The Marxians interpreted it as that concentration of capital which Marx had predicted. They purposely ignored the fact that it was not an outcome of the free evolution of capitalism but the result of government interference, of tariffs and—in the case of some branches, like potash and coal—of direct government compulsion. Some of the less shrewd socialists of the chair (Lujo Brentano, for example) went so far in their inconsistency as to advocate at the same time free trade and a more radical pro-labor policy.

In the thirty years preceding the first World War Germany could eclipse all other European countries in pro-labor policies because it above all indulged in protectionism and subsequently in cartelization.

When, later, in the course of the depression of 1929 and the following years, unemployment figures went up conspicuously because trade-unions would not accept a reduction of boom wage rates, the comparatively mild tariff protectionism turned into the hyper-protectionist policies of the quota system, monetary devaluation, and foreign exchange control. At that time Germany was no longer ahead in pro-labor policies; other countries had surpassed it. Great Britain, once the champion of free trade, adopted the German idea of social protection. So did all other countries. Up-to-date hyper-protectionism is the corollary of present-day Sozialpolitik.

There cannot be any doubt that for nearly sixty years Germany set the example in Europe both of Sozialpolitik and of protectionism. But the problems involved are not Germany's problems alone.

The most advanced countries of Europe have poor domestic resources. They are comparatively overpopulated. They are in a very unlucky position indeed in the present trend toward autarky, migration barriers, and expropriation of foreign investments. Insulation means for them a severe fall in standards of living. After the present war Great Britain—with its foreign assets gone—will be in the same position as Germany. The same will be true for Italy, Belgium, Switzerland. Perhaps France is better off because it has long had a low birth rate. But even the smaller, predominantly agricultural countries of the European East are in a critical position. How should they pay for imports of cotton, coffee, various minerals, and so on? Their soil is much poorer than that of Canada or the American wheat belt; its products cannot compete on the world market.

Thus the problem is not a German one; it is a European problem. It is a German problem only to the extent that the Germans tried—in vain—to solve it by war and conquest.

IV. ETATISM AND NATIONALISM

1. The Principle of Nationality

IN the early nineteenth century the political vocabulary of the citizens of the United Kingdom of Great Britain and Ireland did not differentiate between the concepts state, people, and nation. The conquests which expanded the realm and brought countries and their inhabitants into subjection did not alter the size of the nation and the state. These annexed areas, as well as the overseas settlements of British subjects, remained outside the state and the nation. They were property of the crown under the control of Parliament. The nation and the people were the citizens of the three kingdoms, England, Scotland, and Ireland. England and Scotland had formed a union in 1707; in 1801 Ireland joined this union. There was no intention of incorporating into this body the citizens settled beyond the sea in North America. Every colony had its own parliament and its own local government. When the Parliament of Westminster attempted to include in its jurisdiction the colonies of New England and those south of New England, it kindled the conflict which resulted in American independence. In the Declaration of Independence the thirteen colonies call themselves a people different from the people represented in the Parliament at Westminster. The individual colonies, having proclaimed their right to independence, formed a political union, and thus gave to the new nation, set up by nature and by history, an adequate political organization.

Even at the time of the American conflict British liberals sympathized with the aims of the colonists. In the course of the nineteenth century Great Britain fully recognized the right of the white settlers in overseas possessions to establish autonomous governments. The citizens of the dominions are not members of the British nation. They form nations of their own with all the rights to which civilized peoples are entitled. There has been no effort to expand the territory from which members are returned to the Parliament of Westminster. If autonomy is granted to a part of the Empire, that part becomes a state with its own constitution. The size of the territory whose citizens are represented in the Parliament at London has not expanded since 1801; it was narrowed by the founding of the Irish Free State.

For the French Revolutionists the terms state, nation, and people were also identical. France was for them the country within the historical frontiers. Foreign enclaves (like papal Avignon and the possessions of German princes) were according to natural law parts of France, and therefore to be reunited. The victorious wars of the Revolution and of Napoleon I temporarily relegated these notions to oblivion. But after 1815 they were restored to their previous meaning. France is the country within the frontiers fixed by the Congress of Vienna. Napoleon III later incorporated into this realm Savoy and Nice, districts with French-speaking inhabitants for whom there was no longer room left in the new Italian kingdom in which the state of Savoy-Piedmont-Sardinia had been merged. The French were not enthusiastic about this expansion of their country; the new districts were slow to be assimilated to the French commonwealth. The plans of Napoleon III to acquire Belgium, Luxembourg, and the left bank of the Rhine were not popular in France. The French do not consider the Walloons or the French-speaking Swiss or Canadians members of their nation or people. They are in their eyes French-speaking foreigners, good old friends, but not Frenchmen.

It was different with the German and Italian liberals. The states which they wanted to reform were products of dynastic warfare and intermarriage; they could not be considered natural entities. It would have been paradoxical indeed to destroy the despotism of the prince of *Reuss Junior Branch* in order to establish a democratic government in the scattered territories owned by that potentate. The subjects of such princelings did not consider themselves *Reussians of the Junior Branch* or *Saxe-Weimar-Eisenachians,* but Germans. They did not aim at a liberal *Schaumburg-Lippe.* They wanted a liberal Germany. It was the same in Italy. The Italian liberals did not fight for a free state of Parma or of Tuscany but for a free Italy. As soon as liberalism reached Germany and Italy the problem of the extent of the state and its boundaries was raised. Its solution seemed easy. The nation is the community of all people speaking the same language; the state's frontiers should coincide with the linguistic demarcations. Germany is the country inhabited by German-speaking people; Italy is the land of the people using the Italian idiom. The old border lines drawn by the intrigues of dynasties were doomed to disappear. Thus the right of self-determination and of government by the people, as expounded by Western liberalism, becomes transformed into the principle of nationality as soon as liberalism becomes a political factor in Central Europe. The political terminology begins to differentiate between state and nation (people). The people (the nation) are all men speaking the same idiom; nationality means community of language.

According to these ideas, every nation should form an independent state, including all members of the nation. When this has one day been achieved there will be no more wars. The princes fight each other because they wish to increase their power and wealth by conquest. No such motives are present with nations. The extent of a nation's territory is determined by nature. The national boundaries are the linguistic boundaries. No conquest can make a nation bigger, richer, or more powerful. The principle of nationality is the golden rule of international law which will bring undisturbed peace to Europe. While kings were still planning wars and conquests the revolutionary movements of Young Germany and of Young Italy were already coöperating for the realization of this happy constitution of a New Europe. The Poles and Hungarians joined the choir. Their aspirations also met with the sympathies of liberal Germany. German poets glorified the Polish and Hungarian struggles for independence.

But the aspirations of the Poles and Magyars differed in a very important way from those of the German and Italian liberals. The former aimed at a reconstruction of Poland and Hungary within their old historical boundaries. They did not look forward to a new liberal Europe but backward to the glorious past of their victorious kings and conquerors, as depicted by their historians and writers. Poland was for the Poles all the countries that their kings and magnates had once subjugated, Hungary was for the Magyars all the countries that had been ruled in the Middle Ages by the successors of Saint Stephen. It did not matter that these realms included many people speaking idioms other than Polish and Hungarian. The Poles and the Magyars paid lip service to the principles of nationality and self-determination; and this attitude made the liberals of the West sympathetic to their programs. Yet what they planned was not the liberation but the oppression of other linguistic groups.

So too with the Czechs. It is true that in earlier days some champions of Czech independence proposed a partition of Bohemia according to linguistic demarcations. But they were very soon silenced by their fellow citizens, for whom Czech self-determination was synonymous with the oppression of millions of non-Czechs.

The principle of nationality was derived from the liberal principle of self-determination. But the Poles, the Czechs, and the Magyars substituted for this democratic principle an aggressive nationalism aiming at the domination of people speaking other languages. Very soon German and Italian nationalists and many other linguistic groups adopted the same attitude.

It would be a mistake to ascribe the ascendancy of modern nationalism to human wickedness. The nationalists are not innately aggressive men; they become aggressive through their conception of nationalism. They are confronted with conditions which were unknown to the champions of the old principle of self-determination. And their etatist prejudices prevent them from finding a solution for the problems they have to face other than that provided by aggressive nationalism.

What the Western liberals have failed to recognize is that there are large territories inhabited by people of different idioms. This important fact could once be neglected in Western Europe but it could not be overlooked in Eastern Europe. The principle of nationality cannot work in a country where linguistic groups are inextricably mixed. Here you cannot draw boundaries which clearly segregate linguistic groups. Every territorial division necessarily leaves minorities under foreign rule.

The problem becomes especially fateful because of the changeability of linguistic structures. Men do not necessarily stay in the place of their birth. They have always migrated from comparatively overpopulated into comparatively underpopulated areas. In our age of rapid economic change brought about by capitalism, the propensity to migrate has increased to an unprecedented extent. Millions move from the agricultural districts into the centers of mining, trade, and industry. Millions move from countries where the soil is poor to those offering more favorable conditions for agriculture. These migrations transform minorities into majorities and vice versa. They bring alien minorities into countries formerly linguistically homogeneous.

The principle of nationality was based on the assumption that every individual clings throughout his life to the language of his parents, which he has learned in early childhood. This too is an error. Men can change their language in the course of their life; they can daily and habitually speak a language other than that of their parents. Linguistic assimilation is not always the spontaneous outcome of the conditions under which the individual lives. It is caused not only by environment and cultural factors; governments can encourage it or even achieve it by compulsion. It is an illusion to believe that language is a nonarbitrary criterion for an impartial delimitation of boundaries. The state can, under certain conditions, influence the linguistic character of its citizens.

The main tool of compulsory denationalization and assimilation is education. Western Europe developed the system of obligatory public education. It came to Eastern Europe as an achievement of Western civilization. But in the linguistically mixed territories it turned into a dreadful weapon in the hands of governments determined to change the linguistic allegiance of their subjects.

The philanthropists and pedagogues of England who advocated public education did not foresee what waves of hatred and resentment would rise out of this institution.

But the school is not the only instrument of linguistic oppression and tyranny. Etatism puts a hundred more weapons in the hands of the state. Every act of the government which can and must be done by administrative discretion with regard to the special merits of each case can be used for the achievement of the government's political aims. The members of the linguistic minority are treated like foes or like outlaws. They apply in vain for licenses, for foreign exchange under a system of foreign exchange control, or for import licenses under a quota system. Their shops and plants, their clubhouses, school buildings, and assembly halls are closed by the police because they allegedly do not comply with the rules of the building code or with the regulations for preventing fires. Their sons somehow fail to pass the examinations for civil service jobs. Protection is denied to their property, persons, and lives when they are attacked by armed gangs of zealous members of the ruling linguistic group. They cannot even undertake to defend themselves: the licenses required for the possession of arms are denied to them. The tax collectors always find that they owe the treasury much more than the amount shown on the returns they have filed.

All this indicates clearly why the attempts of the Covenant of the League of Nations to protect minorities by international law and international tribunals were doomed to failure. A law cannot protect anybody against measures dictated by alleged considerations of economic expediency. All sorts of government interference in business, in the countries inhabited by different linguistic groups, are used for the purpose of injuring the pariahs. Custom tariffs, taxation, foreign exchange regulations, subsidies, labor legislation, and so on may be utilized for discrimination, even though this cannot be proved in court procedure. The government can always explain these measures as being dictated by purely economic considerations. With the aid of such measures life for the undesirables, without formal violation of legal equality, can be made unbearable. In an age of interventionism and socialism there is no legal protection available against an ill-intentioned government. Every government interference with business becomes an act of national warfare against the members of the persecuted linguistic groups. With the progress of etatism the antagonism between the linguistic groups becomes more bitter and more implacable.

Thus the meaning of the concepts of Western political terminology underwent a radical change in Central and Eastern Europe. The people differentiate between the good state and the bad state.

They worship the state as do all other etatists. But they mean only the good state—i.e., the state in which their own linguistic group dominates. For them this state is God. The other states in which their own linguistic group does not dominate are, in their opinion, devils. Their concept of fellow citizens includes all people speaking their own language, all *Volksgenossen,* as the Germans say, without any regard to the country where they live; it does not include citizens of their own state who happen to speak another language. These are foes and barbarians. The Volksgenossen living under a foreign yoke must be freed. They are the Irredenta, the unredeemed people.

And every means is believed right and fair, if it can accelerate the coming of the day of redemption. Fraud, felonious assault, and murder are noble virtues if they serve the cause of Irredentism. The war for the liberation of the Volksgenossen is a just war. The greatness of the linguistic group and the glory of the right and true state are the supreme criteria of morality. There is but one thing that counts—their own linguistic group, the community of men speaking the same language, the *Volksgemeinschaft.*

2. The Linguistic Group

Economists, sociologists, and historians have provided us with different definitions of the term nation. But we are not interested here in what meaning social science ought to attach to it. We are inquiring what meaning the European supporters of the principle of nationality attach to the concepts nation and nationality. It is important to establish the way in which these terms are used in the vocabulary of present-day political action and the role they play in actual life and in contemporary conflicts.

The principle of nationality is unknown to American or Australian politics. When the Americans freed themselves from the rule of Great Britain, Spain, and Portugal their aim was self-determination, not the establishment of *national* states in the sense that the principle of nationality gives to the term nation. Linguistically they resembled the old countries overseas from which their ancestors once came to America. The people who now form the United States of America did not want to annex English-speaking Canada. Nor did the French-speaking Canadians who opposed the British system of administration fight for a French-speaking state. Both linguistic groups coöperate in a more or less peaceful way within the Dominion of Canada; there is no Irredenta. Latin America is also free from linguistic problems. What separates Argentina from Chile or Guatemala from Mexico is not the idiom.

There are many racial, social, political, and even religious conflicts in the Western Hemisphere too. But in the past no serious linguistic problem has troubled American political life.

Neither are there any grave linguistic antagonisms in present-day Asia. India is linguistically not homogeneous; but the religious discrepancy between Hinduism and Islam is much more important there than the problem of idioms.

Conditions may perhaps soon change. But at the present moment the principle of nationality is more or less a European concept. It is the main political problem of Europe.

According to the principle of nationality, then, every linguistic group must form an independent state, and this state must embrace all people speaking this language. The prestige of this principle is so great that a group of men who for some reason wish to form a state of their own which would otherwise not conform to the principle of nationality are eager to change their language in order to justify their aspirations in the light of this principle.

The Norwegians now speak and write an idiom that is almost identical with that of Denmark. But they are not prepared to renounce their political independence. To provide linguistic support for their political program, eminent Norwegians have wanted to create a language of their own; to form out of their local dialects a new language, something like a return to the old Norse used up to the fifteenth century. The greatest Norwegian writer, Henrik Ibsen, considered these endeavors lunacy and scorned them as such in *Peer Gynt.**

The people of Ireland speak and write English. Some of the foremost writers of the English language are Irishmen. But the Irish want to be politically independent. Therefore, they reason, it is necessary to return to the Gaelic idiom once used in their country. They have excavated this language from old books and manuscripts and try to revive it. To some extent they have even succeeded.

The Zionists want to create an independent state composed of those professing the Jewish religion. For them the Jews are a people and a nation. We are not concerned here with whether the historical arguments brought forward for the justification of these claims are correct or not, or whether the plan is politically sound or unsound. But it is a fact that the Jews speak many different languages; from the viewpoint of the principle of nationality the aspirations of Zionism are no less irregular than those of the Irish. Therefore the Zionists try to induce the Jews to speak and write Hebrew. These plans are paradoxical in the face of the fact that in the days of Christ the inhabitants of Palestine did not speak He-

* Act IV, scene in the lunatic asylum.

brew; their native tongue was Aramaic. Hebrew was the language of the religious literature only. It was not understood by the people. The second language generally known was Greek.*

These facts demonstrate the meaning and prestige of the principle of nationality. The terms nation and nationality as applied by the advocates of this principle are equivalent to the term "linguistic group." The terms used in the Habsburg Empire for these conflicts were *die nationale Frage* (the national question), and synonymously *die Sprachenfrage* (the linguistic problem), *nationale Kämpfe* (national struggles), and synonymously *Sprachenkämpfe* (linguistic struggles). The main subject of conflict has always been which language should be used by the administration, by the tribunals, and by the army, and which language should be taught in the schools?

It is a serious error of English and French books and newspapers to refer to these conflicts as racial. There is no conflict of races in Europe. No distinct bodily features which an anthropologist could establish with the aid of the scientific methods of anatomy separate the people belonging to different groups. If you presented one of them to an anthropologist he would not be able to decide by biological methods whether he was a German, Czech, Pole, or Hungarian.

Neither have the people belonging to any one of these groups a common descent. The right bank of the Elbe River, the whole of northeastern Germany, eight hundred years ago was inhabited only by Slavs and Baltic tribes. It became German-speaking in the course of the processes which the German historians call the colonization of the East. Germans from the west and south migrated into this area; but in the main its present population is descended from the indigenous Slavs and Baltic peoples who, under the influence of church and school, adopted the German language. Prussian chauvinists, of course, assert that the native Slavs and Balts were exterminated and that the whole population today is descended from German colonists. There is not the slightest evidence for this doctrine. The Prussian historians invented it in order to justify in the eyes of German nationalists Prussia's claim to hegemony in Germany. But even they have never dared to deny that the Slav ancestry of the autochthonous princely dynasties (of Pomerania, Silesia, and Mecklenburg) and of most of the aristocratic

---

* Kenyon, "The Bible as Christ Knew It," *The History of Christianity in the Light of Modern Knowledge* (London, 1929), p. 172. Some Zionists advocated Yiddish as the national language; but they did not succeed in establishing it. Yiddish is a German dialect with some words borrowed from Hebrew and more from the Slavonic languages. It is the dialect spoken by the Jews of German origin in northeastern Europe. The newspapers in Hebrew type printed and distributed in America are not written in Hebrew but in Yiddish.

families is beyond doubt. Queen Louise of Prussia, whom all German nationalists consider the paragon of German womanhood, was a scion of the ducal house of Mecklenburg, whose originally Slav character has never been contested. Many noble families of the German northeast can be traced back to Slav ancestors. The genealogical trees of the middle classes and the peasantry, of course, cannot be established as far back as those of the nobility; this alone explains why the proof of Slav origin cannot be provided for them. It is indeed paradoxical to assume that the Slavonic princes and knights should have exterminated their Slav serfs in order to settle their villages with imported German serfs.

Shifting from one of these linguistic groups to another occurred not only in earlier days. It happened and happens so frequently that nobody remarks upon it. Many outstanding personalities in the Nazi movement in Germany and Austria and in the Slavonic, Hungarian, and Rumanian districts claimed by Nazism were the sons of parents whose language was not German. Similar conditions prevail all over Europe. In many cases the change of loyalties has been accompanied by a change in family name; more often people have retained their foreign-sounding family names. The Belgian poets Maeterlinck and Verhaeren have written in French; their names suggest a Flemish ancestry. The Hungarian poet Alexander Petöfi, who died for the cause of the Hungarian revolution in the battle of Schässburg (1849), was the son of a Slavonic family named Petrovics. Thousands of such cases are known to everyone familiar with European soil and people. Europe too is a melting pot, or rather a collection of melting pots.

Whenever the question is raised whether a group must be considered a distinct nation and therefore entitled to claim political autonomy, the issue is whether the idiom involved is a distinct language or only a dialect. The Russians maintain that the Ukrainian or Ruthenian idiom is a dialect, like *Platt-Deutsch* in northern Germany or Provençal in southern France. The Czechs use the same argument against the political aspirations of the Slovaks, and the Italians against the Rhaeto-Romanic idiom. Only a few years ago the Swiss Government gave to the Romansh the legal status of a national language. Many Nazis declare that Dutch is not a language but a German dialect—a Platt which has arrogated to itself the status of a language.

The principle of nationality has been late in penetrating into the political thought of Switzerland. There are two reasons why Switzerland has up to now successfully resisted its disintegrating power.

The first factor is the quality of the three main languages of Switzerland: German, French, and Italian. For every inhabitant of continental Europe it is a great advantage to learn one of these languages. If a German-Swiss acquires command of French or Italian he not only becomes better equipped for business life but gains access to one of the great literatures of the world. It is the same for the French-Swiss and for the Italian-Swiss when learning Italian or German. The Swiss, therefore, do not object to a bilingual education. They consider it a great help for their children to know one or both of the two other main languages of the country. But what gain can a French-Belgian derive from a knowledge of Flemish, a Slovak from a knowledge of Hungarian, or a Hungarian from a knowledge of Rumanian? It is almost indispensable for an educated Pole or Czech to know German; but for a German it is a waste of time to learn Czech or Polish. This explains why the educational problem is of minor importance under the linguistic conditions of Switzerland.

The second factor is the political structure. The countries of eastern Europe were never liberal. They jumped from monarchical absolutism directly into etatism. Since the 1850's they have clung to the policy of interventionism which only in the last decades has overwhelmed the West. Their intransigent economic nationalism is a consequence of their etatism. But on the eve of the first World War Switzerland was still a predominantly liberal country. Since then it has turned more and more to interventionism; and as that spread the linguistic problem has become more serious. There is Italian Irredentism in the Ticino; there is a pro-Nazi party in the German-speaking parts, and there are French nationalists in the southwest. A victory of the allied democracies will doubtless stop these movements; but in that case Switzerland's integrity will be safeguarded by the same factor to which it owed its origin and its maintenance in the past, namely, the political conditions of its neighbor countries.

There is one instance in continental Europe in which the characteristic feature that separates two nations is not language but religion and the alphabetical types used in writing and printing. The Serbs and the Croats speak the same idiom; but while the Serbs use the Cyrillic alphabet the Croats use the Roman. The Serbs adhere to the orthodox creed of the Oriental Church; the Croats are Roman Catholics.

It must be emphasized again and again that racism and considerations of racial purity and solidarity play no role in these European struggles of linguistic groups. It is true that the nationalists often resort to "race" and "common descent" as catchwords. But that is mere propaganda without any practical effect on policies and political actions. On the contrary, the nationalists consciously and purposely reject racism and racial characteristics of individuals when dealing with *political* problems and activities. The German racists have provided us with an image of the prototype of the noble German or Aryan hero and with a biologically exact description of his bodily features. Every German is familiar with this archetype and most of them are convinced that this portrait is correct. But no German nationalist has ever ventured to use this pattern to draw the distinction between Germans and non-Germans. The criterion of Germanism is found not in a likeness to this standard but in the German tongue.* Breaking up the German-speaking group according to racial characteristics would result in eliminating at least 80 per cent of the German people from the ranks of the Germans. Neither Hitler nor Goebbels nor most of the other champions of German nationalism fit the Aryan prototype of the racial myth.

The Hungarians are proud to be the descendants of a Mongolian tribe which in the early Middle Ages conquered the country they call Hungary. The Rumanians boast their descent from Roman colonists. The Greeks consider themselves scions of the ancient Greeks. Historians are rather skeptical in regard to these claims. The modern political nationalism of these nations ignores them. It finds the practical criterion of the nation in the language instead of in racial characteristics or in the proof of descent from the alleged ancestry.

3. *Liberalism and the Principle of Nationality*

The foes of liberalism have failed in their endeavors to disprove liberalism's teachings concerning the value of capitalism and democratic government. Have they succeeded better in criticizing the third part of the liberal program—namely, the proposals for peaceful coöperation among different nations and states? In answering this question we must emphasize again that the principle of nationality does not represent the liberal solution of the international problem. The liberals urged self-determination. The principle of nationality is an outcome of the interpretation which people in Central and Eastern Europe, who never fully grasped the meaning of liberal ideas, gave to the principle of self-determination. It is a distortion, not a perfection, of liberal thought.

We have already shown that the Anglo-Saxon and the French fathers of liberal ideas did not recognize the problems involved. When these problems became visible, the old liberalism's creative period had already been brought to an end. The great champions were gone. Epigones, unable successfully to combat the growing

* We shall consider in Chapter VIII the alleged racial factors in nationalist Jew baiting.

socialist and interventionist tendencies, filled the stage. These men lacked the strength to deal with new problems.

Yet, the Indian summer of the old classical liberalism produced one document worthy of the great tradition of French liberalism. Ernest Renan, it is true, cannot really be considered a liberal. He made concessions to socialism, because his grasp of economic theories was rather poor; he was consequently too accommodating to the antidemocratic prejudices of his age. But his famous lecture, *Qu'est-ce qu'une nation?*, delivered in the Sorbonne on March 11, 1882, is thoroughly inspired by liberal thought.* It was the last word spoken by the older Western liberalism on the problems of state and nation.

For a correct understanding of Renan's ideas it is necessary to remember that for the French—as for the English—the terms nation and state are synonymous. When Renan asks: What is a nation? he means: What should determine the boundaries of the various states? And his answer is: Not the linguistic community, not the racial kinship founded on parentage from common ancestors, not religious congeniality, not the harmony of economic interests, not geographical or strategical considerations, but—the right of the population to determine its own destiny.† The nation is the outcome of the will of human beings to live together in one state.‡ The greater part of the lecture is devoted to showing how this spirit of nationality originates.

The nation is a soul, a moral principle (*"une âme, un principe spirituel"*).§ A nation, says Renan, daily confirms its existence by manifesting its will to political coöperation within the same state; a daily repeated plebiscite, as it were. A nation, therefore, has no right to say to a province: You belong to me, I want to take you. A province consists of its inhabitants. If anybody has a right to be heard in this case it is these inhabitants. Boundary disputes should be settled by plebiscite.‖

It is important to realize how this interpretation of the right of self-determination differs from the principle of nationality. The right of self-determination which Renan has in mind is not a right of linguistic groups but of individual men. It is derived from the rights of man. "Man belongs neither to his language nor to his race; he belongs to himself." ¶

* Renan, *Qu'est-ce qu'une nation?* (ed. Paris, 1934).
† Renan, *idem*, p. xi.
‡ *Idem*, pp. 84, 88.
§ *Idem*, p. 83.
‖ *Idem*, pp. viii ff.; 89–90, 95 ff.
¶ "L'homme n'appartient ni à sa langue, ni à sa race; il n'appartient qu' à lui-même." *Idem*, p. ix.

Seen from the point of view of the principle of nationality the existence of states like Switzerland, composed of people of different languages, is as anomalous as the fact that the Anglo-Saxons and the French are not eager to unite into one state all the people speaking their own language. For Renan there is nothing irregular in these facts.

More noteworthy than what Renan says is what he does not say. Renan sees neither the fact of linguistic minorities nor that of linguistic changes. Consult the people; let them decide. All right. But what if a conspicuous minority dissents from the will of the majority? To that objection Renan does not make a satisfactory answer. He declares—with regard to the scruple that plebiscites could result in the disintegration of old nations and in a system of small states (we say today Balkanization)—that the principle of self-determination should not be abused but only employed in a general way (*d'une façon très générale*).*

Renan's brilliant exposition proves that the threatening problems of Eastern Europe were unfamiliar to the West. He prefaced his pamphlet with a prophecy: We are rushing into wars of destruction and extermination, because the world has abandoned the principle of free union and has granted to the nations, as it once did to the dynasties, the right to annex provinces contrary to their desires.† But Renan saw only half the problem involved and therefore his solution could be but a half-way one.

Yet it would be wrong to say that liberalism has failed in this field. Liberalism's proposals for the coexistence and coöperation of nations and states are only a part of the total liberal program. They can be realized, they can be made to work only within a liberal world. The main excellence of the liberal scheme of social, economic, and political organization is precisely this—that it makes the peaceful coöperation of nations possible. It is not a shortcoming of the liberal program for international peace that it cannot be realized within an antiliberal world and that it must fail in an age of interventionism and socialism.

In order to grasp the meaning of this liberal program we need to imagine a world order in which liberalism is supreme. Either all the states in it are liberal, or enough are so that when united they are able to repulse an attack of militarist aggressors. In this liberal world, or liberal part of the world, there is private property in the means of production. The working of the market is not hampered by government interference. There are no trade barriers; men can live and work where they want. Frontiers are drawn on the maps

* Renan, *op. cit.*, p. 91.
† *Idem*, p. viii.

but they do not hinder the migrations of men and shipping of commodities. Natives do not enjoy rights that are denied to aliens. Governments and their servants restrict their activities to the protection of life, health, and property against fraudulent or violent aggression. They do not discriminate against foreigners. The courts are independent and effectively protect everybody against the encroachments of officialdom. Everyone is permitted to say, to write, and to print what he likes. Education is not subject to government interference. Governments are like night-watchmen whom the citizens have entrusted with the task of handling the police power. The men in office are regarded as mortal men, not as superhuman beings or as paternal authorities who have the right and duty to hold the people in tutelage. Governments do not have the power to dictate to the citizens what language they must use in their daily speech or in what language they must bring up and educate their children. Administrative organs and tribunals are bound to use each man's language in dealing with him, provided this language is spoken in the district by a reasonable number of residents.

In such a world it makes no difference where the frontiers of a country are drawn. Nobody has a special material interest in enlarging the territory of the state in which he lives; nobody suffers loss if a part of this area is separated from the state. It is also immaterial whether all parts of the state's territory are in direct geographical connection, or whether they are separated by a piece of land belonging to another state. It is of no economic importance whether the country has a frontage on the ocean or not. In such a world the people of every village or district could decide by plebiscite to which state they wanted to belong. There would be no more wars because there would be no incentive for aggression. War would not pay. Armies and navies would be superfluous. Policemen would suffice for the fight against crime. In such a world the state is not a metaphysical entity but simply the producer of security and peace. It is the night-watchman, as Lassalle contemptuously dubbed it. But it fulfills this task in a satisfactory way. The citizen's sleep is not disturbed, bombs do not destroy his home, and if somebody knocks at his door late at night it is certainly neither the Gestapo nor the O.G.P.U.

The reality in which we have to live differs very much from this perfect world of ideal liberalism. But this is due only to the fact that men have rejected liberalism for etatism. They have burdened the state, which could be a more or less efficient night-watchman, with a multitude of other duties. Neither nature, nor the working of forces beyond human control, nor inevitable necessity has led to etatism, but the acts of men. Entangled by dialectic fallacies and fantastic illusions, blindly believing in erroneous doctrines, biased by envy and insatiable greed, men have derided capitalism and have substituted for it an order engendering conflicts for which no peaceful solution can be found.

4. *Aggressive Nationalism*

Etatism—whether interventionism or socialism—must lead to conflict, war, and totalitarian oppression of large populations. The right and true state, under etatism, is the state in which I or my friends, speaking my language and sharing my opinions, are supreme. All other states are spurious. One cannot deny that they too exist in this imperfect world. But they are enemies of my state, of the only righteous state, even if this state does not yet exist outside of my dreams and wishes. Our German Nazi state, says Steding, is the Reich; the other states are deviations from it.* Politics, says the foremost Nazi jurist, Carl Schmitt, is the discrimination between friend and foe.†

In order to understand these doctrines we must look first at the liberal attitude toward the problem of linguistic antagonisms.

He who lives as a member of a linguistic minority, within a community where another linguistic group forms the majority, is deprived of the means of influencing the country's politics. (We are not considering the special case in which such a linguistic minority occupies a privileged position and oppresses the majority as, for example, the German-speaking aristocracy in the Baltic duchies in the years preceding the Russianization of these provinces.) Within a democratic community public opinion determines the outcome of elections, and thereby the political decisions. Whoever wants to make his ideas prevalent in political life must try to influence public opinion through speech and writing. If he succeeds in convincing his fellow citizens, his ideas obtain support and persist.

In this struggle of ideas linguistic minorities cannot take part. They are voiceless spectators of the political debates out of which the deciding vote emerges. They cannot participate in the discussions and negotiations. But the result determines their fate too. For them democracy does not mean self-determination; other people control them. They are second-class citizens. This is the reason why men in a democratic world consider it a disadvantage to be members of a linguistic minority. It explains at the same time why there were no linguistic conflicts in earlier ages, where there was no democracy. In this age of democracy people in the main

* Steding, *Das Reich und die Krankheit der Kultur* (Hamburg, 1938).
† Carl Schmitt-Dorotić, *Der Begriff des Politischen* (Munich, 1932).

prefer to live in a community where they speak the same language as the majority of their fellow citizens. Therefore in plebiscites concerning the question to which state a province should belong, people as *a rule, but not always,* vote in favor of the country where they will not be members of a linguistic minority.

But the recognition of this fact by no means leads liberalism to the principle of nationality. Liberalism does not say: Every linguistic group should form one state and one state only, and each single man belonging to this group should, if at all possible, belong to this state. Neither does it say: No state should include people of several linguistic groups. Liberalism postulates self-determination. That men in the exercise of this right allow themselves to be guided by linguistic considerations is for liberalism simply a fact, not a principle or a moral law. If men decide in another way, which was the case, for example, with the German-speaking Alsatians, that is their own concern. Such a decision, too, must be respected.

But it is different in our age of etatism. The etatist state must necessarily extend its territory to the utmost. The benefits it can grant to its citizens increase in proportion to its territory. Everything that the interventionist state can provide can be provided more abundantly by the larger state than by the smaller one. Privileges become more valuable the larger the territory in which they are valid. The essence of etatism is to take from one group in order to give to another. The more it can take the more it can give. It is to the interest of those whom the government wishes to favor that their state become as large as possible. The policy of territorial expansion becomes popular. The people as well as the governments become eager for conquest. Every pretext for aggression is deemed right. Men then recognize but one argument in favor of peace: that the prospective adversary is strong enough to defeat their attack. Woe to the weak!

The domestic policies of a nationalist state are inspired by the aim of improving the conditions of some groups of citizens by inflicting evils on foreigners and those citizens who use a foreign language. In foreign policy economic nationalism means discrimination against foreigners. In domestic policy it means discrimination against citizens speaking a language which is not that of the ruling group. These pariahs are not always minority groups in a technical sense. The German-speaking people of Meran, Bozen, and Brixen are majorities in their districts; they are minorities only because their country has been annexed by Italy. The same is true for the Germans of the Egerland, for the Ukrainians in Poland, the Magyars of the Szekler district in Transylvania, the Slovenes in Italian-occupied Carniola. He who speaks a foreign mother tongue in a state where another language predominates is an outcast to whom the rights of citizens are virtually denied.

The best example of the political consequences of this aggressive nationalism is provided by conditions in Eastern Europe. If you ask representatives of the linguistic groups of Eastern Europe what they consider would be a fair determination of their national states, and if you mark these boundaries on a map, you will discover that the greater part of this territory is claimed by at least two nations, and not a negligible part by three or even more.* Every linguistic group defends its claims with linguistic, racial, historical, geographical, strategic, economic, social, and religious arguments. No nation is prepared sincerely to renounce the least of its claims for reasons of expediency. Every nation is ready to resort to arms to satisfy its pretensions. Every linguistic group therefore considers its immediate neighbors mortal enemies and relies on its neighbor's neighbors for armed support of its own territorial claims against the common foe. Every group tries to profit from every opportunity to satisfy its claims at the expense of its neighbors. The history of the last decades proves the correctness of this melancholy description.

Take, for example, the case of the Ukrainians. For hundreds of years they were under the yoke of the Russians and the Poles. There has been no Ukrainian national state in our day. One might assume that the spokesmen of a people which has so fully experienced the hardships of ruthless foreign oppression would be prudent in their pretensions. But nationalists simply cannot renounce. Thus the Ukrainians claim an area of more than 360,000 square miles with a total population of some sixty millions, of whom, according even to their own declaration, only "more than forty millions" are Ukrainians.† These oppressed Ukrainians would not be content with their own liberation; they strive at the oppression of twenty or more millions of non-Ukrainians.

In 1918 the Czechs were not satisfied with the establishment of an independent state of their own. They incorporated into their state millions of German-speaking people, all the Slovaks, tens of thousands of Hungarians, the Ukrainians of Carpatho-Russia and —for considerations of railroad management—some districts of Lower Austria. And what a spectacle was the Polish Republic, which in the twenty-one years of its independence tried to rob violently three of its neighbors—Russia, Lithuania, and Czechoslovakia—of a part of their territories!

---

* e.g., the city of Fiume is claimed by the Hungarians, Croats, Yugoslavs, and Italians.

† Hrushevsky, *A History of the Ukraine* (published for the Ukrainian National Association by Yale University Press, New Haven, 1941), p. 574.

These conditions were correctly described by August Strindberg in his trilogy *To Damascus:* *

FATHER MELCHER: "At the Amsteg station, on the Gotthard line, you have probably seen a tower called the castle of Zwing-Uri; it is celebrated by Schiller in *Wilhelm Tell*. It stands there as a monument to the inhuman oppression which the inhabitants of Uri suffered at the hands of the German Kaiser! Lovely! On the Italian side of the Saint Gotthard lies the station of Bellinzona, as you know. There are many towers there, but the most remarkable is the Castel d'Uri. It is a monument to the inhuman oppression, which the Italian canton suffered at the hands of the inhabitants of Uri. Do you understand?"

THE STRANGER: "Liberty! Liberty, give us, in order that we may suppress."

However, Strindberg did not add that the three cantons Uri, Schwyz, and Unterwalden under nineteenth-century liberalism peacefully coöperated with the Ticino whose people they had oppressed for almost three hundred years.

5. Colonial Imperialism

In the fifteenth century the Western nations began to occupy territories in non-European countries peopled by non-Christian populations. They were eager to obtain precious metals and raw materials that could not be produced in Europe. To explain this colonial expansion as a search for markets is to misrepresent the facts. These traders wanted to get colonial products. They had to pay for them; but the profit they sought was the acquisition of commodities that could not be bought elsewhere. As businessmen they were not so foolish as to believe in the absurd teaching of Mercantilism—old and new—that the advantage derived from foreign trade lies in exporting and not in importing. They were so little concerned about exporting that they were glad when they could obtain the goods they wanted without any payment at all. They were often more pirates and slavers than merchants. They had no moral inhibitions in their dealings with the heathen.

It was not in the plans of the kings and royal merchants who inaugurated European overseas expansion to settle European farmers in the occupied territories. They misprized the vast forests and prairies of North America from which they expected neither precious metals nor spices. The rulers of Great Britain were much less

* Part III, Act IV, Scene ii. Authorized translation by Sam E. Davidson, *Poet Lore*, XLII, No. 3 (Boston, Bruce Humphries, Inc., 1935), 259.

enthusiastic about founding settlements in continental America than about their enterprises in the Caribbean, in Africa, and the East Indies, and their participation in the slave trade. The colonists, not the British Government, built up the English-speaking communities in America, and later in Canada, in Australia, New Zealand, and South Africa.

The colonial expansion of the nineteenth century was very different from that of the preceding centuries. It was motivated solely by considerations of national glory and pride. The French officers, poets, and after-dinner speakers—not the rest of the nation—suffered deeply from the inferiority complex which the battles of Leipzig and Waterloo, and later those of Metz and Sedan, left with them. They thirsted for glory and fame; and they could quench their thirst neither in liberal Europe nor in an America sheltered by the Monroe Doctrine. It was the great comfort of Louis Philippe that his sons and his generals could reap laurels in Algeria. The Third Republic conquered Tunis, Morocco, Madagascar, and Tonking in order to reëstablish the moral equilibrium of its army and navy. The inferiority complex of Custozza and Lissa drove Italy to Abyssinia, and the inferiority complex of Aduwa to Tripoli. One of the important motives that made Germany embark on colonial conquests was the turbulent ambition of shabby adventurers like Dr. Karl Peters.

There were other cases too. King Leopold II of Belgium and Cecil Rhodes were belated conquistadors. But the main incentive of modern colonial conquest was the desire for military glory. The defenselessness of the poor aborigines, whose main weapons were the dreariness and impassableness of their countries, was too tempting. It was easy and not dangerous to defeat them and to return home a hero.

The modern world's paramount colonial power was Great Britain. Its East Indian Empire surpassed by far the colonial possessions of all other European nations. In the 1820's it was virtually the only colonial *power*. Spain and Portugal had lost almost their entire overseas territories. The French and the Dutch retained at the end of the Napoleonic Wars as much as the British were willing to leave them; their colonial rule was at the mercy of the British Navy. But British liberalism has fundamentally reformed the meaning of colonial imperialism. It granted autonomy—dominion status —to the British settlers, and ran the East Indies and the remaining Crown colonies on free-trade principles. Long before the Covenant of the League of Nations created the concept of mandates, Great Britain acted virtually as mandatory of European civilization in countries whose population was, as the Britons believed, not qualified for independence. The main blame which can be laid on British East Indian policies is that they respected too much some native customs—that, for example, they were slow to improve the lot of the untouchables. But for the English there would be no India today, only a conglomeration of tyrannically misruled petty principalities fighting each other on various pretexts; there would be anarchy, famines, epidemics.

The men who represented Europe in the colonies were seldom proof against the specific moral dangers of the exalted positions they occupied among backward populations. Their snobbishness poisoned their personal contact with the natives. The marvelous achievements of the British administration in India were overshadowed by the vain arrogance and stupid race pride of the white man. Asia is in open revolt against the gentlemen for whom socially there was but little difference between a dog and a native. India is, for the first time in its history, unanimous on one issue—its hatred for the British. This resentment is so strong that it has blinded for some time even those parts of the population who know very well that Indian independence will bring them disaster and oppression: the 80 millions of Moslems, the 40 millions of untouchables, the many millions of Sikhs, Buddhists, and Indian Christians. It is a tragic situation and a menace to the cause of the United Nations. But it is at the same time the manifest failure of the greatest experiment in benevolent absolutism ever put to work.

Great Britain did not in the last decades seriously oppose the step-by-step liberation of India. It did not hinder the establishment of an Indian protectionist system whose foremost aim is to lock out British manufactures. It connived at the development of an Indian monetary and fiscal system which soon or late will result in a virtual annulment of British investments and other claims. The only task of the British administration in India in these last years has been to prevent the various political parties, religious groups, races, linguistic groups, and castes from fighting one another. But the Hindus do not long for British benefits.

British colonial expansion did not stop in the last sixty years. But it was an expansion forced upon Great Britain by other nations' lust of conquest. Every annexation of a piece of land by France, Germany, or Italy curtailed the market for the products of all other nations. The British were committed to the principles of free trade and had no desire to exclude other people. But they had to take over large blocks of territory if only to prevent them from falling into the hands of exclusive rivals. It was not their fault that under the conditions brought about by French, German,

Italian, and Russian colonial methods only political control could adequately safeguard trade.*

It is a Marxian invention that the nineteenth-century colonial expansion of the European powers was engendered by the economic interests of the pressure groups of finance and business. There have been some cases where governments acted on behalf of their citizens who had made foreign investments; the purpose was to protect them against expropriation or default. But historical research has brought evidence that the initiative for the great colonial projects came not from finance and business but from the governments. The alleged economic interest was a mere blind. The root cause of the Russo-Japanese War of 1904 was not the desire of the Russian Government to safeguard the interests of a group of investors who wanted to exploit the Yalu timber estates. On the contrary, because the government needed a pretext for intervention, it deployed "a fighting vanguard disguised as lumbermen." The Italian Government did not conquer Tripoli on behalf of the Banco di Roma. The bank went to Tripoli because the government wanted it to pave the way for conquest. The bank's decision to invest in Tripoli was the result of an incentive offered by the Italian Government—the privilege of rediscount facilities at the Bank of Italy, and further compensation in the form of a subsidy to its navigation service. The Banco di Roma did not like the risky investment from which at best but very poor returns could be expected. The German Reich did not care a whit for the interests of the Mannesmanns in Morocco. It used the case of this unimportant German firm as a lame excuse for its aspirations. German big business and finance were not at all interested. The Foreign Office tried in vain to induce them to invest in Morocco. "As soon as you mention Morocco," said the German Secretary for Foreign Affairs, Herr von Richthofen, "the banks all go on strike, every last one of them." †

At the outbreak of the first World War a total of less than 25,000 Germans, most of them soldiers and civil servants and their families, lived in the German colonies. The trade of the mother country with its colonies was negligible; it was less than .5 per cent of Germany's total foreign trade. Italy, the most aggressive colonial power,

---

* W. L. Langer, *The Diplomacy of Imperialism* (New York, 1935), I, 75, 95; L. Robbins, *The Economic Causes of War* (London, 1939), pp. 81, 82.

† Staley, *War and the Private Investor* (New York, 1935); Robbins, *op. cit.*; Sulzbach, *"Capitalist Warmongers," A Modern Superstition* (Chicago, 1942). Charles Beard (*A Foreign Policy for America*, New York, 1930, p. 72) says with regard to America: "Loyalty to the facts of historical record must ascribe the idea of imperialist expansion mainly to naval officers and politicians rather than to business men." That is valid for all other nations too.

lacked the capital to develop its domestic resources; its investments in Tripoli and in Ethiopia perceptibly increased the capital shortage at home.

The most modern pretense for colonial conquest is condensed in the slogan "raw materials." Hitler and Mussolini tried to justify their plans by pointing out that the natural resources of the earth were not fairly distributed. As have-nots they were eager to get their fair share from those nations which had more than they should have had. How could they be branded aggressors when they wanted nothing but what was—in virtue of natural and divine right —their own?

In the world of capitalism raw materials can be bought and sold like all other commodities. It does not matter whether they have to be imported from abroad or bought at home. It is of no advantage for an English buyer of Australian wool that Australia is a part of the British Empire; he must pay the same price that his Italian or German competitor pays.

The countries producing the raw materials that cannot be produced in Germany or in Italy are not empty. There are people living in them; and these inhabitants are not ready to become subjects of the European dictators. The citizens of Texas and Louisiana are eager to sell their cotton crops to anyone who wants to pay for them; but they do not long for German or Italian domination. It is the same with other countries and other raw materials. The Brazilians do not consider themselves an appurtenance of their coffee plantations. The Swedes do not believe that their supply of iron ore justifies Germany's aspirations. The Italians would themselves consider the Danes lunatics if they were to ask for an Italian province in order to get their fair share of citrus fruits, red wine, and olive oil.

It would be reasonable if Germany and Italy were to ask for a general return to free trade and laissez passer and for an abandonment of the—up to now unsuccessful—endeavors of many governments to raise the price of raw materials by a compulsory restriction of output. But such ideas are strange to the dictators, who do not want freedom but Zwangswirtchaft and self-sufficiency.

Modern colonial imperialism is a phenomenon by itself. It should not be confused with European nationalism. The great wars of our age did not originate from colonial conflicts but from nationalist aspirations in Europe. Colonial antagonisms kindled colonial campaigns without disturbing the peace between the Western nations. For all the saber rattling, neither Fashoda nor Morocco nor Ethiopia resulted in European war. In the complex of German, Italian, and French foreign affairs, colonial plans were mere byplay. Colonial aspirations were not much more than a peacetime outdoor sport, the colonies a tilting ground for ambitious young officers.

6. Foreign Investment and Foreign Loans

The main requisite of the industrial changes which transformed the world of handicraftsmen and artisans, of horses, sailing ships, and windmills into the world of steam power, electricity, and mass production was the accumulation of capital. The nations of Western Europe brought forth the political and institutional conditions for safeguarding saving and investment on a broader scale, and thus provided the entrepreneurs with the capital needed. On the eve of the industrial revolution the technological and economic structure of Western economy did not differ essentially from conditions in the other parts of the inhabited surface of the earth. By the second quarter of the nineteenth century a broad gulf separated the advanced countries of the West from the backward countries of the East. While the West was on the road of quick progress, in the East there was stagnation.

Mere acquaintance with Western methods of production, transportation, and marketing would have proved useless for the backward nations. They did not have the capital for the adoption of the new processes. It was not difficult to imitate the technique of the West. But it was almost impossible to transplant the mentalities and ideologies which had created the social, legal, constitutional, and political milieu from which these modern technological improvements had sprung. An environment which could make for domestic capital accumulation was not so easy to produce as a modern factory. The new industrial system was but the effect of the new spirit of liberalism and capitalism. It was the outcome of a mentality which cared more about serving the consumer than about wars, conquest, and the preservation of old customs. The essential feature of the advanced West was not its technique but its moral atmosphere which encouraged saving, capital formation, entrepreneurship, business, and peaceful competition.

The backward nations perhaps might have come to understand this basic problem and might have started to transform their social structures in such a way that autochthonous capital accumulation would have resulted. Even then it would have been a slow and troublesome process. It would have required a long time. The gulf between West and East, between advanced nations and backward nations, would have broadened more and more. It would have been hopeless for the East to overtake the head start gained by the West.

But history took another course. A new phenomenon appeared

—the internationalization of the capital market. The advanced West provided all parts of the world with the capital needed for the new investments. Loans and direct investments made it possible to outfit all countries with the paraphernalia of modern civilization. Mahatma Gandhi expresses a loathing for the devices of the petty West and of devilish capitalism. But he travels by railroad or by motor car and, when ill, goes for treatment to a hospital equipped with the most refined instruments of Western surgery. It does not seem to occur to him that Western capital alone made it possible for the Hindus to enjoy these facilities.

The enormous transfer of capital from Western Europe to the rest of the world was one of the outstanding events of the age of capitalism. It has developed natural resources in the remotest areas. It has raised the standard of living of peoples who from time immemorial had not achieved any improvement in their material conditions. It was, of course, not charity but self-interest which pushed the advanced nations to the export of capital. But the profit was not unilateral; it was mutual. The once backward nations have no sound reason to complain because foreign capitalists provided them with machinery and transportation facilities.

Yet in this age of anticapitalism hostility to foreign capital has become general. All debtor nations are eager to expropriate the foreign capitalist. Loans are repudiated, either openly or by the more tricky means of foreign exchange control. Foreign property is liable to discriminatory taxation which reaches the level of confiscation. Even undisguised expropriation without any indemnification is practiced.

There has been much talk about the alleged exploitation of the debtor nations by the creditor nations. But if the concept of exploitation is to be applied to these relations, it is rather an exploitation of the investing by the receiving nations. These loans and investments were not intended as gifts. The loans were made upon solemn stipulation of payment of principal and interest. The investments were made in the expectation that property rights would be respected. With the exception of the bulk of the investments made in the United States, in some of the British dominions, and in some smaller countries, these expectations have been disappointed. Bonds have been defaulted or will be in the next few years. Direct investments have been confiscated or soon will be. The capital-exporting countries can do nothing but wipe off their balances.

Let us look at the problem from the point of view of the predominantly industrial countries of Europe. These comparatively overpopulated countries are poorly endowed by nature. In order to pay for badly needed foodstuffs and raw materials they must export manufactures. The economic nationalism of the nations which are in a position to sell them these foodstuffs and raw materials shuts the doors in their face. For Europe the restriction of exports means misery and starvation. Yet there was one safety valve left, as long as the foreign investments could be relied upon. The debtor nations were obliged to export some quantities of their products as payment of interest and dividends. Even if the goal of present-day foreign-trade policies, the complete prevention of any import of manufactures, were to be attained, the debtor nations would still have to provide the creditor nations with the means to pay for a part of the formers' excess production of food and raw materials. The consumers of the creditor nations would be in a position to buy these goods on the sheltered home market, as it were, from the hands of those receiving the payments from abroad. These foreign investments represented in a certain manner the share of the creditor nations in the rich resources of the debtor nations. The existence of these investments softened to some extent the inequality between the haves and the have-nots.

In what sense was prewar Great Britain a have nation? Surely not in the sense that it "owned" the Empire. But the British capitalists owned a considerable amount of foreign investments, whose yield made it possible for the country to buy a corresponding quantity of foreign products in excess of that quantity which was the equivalent of current British exports. The difference in the economic structures of prewar Great Britain and Austria was precisely that Austria did not own such foreign assets. The British worker could provide for a considerable quantity of foreign food and raw materials by working in factories which sold their products on the sheltered British market to those people who received these payments from abroad. It was as if these foreign wheat fields, cotton and rubber plantations, oil wells and mines had been situated within Great Britain.

After the present war, with their foreign assets gone either through the methods applied in financing the war expenditure or by default and confiscation on the part of the governments of the debtor nations, Great Britain and some other countries of Western Europe will be reduced to the status of comparatively poor nations. This change will affect very seriously the conditions of British labor. Those quantities of foreign food and raw materials which the country could previously procure by means of the interest and dividend payments received from abroad will in the future be sought by desperate attempts to sell manufactures to which every country wants to bar access.

7. Total War

The princes of the ancien régime were eager for aggrandizement. They seized every opportunity to wage war and to conquer. They organized—comparatively small—armies. These armies fought their battles. The citizens detested the wars, which brought mischief to them and burdened them with taxes. But they were not interested in the outcome of the campaigns. It was more or less immaterial to them whether they were ruled by a Habsburg or by a Bourbon. In those days Voltaire declared: "The peoples are indifferent to their rulers' wars." *

Modern war is not a war of royal armies. It is a war of the peoples, a total war. It is a war of states which do not leave to their subjects any private sphere; they consider the whole population a part of the armed forces. Whoever does not fight must work for the support and equipment of the army. Army and people are one and the same. The citizens passionately participate in the war. For it is their state, their God, who fights.

Wars of aggression are popular nowadays with those nations which are convinced that only victory and conquest could improve their material well-being. On the other hand the citizens of the nations assaulted know very well that they must fight for their own survival. Thus every individual in both camps has a burning interest in the outcome of the battles.

The annexation of Alsace-Lorraine by Germany in 1871 did not bring about any change in the wealth or income of the average German citizen. The inhabitants of the annexed province retained their property rights. They became citizens of the Reich, and returned deputies to the Reichstag. The German Treasury collected taxes in the newly acquired territory. But it was, on the other hand, burdened with the expense of its administration. This was in the days of laissez faire.

The old liberals were right in asserting that no citizen of a liberal and democratic nation profits from a victorious war. But it is different in this age of migration and trade barriers. Every wage earner and every peasant is hurt by the policy of a foreign government, barring his access to countries in which natural conditions of production are more favorable than in his native country. Every toiler is hurt by a foreign country's import duties penalizing the sale of the products of his work. If a victorious war destroys such trade and migration walls, the material well-being of the masses concerned is favored. Pressure on the domestic labor market can be relieved by the emigration of a part of the workers. The emigrants

* Benda, *La Trahison des clercs* (Paris, 1927), p. 253.

earn more in their new country, and the restriction of the supply on the domestic labor market tends to raise wage rates at home too. The abolition of foreign tariffs increases exports and thereby the demand on the domestic labor market. Production on the least fertile soil is discontinued at home, and the farmers go to countries in which better soil is still available. The average productivity of labor all over the world increases because production under the least favorable conditions is curtailed in the emigration countries and replaced by an expansion of production in the immigration countries offering more favorable physical opportunities.

But, on the other hand, the interests of the workers and farmers in the comparatively underpopulated countries are injured. For them the tendency toward an equalization of wage rates and farm yields (per capita of the men tilling a unit of land), inherent in a world of free mobility of labor, results, for the immediate future, in a drop of income, no matter how beneficial the later consequences of this free mobility may be.

It would be futile to object that there is unemployment in the comparatively underpopulated countries, foremost among them Australia and America, and that immigration would only result in an increase of unemployment figures, not in an improvement of the conditions of the immigrants. Unemployment as a mass phenomenon is always due to the enforcement of minimum wages higher than the potential wages which the unhampered labor market would have fixed. If the labor unions did not persistently try to raise wage rates above the potential market rates there would be no lasting unemployment of many workers. The problem is not the differences in union minimum rates in different countries, but those in potential market wage rates. If there were no trade-union manipulation of wages, Australia and America could absorb many millions of immigrant workers until an equalization of wages was reached. The market wage rates both in manufacturing and in agriculture are many times higher in Australia, in New Zealand. and in northern America than in continental Europe. This is due to the fact that in Europe poor mines are still exploited while much richer mining facilities remain unused in overseas countries. The farmers of Europe are tilling the rocky and barren soil in the Alps, the Carpathians, the Apennines, and the Balkan Mountains. and the sandy soil of the plains of northeastern Germany, while millions of acres of more fertile soil lie untouched in America and Australia. All these peoples are prevented from moving to places where their toil and trouble would be much more productive and where they could render better services to the consumers.

We can now realize why etatism must result in war whenever the underprivileged believe that they will be victorious. As things are in this age of etatism the Germans, the Italians, and the Japanese *could* possibly derive profit from a victorious war. It is not a warrior caste which drives Japan into ruthless aggression but considerations of wage policies which do not differ from those of the trade-unions. The Australian trade-unions wish to close their ports to immigration in order to raise wage rates in Australia. The Japanese workers wish to open the Australian ports in order to raise wage rates for the workers of their own race.

Pacifism is doomed in an age of etatism. In the old days of royal absolutism philanthropists thus addressed the kings: "Take pity on suffering mankind; be generous and merciful! You, of course, may profit from victory and conquest. But think of the grief of the widows and orphans, the desolation of those maimed, mutilated and crippled, the misery of those whose homes have been destroyed! Remember the commandment: Thou shalt not kill! Renounce glory and aggrandizement! Keep peace! " They preached to deaf ears. Then came liberalism. It did not declaim against war; it sought to establish conditions, in which war would not pay, to abolish war by doing away with the causes. It did not succeed because along came etatism. When the pacifists of our day tell the peoples that war cannot improve their well-being, they are mistaken. The aggressor nations remain convinced that a victorious war could improve the fate of their citizens.

These considerations are not a plea for opening America and the British Dominions to German, Italian, and Japanese immigrants. Under present conditions America and Australia would simply commit suicide by admitting Nazis, Fascists, and Japanese. They could as well directly surrender to the Führer and to the Mikado. Immigrants from the totalitarian countries are today the vanguard of their armies, a fifth column whose invasion would render all measures of defense useless. America and Australia can preserve their freedom, their civilizations, and their economic institutions only by rigidly barring access to the subjects of the dictators. But these conditions are the outcome of etatism. In the liberal past the immigrants came not as pacemakers of conquest but as loyal citizens of their new country.

However, it would be a serious omission not to mention the fact that immigration barriers are recommended by many contemporaries without any reference to the problem of wage rates and farm yields. Their aim is the preservation of the existing geographical segregation of various races. They argue this: Western civilization is an achievement of the Caucasian races of Western and Central Europe and their descendants in overseas countries. It would perish if the countries peopled by these Westerners were to be overflowed by the natives of Asia and Africa. Such an invasion would harm both the Westerners and the Asiatics and Africans. The segregation of various races is beneficial to all mankind because it prevents a disintegration of Western civilization. If the Asiatics and Africans remain in that part of the earth in which they have been living for many thousands of years, they will be benefited by the further progress of the white man's civilization. They will always have a model before their eyes to imitate and to adapt to their own conditions. Perhaps in a distant future they themselves will contribute their share to the further advancement of culture. Perhaps at that time it will be feasible to remove the barriers of segregation. In our day —they say—such plans are out of the question.

We must not close our eyes to the fact that such views meet with the consent of the vast majority. It would be useless to deny that there exists a repugnance to abandoning the geographical segregation of various races. Even men who are fair in their appraisal of the qualities and cultural achievements of the colored races and severely object to any discrimination against those members of these races who are already living in the midst of white populations, are opposed to a mass immigration of colored people. There are few white men who would not shudder at the picture of many millions of black or yellow people living in their own countries.

The elaboration of a system making for harmonious coexistence and peaceful economic and political coöperation among the various races is a task to be accomplished by coming generations. But mankind will certainly fail to solve this problem if it does not entirely discard etatism. Let us not forget that the actual menace to our civilization does not originate from a conflict between the white and colored races but from conflicts among the various peoples of Europe and of European ancestry. Some writers have prophesied the coming of a decisive struggle between the white race and the colored races. The reality of our time, however, is war between groups of white nations and between the Japanese and the Chinese who are both Mongolians. These wars are the outcome of etatism.

8. Socialism and War

The socialists insist that war is but one of the many mischiefs of capitalism. In the coming paradise of socialism, they hold, there will no longer be any wars. Of course, between us and this peaceful utopia there are still some bloody civil wars to be fought. But with the inevitable triumph of communism all conflicts will disappear.

It is obvious enough that with the conquest of the whole surface of the earth by a single ruler all struggles between states and nations would disappear. If a socialist dictator should succeed in conquering every country there would no longer be external wars, provided that the O.G.P.U. were strong enough to hinder the disintegration of this World State. But the same holds true for any other conqueror. If the Mongol Great Khans had accomplished their ends, they too would have made the world safe for eternal peace. It is too bad that Christian Europe was so obstinate as not to surrender voluntarily to their claims of world supremacy.*

However, we are not considering projects for world pacification through universal conquest and enslavement, but how to achieve a world where there are no longer any causes of conflict. Such a possibility was implied in liberalism's project for the smooth coöperation of democratic nations under capitalism. It failed because the world abandoned both liberalism and capitalism.

There are two possibilities for world-embracing socialism: the coexistence of independent socialist states on the one hand, or the establishment of a unitary world-embracing socialist government on the other.

The first system would stabilize existing inequalities. There would be richer nations and poorer ones, countries both under-populated and overpopulated. If mankind had introduced this system a hundred years ago, it would have been impossible to exploit the oil fields of Mexico or Venezuela, to establish the rubber plantations in Malaya, or to develop the banana production of Central America. The nations concerned lacked both the capital and trained men to utilize their own natural resources. A socialist scheme is not compatible with foreign investment, international loans, payments of dividends and interest, and all such capitalist institutions.

Let us consider what some of the conditions would be in such a world of coördinate socialist nations. There are some overcrowded countries peopled by white workers. They labor to improve their standard of living, but their endeavors are handicapped by inadequate natural resources. They badly need raw materials and foodstuffs that could be produced in other, better endowed countries. But these countries which nature has favored are thinly populated and lack the capital required to develop their resources. Their inhabitants are neither industrious nor skillful enough to profit from the riches which nature has lavished upon them. They are without initiative; they cling to old-fashioned methods of production; they

---

* Voegelin, "The Mongol Orders of Submission to the European Powers 1245–1255," *Byzantion*, XV, 378–413.

are not interested in improvement. They are not eager to produce more rubber, tin, copra, and jute and to exchange these products for goods manufactured abroad. By this attitude they affect the standard of living of those peoples whose chief asset is their skill and diligence. Will these peoples of countries neglected by nature be prepared to endure such a state of things? Will they be willing to work harder and to produce less because the favored children of nature stubbornly abstain from exploiting their treasures in a more efficient way?

Inevitably war and conquest result. The workers of the comparatively overpopulated areas invade the comparatively underpopulated areas, conquer these countries, and annex them. And then follow wars between the conquerors for the distribution of the booty. Every nation is prepared to believe that it has not obtained its fair share, that other nations have got too much and should be forced to abandon a part of their plunder. Socialism in independent nations would result in endless wars.

These considerations prepare for a disclosure of the nonsensical Marxian theories of imperialism. All these theories, however much they conflict with each other, have one feature in common: they all maintain that the capitalists are eager for foreign investment because production at home tends, with the progress of capitalism, to a reduction in the rate of profit, and because the home market under capitalism is too narrow to absorb the whole volume of production. This desire of capitalists for exports and for foreign investment, it is held, is detrimental to the class interests of the proletarians. Besides, it leads to international conflict and war.

Yet the capitalists did not invest abroad in order to withhold goods from home consumption. In the contrary, they did so in order to supply the home market with raw materials and foodstuffs which could otherwise not be obtained at all, or only in insufficient quantities or at higher costs. Without export trade and foreign investment European and American consumers would never have enjoyed the high standard of living that capitalism gave them. It was the wants of the domestic consumers that pushed the capitalists and entrepreneurs toward foreign markets and foreign investment. If the consumers had been more eager for the acquisition of a greater quantity of goods that could be produced at home without the aid of foreign raw materials than for imported food and raw materials, it would have been more profitable to expand home production further than to invest abroad.

The Marxian doctrinaires shut their eyes purposely to the inequality of natural resources in different parts of the world. And yet these inequalities are the essential problem of international relations.* But for them the Teutonic tribes and later the Mongols would not have invaded Europe. They would have turned toward the vast empty areas of the Tundra or of northern Scandinavia. If we do not take into account these inequalities of natural resources and climates we can discover no motive for war but some devilish spell, for example—as the Marxians say—the sinister machinations of capitalists, or—as the Nazis say—the intrigues of world Jewry.

These inequalities are natural and can never disappear. They would present an insoluble problem for a unitary world socialism also. A socialist world-embracing management could, of course, consider a policy under which all human beings are treated alike; it could try to ship workers and capital from one area to another, without considering the vested interests of the labor groups of different countries or of different linguistic groups. But nothing can justify the illusion that these labor groups, whose per capita income and standard of living would be reduced by such a policy, would be prepared to tolerate it. No socialist of the Western nations considers socialism to be a scheme which (even if we were to grant the fallacious expectations that socialist production would increase the productivity of labor) must result in lowering living standards in those nations. The workers of the West are not striving for equalization of their earnings with those of the more than 1,000 million extremely poor peasants and workers of Asia and Africa. For the same reason that they oppose immigration under capitalism, these workers would oppose such a policy of labor transfer on the part of a socialist world management. They would rather fight than agree to abolition of the existing discriminations between the lucky inhabitants of comparatively underpopulated areas and the unfortunate inhabitants of the overpopulated areas. Whether we call such struggles civil wars or foreign wars is immaterial.

The workers of the West favor socialism because they hope to improve their condition by the abolition of what they describe as *unearned* incomes. We are not concerned with the fallacies of these expectations. We have only to emphasize that these Western socialists do not want to share their incomes with the underprivileged masses of the East. They are not prepared to renounce the most valuable privilege which they enjoy under etatism and economic

* We have dealt only with those types of foreign investment that were intended to develop the natural resources of the backward countries, i.e., investment in mining and agriculture and their auxiliaries such as transportation facilities, public utilities, and so on. The investment in foreign manufacturing was to a great extent due to the influence of economic nationalism; it would not have happened within a world of free trade. It was protectionism that forced the American motor-car producers and the German electrical plants to establish branch factories abroad.

nationalism—the exclusion of foreign labor. The American workers are for the maintenance of what they call "the American way of life," not for a world socialist way of life, which would lie somewhere between the present American and the coolie level, probably much nearer to the latter than to the former. This is stark reality that no socialist rhetoric can conjure away.

The same selfish group interests which through migration barriers have frustrated the liberal plans for world-wide peaceful cooperation of nations, states, and individuals would destroy the internal peace within a socialist world state. The peace argument is just as baseless and erroneous as all the other arguments brought forward to demonstrate the practicability and expediency of socialism.

V. REFUTATION OF SOME FALLACIOUS EXPLANATIONS

1. The Shortcomings of Current Explanations

THE current explanations of modern nationalism are far from recognizing that nationalism within our world of international division of labor is the inevitable outcome of etatism. We have already exposed the fallacies of the most popular of these explanations, namely, of the Marxian theory of imperialism. We have now to pass in review some other doctrines.

The faultiness of the Marxian theory is due to its bad economics. Most of the theories with which we shall deal now do not take economic factors into account at all. For them nationalism is a phenomenon in a sphere not subject to the influence of factors commonly called economic. Some of these theories even go so far as to assert that nationalistic motivations arise from an intentional neglect of economic matters for the other matters.

A thorough scrutiny of all these dissenting opinions would require an examination of all the fundamental problems of social life and social philosophy. We cannot achieve this in a study devoted to nationalism and the conflicts it has aroused, but must limit ourselves to the problems under investigation.

With regard to prevalent mistakes it may be necessary to emphasize again that we are considering policies and political actions and the doctrines influencing them, not mere views and opinions without practical effect. Our purpose is not to answer such questions as: In what respect do people of various nations, states, linguistic, and other social groups differ from one another? Or: Do they love or hate one another? We wish to know why they prefer a policy of economic nationalism and war to one of peaceful coöperation. Even nations bitterly hating one another would cling to peace and free trade if they were convinced that such a policy best promoted their own interests.

2. The Alleged Irrationality of Nationalism

There are people who believe that they have satisfactorily explained nationalism by establishing its irrationality. They hold it a serious mistake, common mostly to economists, to assume that human action is always rational. Man is not, they say, a rational being. The ultimate goals of his actions are often if not always irrational.

The glory and the greatness of their own nation, state, race, linguistic group, or social class are such irrational goals, which men prefer to increase in wealth and welfare or to the improvement of their standard of living. Men do not like peace, security, and a quiet life. They long for the vicissitudes of war and conquest, for change, adventure, and danger. They enjoy killing, robbing, and destroying. They yearn to march against the enemy when the drums beat, when the trumpets sound, and flags flutter in the wind.

We must recognize, however, that the concepts rational and irrational apply only to means, never to ultimate ends. The judgments of value through which people make their choice among conflicting ultimate ends are neither rational nor irrational. They are arbitrary, subjective, and the outcome of individual points of view. There are no such things as objective absolute values, independent of the individual's preferences. The preservation of life is as a rule considered an ultimate goal. But there have always been men who preferred death to life, when life could be preserved only under conditions that they considered unbearable. Human actions consist always in a choice between two goods or two evils which are not deemed equivalent. Where there is perfect equivalence, man stays neutral; and no action results. But what is good and what is better, or what is bad and what is worse, is decided according to subjective standards, different with different individuals, and changing with the same individuals according to circumstances.

As soon as we apply the concepts rational and irrational to judgments of value we reduce ends to means. We are referring to something which we have set as a provisional end, and considering the choice made on the basis of whether it is an efficient means to attain this end. If we are dealing with other people's actions we are substituting our own judgment for theirs, and if we are dealing with our own past actions we are substituting our present valuations for our valuations at the instant in which we acted.

Rational and irrational always mean: reasonable or not from the point of view of the ends sought. There is no such thing as absolute rationality or irrationality.

We may now understand what people are trying to say when they ascribe irrational motives to nationalism. They mean that liberalism was wrong in assuming that men are more eager to improve the material conditions of their well-being than to attain other ends, e.g., national glory, the enjoyment of the dangerous life, or an indulgence in a taste for sadistic pleasures. Men, they say, have rejected capitalism and free trade because they aim at goals other than those that liberalism considers supreme. They do not seek a life free from want and fear, or one of steadily increasing security and riches, but the particular satisfactions with which the totalitarian dictators provide them.

Whether these statments are true or untrue cannot be determined by philosophical or a priori considerations. These are statements about facts. We need to ask whether the attitude of our contemporaries is really such as these explanations would have us believe.

There is no doubt that there really are some people, who prefer the attainment of other ends to the improvement of their own material well-being. There have always been men who voluntarily renounced many pleasures and satisfactions in order to do what they considered right and moral. Men have preferred martyrdom to the renunciation of what they believed to be true. They have chosen poverty and exile because they wanted to be free in the search for truth and wisdom. All that is noblest in the progress of civilization, welfare, and enlightenment has been the achievement of such men, who braved every danger and defied the tyranny of powerful kings and fanatical masses. The pages of history tell us the epic of heretics burned at the stake, of philosophers put to death from Socrates to Giordano Bruno, of Christians and Jews heroically clinging to their faith in spite of murderous persecutions, and of many other champions of honesty and fidelity whose martyrdom was less spectacular but no less genuine. But these examples of self-denial and readiness to sacrifice have always been exceptional; they have been the privilege of a small elite.

It is furthermore true that there have always been people who sought power and glory. But such aspirations are not contrary to the common longing for more wealth, higher income, and more luxuries. The thirst for power does not involve the renunciation of material improvement. On the contrary, men want to be powerful in order to acquire more wealth than they could get by other methods. Many expect to acquire more treasures by robbing others than they could get by serving consumers. Many chose an adventurous career because they were confident that they could succeed better that way. Hitler, Goebbels, and Goering were simply unfit for any honest job. They were complete failures in the peaceful business of capitalist society. They strove for power, glory, and leadership, and thus became the richest men in present-day Germany. It is nonsense to assert that the "will to power" with them is something contrary to the longing for more material well-being.

The explanation of modern nationalism and war with which we have to deal at this point in our investigation refers not only to the leaders but also to their followers. With regard to these the question is: Is it true that people—the voters, the masses of our contemporaries—have intentionally abandoned liberalism, capitalism, and free trade and substituted for them etatism—interventionism or socialism—economic nationalism and wars and revolutions, because they care more for a dangerous life in poverty than for a good life in peace and security? Do they really prefer being poorer in an environment where no one is better off than they to being richer within a market society where there are people wealthier than they? Do they choose the chaos of interventionism, socialism, and endless wars although they are fully aware that this must mean poverty and hardships for them? Only a man lacking all sense of reality or common observation could venture to answer these questions in the affirmative. Clearly men have abandoned liberalism and are fighting capitalism because they believe that interventionism, socialism, and economic nationalism will make them richer, not poorer. The socialists did not and do not say to the masses: We want to lower your standard of living. The protectionists do not say: Your material well-being will suffer by import duties. The interventionists do not recommend their measures by pointing out their detrimental effects for the commonweal. On the contrary, all these groups insist again and again that their policy will make their partisans richer. People favor etatism because they believe that it will make them richer. They denounce capitalism because they believe that it deprives them of their fair share.

The main point in the propaganda of Nazism between 1919 and 1933 was: World Jewry and Western capitalism have caused your misery; we will fight these foes, thus rendering you more prosperous. German Nazis and Italian Fascists fought for raw materials and fertile soil, and they promised their followers a life of wealth and luxury. The *sacro egoismo* of the Italians is not the mentality of idealists but that of robbers. Mussolini did not praise the dangerous life for its own sake but as a means of getting rich booty. When Goering said that guns are more important than butter he explained that Germans in the immediate future had to restrict their consumption of butter in order to get the guns necessary for the conquest of all the treasures of the world. If this is altruism, self-denial, or irrational idealism, then the gentlemen of Brooklyn's Murder Syndicate were the most perfect altruists and idealists.

The nationalists of all countries have succeeded in convincing their followers that only the policies they recommend are really advantageous to the well-being of the whole nation and of all its honest citizens, of the *we;* and that all other parties are treacherously ready to sell their own nation's prosperity to foreigners, to the *they*. By taking the name "nationalist" they insinuate that the other parties favor foreign interests. The German nationalists in the first World War called themselves the party of the Fatherland, thus labeling all those who favored a negotiated peace, a sincere declaration that Germany did not want to annex Belgium, or no more sinking of liners by submarines, as treacherous foes of the nation. They were not prepared to admit that their adversaries also were honest in their affection for the commonweal. Whoever was not a nationalist was in their eyes an apostate and traitor.

This attitude is common to all contemporary antiliberal parties. The so-called "labor parties," for example, pretend to recommend the only means favorable to the—of course—material interests of labor. Whoever opposes their program becomes for them a foe of labor. They do not permit rational discussion concerning the expediency of their policies for the workers. They are infatuated enough to pay no attention at all to the objections raised against them by economists. What they recommend is good, what their critics urge is bad, for labor.

This intransigent dogmatism does not mean that nationalists or labor leaders are in favor of goals other than those of the material well-being of their nations or classes. It merely illustrates a characteristic feature of our day, the replacement of reasonable discussion by the errors of polylogism. We will deal with this phenomenon in a later chapter.

3. The Aristocratic Doctrine

Among the infinity of fallacious statements and factual errors that go to form the structure of Marxian philosophy there are two that are especially objectionable. Marx asserts that capitalism causes increasing pauperization of the masses, and blithely contends that the proletarians are intellectually and morally superior to the narrow-minded, corrupt, and selfish bourgeoisie. It is not worth while to waste time in a refutation of these fables.

The champions of a return to oligarchic government see things from a quite different angle. It is a fact, they say, that capitalism has poured a horn of plenty for the masses, who do not know why they become more prosperous from day to day. The proletarians have done everything they could to hinder or slow down the pace of technical innovations—they have even destroyed newly invented machines. Their unions today still oppose every improvement in methods of production. The entrepreneurs and capitalists have had to push the reluctant and unwilling masses toward a system of production which renders their lives more comfortable.

Within an unhampered market society, these advocates of aristocracy go on to say, there prevails a tendency toward a diminution of the inequality of incomes. While the average citizen becomes wealthier, the successful entrepreneurs seldom attain wealth which raises them far above the average level. There is but a small group of high incomes, and the total consumption of this group is too insignificant to play any role in the market. The members of the upper middle class enjoy a higher standard of living than the masses but their demands also are unimportant in the market. They live more comfortably than the majority of their fellow citizens but they are not rich enough to afford a style of life substantially different. Their dress is more expensive than that of the lower strata but it is of the same pattern and is adjusted to the same fashions. Their bathrooms and their cars are more elegant but the service they render is substantially the same. The old discrepancies in standards have shrunk to differences that are mostly but a matter of ornament. The private life of a modern entrepreneur or executive differs much less from that of his employees than, centuries ago, the life of a feudal landlord differed from that of his serfs.

It is, in the eyes of these pro-aristocratic critics, a deplorable consequence of this trend toward equalization and a rise in mass standards that the masses take a more active part in the nation's mental and political activities. They not only set artistic and literary standards; they are supreme in politics also. They now have comfort and leisure enough to play a decisive role in communal matters. But they are too narrow-minded to grasp the sense in sound policies. They judge all economic problems from the point of view of their own position in the process of production. For them the entrepreneurs and capitalists, indeed most of the executives, are simply idle people whose services could easily be rendered by "anyone able to read and write." * The masses are full of envy and resentment; they want to expropriate the capitalists and entrepreneurs whose fault is to have served them too well. They are absolutely unfit to conceive the remoter consequences of the measures they are advocating. Thus they are bent on destroying the sources from which their prosperity stems. The policy of democracies is suicidal. Turbulent mobs demand acts which are contrary to society's and their own best interests. They return to Parliament corrupt demagogues, adventurers, and quacks who praise patent medicines and idiotic remedies. Democracy has resulted in an upheaval of the domestic barbarians against reason, sound policies, and civilization. The masses have firmly established the dictators in many European countries. They may succeed very soon in America too. The great experiment of liberalism and democracy has proved to be self-liquidating. It has brought about the worst of all tyrannies.

Not for the sake of the elite but for the salvation of civilization

* See the characteristic ideas of Lenin about the problems of entrepreneurship and management in his pamphlet *State and Revolution* (New York, 1917), pp. 83–84.

and for the benefit of the masses a radical reform is needed. The incomes of the proletarians, say the advocates of an *aristocratic revolution,* have to be cut down; their work must be made harder and more tedious. The laborer should be so tired after his daily task is fulfilled that he cannot find leisure for dangerous thoughts and activities. He must be deprived of the franchise. All political power must be vested in the upper classes. Then the populace will be rendered harmless. They will be serfs, but as such happy, grateful, and subservient. What the masses need is to be held under tight control. If they are left free they will fall an easy prey to the dictatorial aspirations of scoundrels. Save them by establishing in time the oligarchic paternal rule of the best, of the elite, of the aristocracy.

These are the ideas that many of our contemporaries have derived from the writings of Burke, Dostoievsky, Nietzsche, Pareto, and Michels, and from the historical experience of the last decades. You have the choice, they say, between the tyranny of men from the scum and the benevolent rule of wise kings and aristocracies. There has never been in history a lasting democratic system. The ancient and medieval republics were not genuine democracies; the masses—slaves and metics—never took part in government. Anyway, these republics too ended in demagogy and decay. If the rule of a Grand Inquisitor is inevitable, let him rather be a Roman cardinal, a Bourbon prince, or a British lord than a sadistic adventurer of low breeding.

The main shortcoming of this reasoning is that it greatly exaggerates the role played by the lower strata of society in the evolution toward the detrimental present-day policies. It is paradoxical to assume that the masses whom the friends of oligarchy describe as riffraff should have been able to overpower the upper classes, the elite of entrepreneurs, capitalists, and intellectuals, and to impose on them their own mentality.

Who is responsible for the deplorable events of the last decades? Did perhaps the lower classes, the proletarians, evolve the new doctrines? Not at all. No proletarian contributed anything to the construction of antiliberal teachings. At the root of the genealogical tree of modern socialism we meet the name of the depraved scion of one of the most eminent aristocratic families of royal France. Almost all the fathers of socialism were members of the upper middle class or of the professions. The Belgian Henri de Man, once a radical Left-wing socialist, today a no less radical pro-Nazi socialist, was quite right in asserting: "If one accepted the misleading Marxist expression which attaches every social ideology to a definite class, one would have to say that socialism as a doctrine, even Marxism, is of bourgeois origin." * Neither did interventionism and nationalism come from the "scum." They also are products of the well-to-do.

The overwhelming success of these doctrines which have proved so detrimental to peaceful social coöperation and now shake the foundations of our civilization is not an outcome of lower-class activities. The proletarians, the workers, and the farmers are certainly not guilty. Members of the upper classes were the authors of these destructive ideas. The intellectuals converted the masses to this ideology; they did not get it from them. If the supremacy of these modern doctrines is a proof of intellectual decay, it does not demonstrate that the lower strata have conquered the upper ones. It demonstrates rather the decay of the intellectuals and of the bourgeoisie. The masses, precisely because they are dull and mentally inert, have never created new ideologies. This has always been the prerogative of the elite.

The truth is that we face a degeneration of a whole society and not an evil limited to some parts of it.

When liberals recommend democratic government as the only means of safeguarding permanent peace both at home and in international relations, they do not advocate the rule of the mean, of the lowbred, of the stupid, and of the domestic barbarians, as some critics of democracy believe. They are liberals and democrats precisely because they desire government by the men best fitted for the task. They maintain that those best qualified to rule must prove their abilities by convincing their fellow citizens, so that they will voluntarily entrust them with office. They do not cling to the militarist doctrine, common to all revolutionaries, that the proof of qualification is the seizure of office by acts of violence or fraud. No ruler who lacks the gift of persuasion can stay in office long; it is the indispensable condition of government. It would be an idle illusion to assume that any government, no matter how good, could lastingly do without public consent. If our community does not beget men who have the power to make sound social principles generally acceptable, civilization is lost, whatever the system of government may be.

It is not true that the dangers to the maintenance of peace, democracy, freedom, and capitalism are a result of a "revolt of the masses." They are an achievement of scholars and intellectuals, of sons of the well-to-do, of writers and artists pampered by the best society. In every country of the world dynasties and aristocrats have worked with the socialists and interventionists against freedom.

* De Man, *Die Psychologie des Sozialismus* (rev. ed. Jena, 1927), pp. 16–17. Man wrote this at a time when he was a favorite of German Left-wing socialism.

Virtually all the Christian churches and sects have espoused the principles of socialism and interventionism. In almost every country the clergy favor nationalism. In spite of the fact that Catholicism is world embracing, even the Roman Church offers no exception. The nationalism of the Irish, the Poles, and the Slovaks is to a great extent an achievement of the clergy. French nationalism found most effective support in the Church.

It would be vain to attempt to cure this evil by a return to the rule of autocrats and noblemen. The autocracy of the czars in Russia or that of the Bourbons in France, Spain, and Naples was not an assurance of sound administration. The Hohenzollerns and the Prussian Junkers in Germany and the British ruling groups have clearly proved their unfitness to run a country.

If worthless and ignoble men control the governments of many countries, it is because eminent intellectuals have recommended their rule; the principles according to which they exercise their powers have been framed by upper-class doctrinaires and meet with the approval of intellectuals. What the world needs is not constitutional reform but sound ideologies. It is obvious that every constitutional system can be made to work satisfactorily when the rulers are equal to their task. The problem is to find the men fit for office. Neither a priori reasoning nor historical experience has disproved the basic idea of liberalism and democracy that the consent of those ruled is the main requisite of government. Neither benevolent kings nor enlightened aristocracies nor unselfish priests or philosophers can succeed when lacking this consent. Whoever wants lastingly to establish good government must start by trying to persuade his fellow citizens and offering them sound ideologies. He is only demonstrating his own incapacity when he resorts to violence, coercion, and compulsion instead of persuasion. In the long run force and threat cannot be successfully applied against majorities. There is no hope left for a civilization when the masses favor harmful policies. The elite should be supreme by virtue of persuasion, not by the assistance of firing squads.

4. Misapprehended Darwinism

Nothing could be more mistaken than the now fashionable attempt to apply the methods and concepts of the natural sciences to the solution of social problems. In the realm of nature we cannot know anything about final causes, by reference to which events can be explained. But in the field of human actions there is the finality of acting men. Men make choices. They aim at certain ends and they apply means in order to attain the ends sought.

Darwinism is one of the great achievements of the nineteenth century. But what is commonly called Social Darwinism is a garbled distortion of the ideas advanced by Charles Darwin.

It is an ineluctable law of nature, say these pseudo-Darwinists, that each living being devours the smaller and weaker ones and that, when its turn comes, it is swallowed by a still bigger and stronger one. In nature there are no such things as peace or mutual friendship. In nature there is always struggle and merciless annihilation of those who do not succeed in defending themselves. Liberalism's plans for eternal peace are the outcome of an illusory rationalism. The laws of nature cannot be abolished by men. In spite of the liberal's protest we are witnessing a recurrence of war. There have always been wars, there will always be wars. Thus modern nationalism is a return from fallacious ideas to the reality of nature and life.

Let us first incidentally remark that the struggles to which this doctrine refers are struggles between animals of different species. Higher animals devour lower animals; for the most part they do not feed in a cannibalistic way on their own species. But this fact is of minor importance.

The only equipment which the beasts have to use in their struggles is their physical strength, their bodily features, and their instincts. Man is better armed. Although bodily much weaker than many beasts of prey, and almost defenseless against the more dangerous microbes, man has conquered the earth through his most valuable gift, reason. Reason is the main resource of man in his struggle for survival. It is foolish to view human reason as something unnatural or even contrary to nature. Reason fulfills a fundamental biological function in human life. It is the specific feature of man. When man fights he nearly always makes use of it as his most efficient weapon. Reason guides his steps in his endeavors to improve the external conditions of his life and well-being. Man is the reasonable animal, homo sapiens.

Now the greatest accomplishment of reason is the discovery of the advantages of social coöperation, and its corollary, the division of labor. Thanks to this achievement man has been able to centuple his progeny and still provide for each individual a much better life than nature offered to his nonhuman ancestors some hundred thousand years ago. In this sense—that there are many more people living today and that each of them enjoys a much richer life than his fathers did—we may apply the term progress. It is, of course, a judgment of value, and as such arbitrary. But it is made from a point of view which practically all men accept, even if they—like Count Tolstoi or Mahatma Gandhi—seem unconditionally to disparage all our civilization. Human civilization is not something achieved against nature; it is rather the outcome of the working of the innate qualities of man.

Social coöperation and war are in the long run incompatible. Self-sufficient individuals may fight each other without destroying the foundations of their existence. But within the social system of coöperation and division of labor war means disintegration. The progressive evolution of society requires the progressive elimination of war. Under present conditions of international division of labor there is no room left for wars. The great society of world-embracing mutual exchange of commodities and services demands a peaceful coexistence of states and nations. Several hundred years ago it was necessary to eliminate the wars between the noblemen ruling various countries and districts, in order to pave the way for a peaceful development of domestic production. Today it is indispensable to achieve the same for the world community. To abolish international war is not more unnatural than it was five hundred years ago to prevent the barons from fighting each other, or two thousand years ago to prevent a man from robbing and killing his neighbor. If men do not now succeed in abolishing war, civilization and mankind are doomed.

From a correct Darwinist viewpoint it would be right to say: Social coöperation and division of labor are man's foremost tools in his struggle for survival. The intensification of this mutuality in the direction of a world-embracing system of exchange has considerably improved the conditions of mankind. The maintenance of this system requires lasting peace. The abolition of war is therefore an important item in man's struggle for survival.

5. The Role of Chauvinism

Confusing nationalism and chauvinism or explaining nationalism as a consequence of chauvinism is a widespread error.

Chauvinism is a disposition of character and mind. It does not result in action. Nationalism is, on the one hand, a doctrine recommending a certain type of action and, on the other hand, the policy by which this action is consummated. Chauvinism and nationalism are therefore two entirely different things. The two are not necessarily linked together. Many old liberals were also chauvinists. But they did not believe that inflicting harm upon other nations was the proper means of promoting the welfare of their own nation. They were chauvinists but not nationalists.

Chauvinism is a presumption of the superiority of the qualities and achievements of one's own nation. Under present conditions this means, in Europe, of one's own linguistic group. Such arrogance is a common weakness of the average man. It is not too difficult to explain its origin.

Nothing links men more closely together than a community of language, and nothing segregates them more effectively than a difference of language. We may just as well invert this statement by asserting that men who associate with each other use the same idiom, and men between whom there is no direct intercourse do not. If the lower classes of England and of Germany had more in common with each other than with the upper strata of the society of their own countries, then the proletarians of both countries would speak the same idiom, a language different from that of the upper classes. When under the social system of the eighteenth century the aristocracies of various European countries were more closely linked with each other than with the commoners of their own nation, they used a common upper-class language—French.

The man who speaks a foreign language and does not understand our language is a "barbarian," because we cannot communicate with him. A "foreign" country is one where our own idiom is not understood. It is a great discomfort to live in such a country; it brings about uneasiness and homesickness. When people meet other people speaking a foreign language, they regard them as strangers; they come to consider those speaking their own tongue as more closely connected, as friends. They transfer the linguistic designations to the people speaking the languages. All those speaking Italian as their main and daily language are called Italians. Next the linguistic terminology is used to designate the country in which the Italians live, and finally to designate everything in this country that differs from other countries. People speak of Italian cooking, Italian wine, Italian art, Italian industry, and so on. Italian institutions are naturally more familiar to the Italians than foreign ones. As they call themselves Italians, in speaking of these institutions they use the possessive pronouns "mine" and "our."

Overestimation of one's own linguistic community, and of everything commonly called by the same adjective as the language, is psychologically not more difficult to explain than the overvaluation of an individual's own personality or underestimation of that of other persons. (The contrary—undervaluation of a man's own personality and nation, and overestimation of other people and of foreign countries—may sometimes happen too, although more rarely.) At any rate it must be emphasized that chauvinism was more or less restricted up to the beginning of the nineteenth century. Only a small minority had a knowledge of foreign countries, languages, and institutions, and these few were in the

main educated enough to judge foreign things in a relatively objective way. The masses knew nothing about foreign lands. To
them the foreign world was not inferior but merely unfamiliar.
Whoever was conceited in those days was proud of his rank, not of
his nation. Differences in caste counted more than national or
linguistic ones.

With the rise of liberalism and capitalism conditions changed
quickly. The masses became better educated. They acquired a
better knowledge of their own language. They started reading and
learned something about foreign countries and habits. Travel became cheaper, and more foreigners visited the country. The schools
included more foreign languages in their curriculum. But nevertheless for the masses a foreigner is still in the main a creature
whom they know only from books and newspapers. Even today
there are living in Europe millions who have never had the opportunity of meeting or speaking with a foreigner, except on a battlefield.

Conceit and overvaluation of one's own nation are quite common. But it would be wrong to assume that hatred and contempt
of foreigners are natural and innate qualities. Even soldiers fighting
to kill their enemies do not hate the individual foe, if they happen
to meet him apart from the battle. The boastful warrior neither
hates nor despises the enemy; he simply wants to display his own
valor in a glorious light. When a German manufacturer says that
no other country can produce as cheap and good commodities as
Germany, it is no different from his assertion that the products of
his domestic competitors are worse than his own.

Modern chauvinism is a product of literature. Writers and ora-
tors strive for success by flattering their public. Chauvinism spread
therefore with the mass production of books, periodicals, and newspapers. The propaganda of nationalism favors it. Nevertheless, it
has comparatively slight political significance, and must in any case
be clearly distinguished from nationalism.

The Russians are convinced that physics is taught in the schools
of Soviet Russia only, and that Moscow is the only city equipped
with a subway system. The Germans assert that only Germany has
true philosophers; they picture Paris as an agglomeration of amuse-
ment places. The British believe that adultery is quite usual in
France, and the French style homosexuality *le vice allemand*. The
Americans doubt whether the Europeans use bathtubs. These are
sad facts. But they do not result in war.

It is paradoxical that French boors pride themselves on the fact
that Descartes, Voltaire, and Pasteur were Frenchmen and take a
part of Molière's and Balzac's glory to themselves. But it is politi-

cally innocuous. The same is true of the overestimation of one's own country's military achievements and of the eagerness of historians to interpret lost battles, after decades or even centuries, as victories. It gives an impartial observer a curious feeling when Hungarians or Rumanians speak of their nation's civilization in epithets which would be grotesquely incongruous even if the Bible, the Corpus Juris Civilis, the Declaration of the Rights of Man, and the works of Shakespeare, Newton, Goethe, Laplace, Ricardo, and Darwin were written by Hungarians or Rumanians in Hungarian or Rumanian. But the political antagonism of these two nations has nothing to do with such statements.

Chauvinism has not begotten nationalism. Its chief function in the scheme of nationalist policies is to adorn the shows and festivals of nationalism. People overflow with joy and pride when the official speakers hail them as the elite of mankind and praise the immortal deeds of their ancestors and the invincibility of their armed forces. But when the words fade away and the celebration reaches its end, people return home and go to bed. They do not mount the battle-horse.

From the political point of view it is no doubt dangerous that men are so easily stirred by bombastic talk. But the political actions of modern nationalism cannot be explained or excused by chauvinist intoxication. They are the outcome of cool though misguided reasoning. The carefully elaborated, although erroneous, doctrines of scholarly and thoughtful books have led to the clash of nations, to bloody wars, and destruction.

6. The Role of Myths

The term "myths" has long been used to signify purely fictitious narratives and doctrines. In this sense Christians call the teachings and stories of paganism myths. In this sense those who do not share the Christian faith call the biblical tales mythical. For the Christian they are not myths but truth.

This obvious fact has been distorted by writers who maintain that doctrines which cannot stand the criticism of reason can nonetheless be justified by ascribing to them a mythical character. They have tried to build up a rationalistic theory for the salvation of error and its protection against sound reasoning.

If a statement can be disproved, you cannot justify it by giving it the status of a myth and thus making it proof against reasonable objections. It is true that many fictions and doctrines, today generally or in the main refuted and therefore called myths, have played a great role in history. But they played this role not as myths but as doctrines considered true. In the eyes of their supporters they were entirely authentic; they were their honest convictions. They turned to myths in the eyes of those who considered them fictitious and contrary to fact, and who therefore did not let their actions be influenced by them.

For Georges Sorel a myth is the imaginary construction of a future successful action.* But, we must add, to estimate the value of a method of procedure one point only has to be taken into account, namely, whether or not it is a suitable means to attain the end sought. If reasonable examination demonstrates that it is not, it must be rejected. It is impossible to render an unsuitable method of procedure more expedient by ascribing to it the quality of a myth. Sorel says: "If you place yourself on this ground of myths, you are proof against any kind of critical refutation." † But the problem is not to succeed in polemic by taking recourse to subtleties and tricks. The only question is whether or not action guided by the doctrine concerned will attain the ends sought. Even if one sees, as Sorel does, the task of myths to be that of equipping men to fight for the destruction of what exists,‡ one cannot escape the question: Do these myths represent an adequate means to achieve this task? It needs to be pointed out, incidentally, that destruction of existing conditions alone cannot be considered as a goal; it is necessary to build up something new in the place of what is destroyed.

If it is proved by reasonable demonstration that socialism as a social system cannot realize what people wish or expect to realize through it, or that the general strike is not the appropriate means for the attainment of socialism, you cannot change these facts by declaring—as Sorel did—that socialism and the general strike are myths. People who cling to socialism and the general strike wish to attain certain aims through them. They are convinced that they will succeed by these methods. It is not as myths but as doctrines considered to be correct and well founded that socialism and the general strike are supported by millions of men.

Some free thinkers say: Christianity is an absurd creed, a myth; yet it is useful that the masses should adhere to the Christian dogmas. But the advantage that these free thinkers expect depends upon the masses actually taking the Gospels as truth. It could not be attained if they were to regard the Commandments as myths.

* Sorel, *Réflexions sur la violence* (3d ed. Paris, 1912), p. 32: "Les hommes qui participent aux grands mouvements sociaux se représentent leur action prochaine sous formes d'images de batailles assurant le triomphe de leur cause. Je propose de nommer *mythes* ces constructions."

† *Idem*, p. 49.

‡ *Idem*, p. 46.

Whoever rejects a political doctrine as wrong agrees with the generally accepted terminology in calling it a myth.* But if he wants to profit from a popular superstition in order to attain his own ends, he must be careful not to disparage it by calling it a myth openly. For he can make use of this doctrine only so long as others consider it to be truth. We do not know what those princes of the sixteenth century believed who joined the religious Reformation. If not sincere conviction but the desire for enrichment guided them, then they abused the faith of other people for the sake of their own selfish appetites. They would have prejudiced their own interests, however, if they had called the new creed mythical. Lenin was cynical enough to say that revolutions must be achieved with the catchwords of the day. And he achieved his own revolution by affirming publicly—against his better conviction—the catchwords that had taken hold of public opinion. Some party leaders may be capable of being convinced of the falsehood of their party's doctrine. But doctrines can have real influence only so far as people consider them right.

Socialism and interventionism, etatism and nationalism, are not myths, in the eyes of their advocates, but doctrines indicating the proper way to the attainment of their aims. The power of these teachings is based on the firm belief of the masses that they will effectively improve their lot by applying them. Yet they are fallacious; they start from false assumptions and their reasoning is full of paralogisms. Those who see through these errors are right in calling them myths. But as long as they do not succeed in convincing their fellow citizens that these doctrines are untenable, the doctrines will dominate public opinion and politicians and statesmen will be guided by them. Men are always liable to error. They have erred in the past; they will err in the future. But they do not err purposely. They want to succeed, and they know very well that the choice of inappropriate means will frustrate their actions. Men do not ask for myths but for working doctrines that point the right means for the ends sought.

Nationalism in general and Nazism in particular are neither intentional myths nor founded or supported by intentional myths. They are political doctrines and policies (though faulty) and are even "scientific" in intent.

If somebody were prepared to call myths the variations on themes like "We are the salt of the earth," or "We are the chosen people," in which all nations and castes have indulged in one way or another,

* Perroux, *Les Mythes hitleriens* (Lyon, 1935); Rougier, *Les Mystiques politiques contemporaines* (Paris, 1935); Rougier, *Les Mystiques économiques* (Paris, 1938).

we should have to refer to what has been said about chauvinism. This is music for the enchantment and gratification of the community, mere pastime for the hours not devoted to political business. Politics is activity and striving toward aims. It should not be confused with mere indulgence in self-praise and self-adulation.

PART III

GERMAN NAZISM

VI. THE PECULIAR CHARACTERISTICS OF GERMAN NATIONALISM

1. The Awakening

GERMAN nationalism did not differ from other peoples' nationalism until—in the late 1870's and early '80's—the German nationalists made what they believed to be a great discovery. They discovered that their nation was the strongest in Europe. They concluded that Germany was therefore powerful enough to subdue Europe or even the whole world. Their reasoning ran as follows:

The Germans are the most numerous people in Europe, Russia excepted. The Reich itself has within the boundaries drawn by Bismarck more inhabitants than any other European country, with the same exception. Outside the Reich's borders many millions of German-speaking people are living, all of whom, according to the principle of nationality, should join the Reich. Russia, they said, should not be considered since it is not a homogeneous nation but a conglomeration of many different nationalities. If you deduct from Russia's population figures the Poles, Finns, Estonians, Letts, Lithuanians, White Russians, the Caucasian and Mongolian tribes, the Georgians, the Germans in the Baltic provinces and on the banks of the Volga, and especially the Ukrainians, there remain only the Great Russians, who are fewer in number than the Germans. Besides, Germany's population is increasing faster than that of other European nations and much faster than that of the "hereditary" foe, France.

The German nation enjoys the enormous advantage of occupying the central part of Europe. It thus dominates strategically the whole of Europe and some parts of Asia and Africa. It enjoys in warfare the advantages of standing on interior lines.

The German people are young and vigorous, while the Western nations are old and degenerate. The Germans are diligent, virtuous, and ready to fight. The French are morally corrupt, the idol of the

British is mammon and profit, the Italians are weaklings, the Russians are barbarians.

The Germans are the best warriors. That the French are no match for them has been proved by the battles of Rossbach, Katzbach, Leipzig, Waterloo, St. Privat, and Sedan. The Italians always take to their heels. The military inferiority of Russia was evidenced in the Crimea and in the last war with the Turks. English land power has always been contemptible. Britain rules the waves only because the Germans, politically disunited, have in the past neglected the establishment of sea power. The deeds of the old Hanse clearly proved Germany's maritime genius.

It is therefore obvious that the German nation is predestined for hegemony. God, fate, and history chose the Germans when they endowed them with their great qualities. But unfortunately this blessed nation has not yet discovered what its right and its duty demand. Oblivious of their historic mission, the Germans have indulged in internal antagonisms. Germans have fought each other. Christianity has weakened their innate warlike ardor. The Reformation has split the nation into two hostile camps. The Habsburg emperors have misused the Empire's forces for the selfish interests of their dynasty. The other princes have betrayed the nation by supporting the French invaders. The Swiss and the Dutch have seceded. But now finally the day of the Germans has dawned. God has sent to his chosen people their saviors, the Hohenzollerns. They have revived the genuine Teutonic spirit, the spirit of Prussia. They have freed the people from the yoke of the Habsburgs and of the Roman Church. They will march on and on. They will establish the German *imperium mundi*. It is every German's duty to support them to the extent of his own ability; thus he serves his own best interests. Every doctrine by which Germany's foes attempt to weaken the German soul and hinder it in accomplishing its task must be radically weeded out. A German who preaches peace is a traitor and must be treated as such.

The first step of the new policy must consist in the reincorporation of all Germans now outside. The Austrian Empire must be dismembered. All its countries which until 1866 were parts of the German Federation must be annexed (this includes all Czechs and Slovenes). The Netherlands and Switzerland must be reunited with the Reich, and so must the Flemings of Belgium, and the Baltic provinces of Russia, whose upper classes speak German. The army must be strengthened until it can accomplish these conquests. A navy has to be built strong enough to smash the British fleet. Then the most valuable British and French colonies must be annexed. The Dutch East Indies and the Congo State will come automatically under German rule with the conquest of the mother countries. In South America the Reich must occupy a vast area where at least thirty million Germans can settle.*

This program assigned a special task to the German emigrants living in different foreign countries. They were to be organized by nationalist emissaries, to whom the consular service of the Reich should give moral and financial backing. In countries which were to be conquered by the Reich they were to form a vanguard. In the other countries they were by political action to bring about a sympathetic attitude on the part of the government. This was especially planned in regard to the German-Americans, as the plan was to keep the United States neutral as long as possible.

2. *The Ascendancy of Pan-Germanism*

Pan-Germanism was an achievement of intellectuals and writers. The professors of history, law, economics, political science, geography, and philosophy were its most uncompromising advocates. They converted the students of the universities to their ideas. Very soon the graduates made more converts. As teachers in the field of higher education (in the famous German *Gymnasium* and educational institutions of the same rank), as lawyers, judges, civil servants, and diplomats they had ample opportunity to serve their cause.

---

* In order to demonstrate that this last demand, which could be realized only by a victorious war against the United States, was endorsed not only by hotspurs but also by more moderate men, whom the radical nationalists scorned for their leniency and indifference, we need only quote a dictum of Gustav von Schmoller. Schmoller was the universally recognized head of the German socialists of the chair, professor of political science at the University of Berlin, permanent adviser of the Reich government on economic problems, member of the Prussian chamber of Lords and of the Prussian Academy. His compatriots and German officialdom considered him the greatest economist of the age and a great economic historian. The words which we quote are to be found in a book published in Stuttgart in 1900 under the title, *Handels- und Machtpolitik, Reden und Aufsätze im Auftrage der Freien Vereinigung für Flottenvorträge,* edited by Gustav Schmoller, Adolf Wagner, and Max Sering, Professors of Political Science at the University of Berlin, in I, 35, 36. They are: "I cannot dwell on the details of the commercial and colonial tasks for which we need the navy. Only some points may be mentioned briefly. We are bound to wish at all costs that in the coming century a German country of twenty or thirty million Germans be established in Southern Brazil. It is immaterial whether this remain a part of Brazil, whether it be an independent state, or whether it be more closely connected with our Reich. Without communications continually safeguarded by battleships, without Germany's standing ready for vigorous interference in these countries, this evolution would be exposed to peril."

Still more outspoken than Schmoller was his colleague Adolf Wagner, whose fame and official prestige were almost as great. Speaking of the wars to which the endeavor to find dwelling places for the excess German population is bound to lead, of the coming "struggle for space," he adds: "Idle pretensions like the American Monroe Doctrine . . . are not an insurmountable obstacle." (*Agrar- und Industriestaat,* 2d ed. Jena, 1902, p. 83.) Such were the views of old professors, not of boasting youths. It would be easy to quote hundreds of similar comments.

All other strata of the population resisted the new ideas for some time. They did not want more wars and conquests; they wanted to live in peace. They were, as the nationalists scornfully observed, selfish people, not eager to die but to enjoy life.

The popular theory that the Junkers and officers, big business and finance, and the middle classes were the initiators of German nationalism is contrary to fact. All these groups were at first strongly opposed to the aspirations of Pan-Germanism. But their resistance was vain because it lacked an ideological backing. There were no longer any liberal authors in Germany. Thus the nationalist writers and professors easily conquered. Very soon the youth came back from the universities and lower schools convinced Pan-Germans. By the end of the century Germany was almost unanimous in its approval of Pan-Germanism.

Businessmen and bankers were for many years the sturdiest opponents of Pan-Germanism. They were more familiar with foreign conditions than were the nationalists. They knew that France and Great Britain were not decadent, and that it would be very difficult to conquer the world. They did not want to imperil their foreign trade and investments through wars. They did not believe that armored cruisers could accomplish the tasks of commercial travelers and bring them higher profits. They were afraid of the budgetary consequences of greater armaments. They wanted increased sales, not booty. But it was easy for the nationalists to silence these plutocratic opponents. All important offices soon came into the hands of men whom university training had imbued with nationalist ideas. In the etatist state entrepreneurs are at the mercy of officialdom. Officials enjoy discretion to decide questions on which the existence of every firm depends. They are practically free to ruin any entrepreneur they want to. They had the power not only to silence these objectors but even to force them to contribute to the party funds of nationalism. In the trade associations of businessmen the syndics (executives) were supreme. Former pupils of the Pan-German university teachers, they tried to outdo each other in nationalist radicalism. Thus they sought to please the government officials and further their own careers through successful intercession on behalf of the interests of their members.

German nationalism was not, as the Marxians insist, the "ideological superstructure of the selfish class interests of the armaments industry." In the 1870's Germany possessed—apart from the Krupp plant—only comparatively small and not very profitable armament works. There is not the slightest evidence for the assumption that they subsidized the contemporary nationalist free-lance writers. They had nothing whatever to do with the much more effective propaganda of the university teachers. The large capital invested in munitions works since the 'eighties has been rather a consequence than the cause of German armaments.* Of course every business-man is in favor of tendencies that may result in an increase in his sales. "Soap capital" desires more cleanliness, "building capital" a greater demand for homes, "publishing capital" more and better education, and "armaments capital" bigger armaments. The short-run interests of every branch of business encourage such attitudes. In the long run, however, increased demand results in an inflow of more capital into the booming branch, and the competition of the new enterprises cuts down the profits.

The dedication of a greater part of Germany's national income to military expenditure correspondingly reduced that part of the na-tional income that could be spent by individual consumers for their own consumption. In proportion as armaments increased the sales of munition plants, they reduced the sales of all other industries. The more subtle Marxians do not maintain that the nationalist authors have been bribed by munitions capital but that they have "unconsciously" supported its interests. But this implies that they have to the same extent "unconsciously" hurt the interests of the greater part of the German entrepreneurs and capitalists. What made the "world soul," which directs the working of philosophers and writers against their will, and forces them to adjust their ideas to the lines prescribed by inevitable trends of evolution, so partial as to favor some branches of business at the expense of other, more numerous branches?

It is true that since the beginning of our century almost all Ger-man capitalists and entrepreneurs have been nationalists. But so were, even to a greater degree, all other strata, groups, and classes of Germany. This was the result of nationalist education. This was an achievement of authors like Lagarde, Peters, Langbehn, Treitschke, Schmoller, Houston Stewart Chamberlain, and Naumann.

It is not true that the Berlin court, the Junkers, and the aristo-cratic officers sympathized from the beginning with the Pan-German ideas. The Hohenzollerns and their retainers had sought Prussian hegemony in Germany and at an increase in German prestige in Europe. They had attained these goals and were satisfied. They did not want more. They were anxious to preserve the German caste system, with the privileges of the dynasties and of the aristocracy; this was more important for them than the struggle for world dom-ination. They were not enthusiastic about the construction of a

* Of the five iron armored battleships which the Germans had in the Franco-German war of 1870, three were built in England and two in France. It was only late that Germany developed a domestic industry of naval armaments.

strong navy or about colonial expansion. Bismarck yielded unwillingly to colonial plans.

But courts and noblemen were unable to offer successful resistance to a popular movement supported by intellectuals. They had long since lost all influence on public opinion. They derived an advantage from the defeat of liberalism, the deadly foe of their own privileges. But they themselves had contributed nothing to the ascendancy of the new etatist ideas; they simply profited by the change of mentality. They regarded the nationalist ideas as somewhat dangerous. Pan-Germanism was full of praise for old Prussia and its institutions, for the conservative party in its capacity as adversary of liberalism, for the army and the navy, for the commissioned officers and for the nobility. But the Junkers disliked one point in the nationalist mentality which seemed to them democratic and revolutionary. They considered the nationalist commoners' interference with foreign policy and military problems a piece of impudence. In their eyes these two fields were the exclusive domain of the sovereign. While the support which the nationalists granted to the government's domestic policies pleased them, they regarded as a kind of rebellion the fact that the Pan-Germans had views of their own about "higher politics." The court and the nobles seemed to doubt the right of the people even to applaud their achievements in these fields.

But all such qualms were limited to the older generations, to the men who had reached maturity before the foundation of the new Empire. William II and all his contemporaries were already nationalists. The rising generation could not protect itself from the power of the new ideas. The schools taught them nationalism. They entered the stage of politics as nationalists. True, when in public office, they were obliged to maintain a diplomatic reserve. Thus it happened time and again that the government publicly rebuked the Pan-Germans and sharply rejected suggestions with which it secretly sympathized. But as officialdom and Pan-Germans were in perfect agreement about ultimate aims, such incidents were of little importance.

The third group which opposed radical nationalism was Catholicism. But Catholicism's political organization, the Center party, was neither prepared nor mentally fitted to combat a great intellectual evolution. Its method consisted simply in yielding to every popular trend and trying to use it for its own purposes, the preservation and improvement of the Church's position. The Center's only principle was Catholicism. For the rest it had neither principles nor convictions, it was purely opportunist. It did everything from which success in the next election campaign could be expected. It coöperated, according to changing conditions, at one time with the Protestant conservatives, at another with the nationalists, at another with the Social Democrats. It worked with the Social Democrats in 1918 to overthrow the old system and later in the Weimar Republic. But in 1933 the Center was ready to share power in the Third Reich with the Nazis. The Nazis frustrated these designs. The Center was not only disappointed but indignant when its offer was refused.

The Center party had organized a powerful system of Christian labor unions which formed one of its most valuable auxiliaries and was eager to call itself a working man's party. As such it considered it its duty to further Germany's export trade. The economic ideas generally accepted by German public opinion maintained that the best means of increasing exports was a great navy and an energetic foreign policy. Since the German pseudo-economists viewed every import as a disadvantage and every export as an advantage, they could not imagine how foreigners could be induced to buy more German products by other means than by "an impressive display of German naval power." As most of the professors taught that who-ever opposes increased armaments furthers unemployment and a lowering of the standard of living, the Center in its capacity as a labor party could not vigorously resist the nationalist extremists. Besides, there were other considerations. The territories marked first for annexation in Pan-Germanism's program for conquest were inhabited mainly by Catholics. Their incorporation was bound to strengthen the Reich's Catholic forces. Could the Center regard such plans as unsound?

Only liberalism would have had the power to antagonize Pan-Germanism. But there were no more liberals left in Germany.

3. German Nationalism Within an Etatist World

German nationalism differs from that of other European coun-tries only in the fact of the people's believing itself to be the strong-est in Europe. Pan-Germanism and its heir, Nazism, are the applica-tion of general nationalist doctrines to the special case of the most populous and most powerful nation, which is, however, in the un-lucky position of being dependent on imported foodstuffs and raw materials.

German nationalism is not the outcome of innate Teutonic bru-tality or rowdyism. It does not stem from blood or inheritance. It is not a return of the grandsons to the mentality of their Viking ancestors; the Germans are not the descendants of the Vikings. The forefathers of the Germans of our day were German tribes (who did *not* participate in the invasions which gave the last blow to ancient civilization), Slavonic and Baltic tribes of the northeast, and Celtic aborigines of the Alps. There is more non-German than German "blood" in the veins of present-day Germans. The Scandinavians, the genuine scions of the Vikings, have a different type of nationalism and apply different political methods from those of the Germans. No one can tell whether the Swedes, if they were as numerous as the Germans are today, would in our age of nationalism have adopted the methods of Nazism. Certainly the Germans, if they had not been more numerous than the Swedes, would not have succumbed to the mentality of world conquest.

The Germans invented neither interventionism nor etatism, with their inevitable result, nationalism. They imported these doctrines from abroad. They did not even invent the most conspicuous chauvinistic adornment of their own nationalism, the fable of Aryanism.

It is easy to expose the fundamental errors, fallacies, and paralogisms of German nationalism if one places oneself on the sound basis of scientific praxeology and economics and the practical philosophy of liberalism derived from them. But etatists are helpless when trying to refute the essential statements of Pan-Germanism and Nazism. The only objection they can consistently raise to the teachings of German nationalism is that the Germans were mistaken when they assumed they could conquer all other nations. And the only weapons they can use against Nazism are military ones.

It is inconsistent for an etatist to object to German nationalism on the ground that it means coercion. The state always means coercion. But while liberalism seeks to limit the application of coercion and compulsion to a narrow field, etatists do not recognize these restrictions. For etatism coercion is the essential means of political action, indeed the only means. It is considered proper for the government of Atlantis to use armed men—i.e., customs and immigration officers —in order to hinder the citizens of Thule from selling commodities on the markets of Atlantis or from working in the factories of Atlantis. But if this is so, then no effective logical argument can be brought forward against the plans of the government of Thule to defeat the armed forces of Atlantis and thus to prevent them from inflicting harm on the citizens of Thule. The only working argument for Atlantis is to repulse the aggressors.

We can see this essential matter clearly by comparing the social effects of private property and those of territorial sovereignty. Both private property and territorial sovereignty can be traced back to a point where somebody either appropriated ownerless goods or land or violently expropriated a predecessor whose title had been based on appropriation. To law and legality no other origin can be ascribed. It would be contradictory or nonsensical to assume a "legitimate" beginning. The factual state of affairs became a legitimate one by its acknowledgment by other people. Lawfulness consists in the general acceptance of the rule that no *further* arbitrary appropriations or violent expropriations shall be tolerated. For the sake of peace, security, and progress, it is agreed that in the future every change of property shall be the outcome of voluntary exchange by the parties directly concerned.

This, of course, involves the recognition of the appropriations and expropriations effected in the past. It means a declaration that the present state of distribution, although arbitrarily established, must be respected as the legal one. There was no alternative. To attempt to establish a fair order through the expropriation of all owners and an entirely new distribution would have resulted in endless wars.

Within the framework of a market society the fact that legal formalism can trace back every title either to arbitrary appropriation or to violent expropriation has lost its significance. Ownership in the market society is no longer linked up with the remote origin of private property. Those events in a far-distant past, hidden in the darkness of primitive mankind's history, are no longer of any concern for our present life. For in an unhampered market society the consumers decide by their daily buying or not buying who should own and what he should own. The working of the market daily allots anew the ownership of the means of production to those who know how to use them best for the satisfaction of consumers. Only in a legal and formalistic sense can the owners be considered the successors of appropriators and expropriators. In fact, they are the mandataries of the consumers, bound by the laws of the market to serve the wants or whims of the consumers. The market is a democracy. Capitalism is the consummation of the self-determination of consumers. Mr. Ford is richer than Mr. X because he succeeded better in serving the consumers.

But all this is not true of territorial sovereignty. Here the fact that once in a remote past a Mongolian tribe occupied the country of Tibet still has its full importance. If there should one day be discovered in Tibet precious resources that could improve the lot of every human being it would depend on the Dalai Lama's discretion whether the world should be allowed to make use of these treasures or not. His is the sovereignty of this country; his title, derived from a bloody conquest thousands of years ago, is still supreme and exclusive. This unsatisfactory state of things can be remedied only by violence, by war. Thus war is inescapable; it is the *ultima ratio*; it is the only means of solving such antagonisms—unless people have recourse to the principles of liberalism. It is precisely in order to make war unnecessary that liberalism recommends laissez faire and laissez passer, which would render political boundaries innocuous. A liberal government in Tibet would not hinder anyone from making the best use of the country's resources. If you want to abolish war, you must eliminate its causes. What is needed is to restrict government activities to the preservation of life, health, and private property, and thereby to safeguard the working of the market. Sovereignty must not be used for inflicting harm on anyone, whether citizen or foreigner.

In the world of etatism sovereignty once more has disastrous implications. Every sovereign government has the power to use its apparatus of coercion and compulsion to the disadvantage of citizens and foreigners. The gendarmes of Atlantis apply coercion against the citizens of Thule. Thule orders its army to attack the forces of Atlantis. Each country calls the other aggressor. Atlantis says: "This is our country; we are free to act within its boundaries as we like; you, Thule, have no right to interfere." Thule answers: "You have no title but earlier conquest; now you take advantage of your sovereignty to discriminate against our citizens; but we are strong enough to annul your title by superior force."

Under such conditions there is but one means to avoid war: to be so strong that no one ventures aggression against you.

4. A Critique of German Nationalism

No further critique of nationalism is needed than that provided by liberalism, which has refuted in advance all its contentions. But the plans of *German* nationalism must be considered impracticable even if we omit any reference to the doctrines of liberalism. It is simply not true that the Germans are strong enough to conquer the world. It is moreover not true that they could enjoy the victory if they succeeded.

Germany built up a tremendous military machine while other nations foolishly neglected to organize their defenses. Nevertheless Germany is much too weak, even when supported by allies, to fight the world. The arrogance of the Pan-Germans and of the Nazis was founded upon the vain hope that they would be able to fight each foreign nation as an isolated enemy in a sequence of successful wars. They did not consider the possibility of a united front of the menaced nations.

Bismarck succeeded because he was able to fight first Austria and then France, while the rest of the world kept its neutrality. He was wise enough to realize that this was due to extraordinarily fortunate circumstances. He did not expect that fate would always favor his country in the same way, and he freely admitted that the *cauchemar des coalitions* disturbed his sleep. The Pan-Germans were less cautious. But in 1914 the coalition which Bismarck had feared became a fact. And so it is again today.

Germany did not learn the lesson taught by the first World War. We shall see later, in the chapter dealing with the role of anti-Semitism, what ruse the Nazis used to disguise the meaning of this lesson.

The Nazis are convinced that they must finally conquer because they have freed themselves from the chains of morality and humanity. Thus they argue: "If we conquer, this war will be the last one, and we will establish our hegemony forever. For when we are victorious we will exterminate our foes, so that a later war of revenge or a rebellion of the subdued will be impossible. But if the British and the Americans conquer, they will grant us a passable peace. As they feel themselves bound by moral law, divine commandments, and other nonsense, they will impose on us a new Versailles, maybe something better or something worse, at any rate not extermination, but a treaty which will enable us to renew the fighting after some lapse of time. Thus we will fight again and again, until one day we will have reached our goal, the radical extermination of our foes."

Let us assume for the sake of argument that the Nazis succeed and that they impose on the world what they call a German peace. Will the satisfactory functioning of the German state be possible in such a world, whose moral foundations are not mutual understanding but oppression? Where the principles of violence and tyranny are supreme, there will always be some groups eager to gain advantage from the subjugation of the rest of the nation. Perpetual wars will result among the Germans themselves. The subdued non-German slaves may profit from these troubles in order to free themselves and to exterminate their masters. The moral code of Nazism supported Hitler's endeavors to smash by the weapons of his bands all opposition that his plans encountered in Germany. The Storm Troopers are proud of "battles" fought in beer saloons, assembly halls, and back streets,* of assassinations and felonious assaults. Whoever deemed himself strong enough would in the future too take recourse to such stratagems. The Nazi code results in endless civil wars.

The strong man, say the Nazis, is not only entitled to kill. He has

---

* The old Storm Troopers call themselves proudly *Saalkämpfer*, i.e., beer-hall fighters.

the right to use fraud, lies, defamation, and forgery as legitimate weapons. Every means is right that serves the German nation. But who has to decide what is good for the German nation?

To this question the Nazi philosopher replies quite candidly: Right and noble are what I and my comrades deem such, are what the sound feelings of the people (*das gesunde Volksempfinden*) hold good, right, and fair. But whose feelings are sound and whose unsound? About that matter, say the Nazis, there can be no dispute between genuine Germans. But who is a genuine German? Whose thoughts and feelings are genuinely German and whose are not? Whose ideas are German ones—those of Lessing, Goethe, and Schiller, or those of Hitler and Goebbels? Was Kant, who wanted eternal peace, genuinely German? Or are Spengler, Rosenberg, and Hitler, who call pacifism the meanest of all ideas, genuine Germans? There is dissension among men to whom the Nazis themselves do not deny the appellation German. The Nazis try to escape from this dilemma by admitting that there are some Germans who unfortunately have un-German ideas. But if a German does not always necessarily think and feel in a correct German way, who is to decide which German's ideas are German and which un-German? It is obvious that the Nazis are moving in a circle. Since they abhor as manifestly un-German decision by majority vote, the conclusion is inescapable that according to them German is whatever those who have succeeded in civil war consider to be German.

5. Nazism and German Philosophy

It has been asserted again and again that Nazism is the logical outcome of German idealistic philosophy. This too is an error. German philosophical ideas played an important role in the evolution of Nazism. But the character and extent of these influences have been grossly misrepresented.

Kant's moral teachings, and his concept of the categorical imperative, have nothing at all to do with Prussianism or with Nazism. The categorical imperative is not the philosophical equivalent of the regulations of the Prussian military code. It was not one of the merits of old Prussia that in a far-distant little town a man like Kant occupied a chair of philosophy. Frederick the Great did not care a whit for his great subject. He did not invite him to his philosophical breakfast table whose shining stars were the Frenchmen Voltaire and Alembert. The concern of his successor, Frederick William II, was to threaten Kant with dismissal if he were once more insolent enough to write about religious matters. Kant submitted. It is nonsensical to consider Kant a precursor of Nazism. Kant advocated eternal peace between nations. The Nazis praise war "as the eternal shape of higher human existence" * and their ideal is "to live always in a state of war." †

The popularity of the opinion that German nationalism is the outcome of the ideas of German philosophy is mainly due to the authority of George Santayana. However, Santayana admits that what he calls "German philosophy" is "not identical with philosophy in Germany," and that "the majority of intelligent Germans held views which German philosophy proper must entirely despise." ‡ On the other hand, Santayana declares that the first principle of German philosophy is "borrowed, indeed, from non-Germans." § Now, if this nefarious philosophy is neither of German origin nor the opinion held by the majority of intelligent Germans, Santayana's statements shrink to the establishment of the fact that some German philosophers adhered to teachings first developed by non-Germans || and rejected by the majority of intelligent Germans, in which Santayana believes he has discovered the intellectual roots of Nazism. But he does not explain why these ideas, although foreign to Germany and contrary to the convictions of its majority, have begotten Nazism just in Germany and not in other countries.

Then, again, speaking of Fichte and Hegel he says: "Theirs is a revealed philosophy. It is the heir of Judaism. It could never have been founded by free observation of life and nature, like the philosophy of Greece or of the Renaissance. It is Protestant theology rationalized." ¶ Exactly the same could be said with no less justification of the philosophy of many British and American philosophers.

According to Santayana the main source of German nationalism is egotism. Egotism should "not be confused with the natural egoism or self-assertion proper to every living creature." Egotism "assumes, if it does not assert, that the source of one's being and power lies in oneself, that will and logic are by right omnipotent, and that nothing should control the mind or the conscience except the mind or the conscience itself.** But egotism, if we are prepared to use the term as defined above by Santayana, is the starting point of the utilitarian philosophy of Adam Smith, Ricardo, Bentham, and the two Mills, father and son. Yet, these British scholars did not derive from their first principle conclusions of a Nazi character.

---

* Spengler, *Preussentum und Sozialismus* (Munich, 1925), p. 54.

† Th. Fritsch in "Hammer" (1914), p. 541, as quoted by Hertz, *Nationalgeist und Politik* (Zurich, 1937), I, 467.

‡ Santayana, *Egotism in German Philosophy* (new ed. London, 1939), p. 1.

§ Santayana, *op. cit.*, p. 9.

|| Speaking of Fichte, Mr. Santayana (*op. cit.*, p. 21) says that his philosophy "was founded on one of Locke's errors."

¶ Santayana, *op. cit.*, p. 11.

** *Idem*, p. 151.

Theirs is a philosophy of liberalism, democratic government, social coöperation, good will and peace among nations.

Neither egoism nor egotism is the essential feature of German nationalism, but rather its ideas concerning the means through which the supreme good is to be attained. German nationalists are convinced that there is an insoluble conflict between the interests of the individual nations and those of a world-embracing community of all nations. This also is not an idea of German origin. It is a very old opinion. It prevailed up to the age of enlightenment, when the above-mentioned British philosophers developed the fundamentally new concept of the harmony of the—rightly understood—interests of all individuals and of all nations, peoples, and races. As late as 1764 no less a man than Voltaire could blithely say, in the article "Fatherland" of his *Dictionary of Philosophy:* "To be a good patriot means to wish that one's own community shall acquire riches through trade and power through its arms. It is obvious that a country cannot profit but by the disadvantage of another country, and cannot be victorious but by making other peoples miserable." This identification of the effects of peaceful human coöperation and the mutual exchange of commodities and services with the effects of war and destruction is the main vice of the Nazi doctrines. Nazism is neither simple egoism nor simple egotism; it is *misguided* egoism and egotism. It is a relapse into errors long ago refuted, a return to Mercantilism and a revival of ideas described as militarism by Herbert Spencer. It is, in short, the abandonment of the liberal philosophy, today generally despised as the philosophy of Manchester and laissez faire. And its ideas are, in this respect, unfortunately not limited to Germany.

The contribution of German philosophy to the ascendancy of Nazi ideas had a character very different from that generally ascribed to it. German philosophy always rejected the teachings of utilitarian ethics and the sociology of human coöperation. German political science never grasped the meaning of social coöperation and division of labor. With the exception of Feuerbach all German philosophers scorned utilitarianism as a mean system of ethics. For them the basis of ethics was intuition. A mystical voice in his soul makes man know what is right and what is wrong. The moral law is a restraint imposed upon man for the sake of other people's or society's interests. They did not realize that each individual serves his own—rightly understood, i.e., long-run—interests better by complying with the moral code and by displaying attitudes which further society than by indulging in activities detrimental to society. Thus they never understood the theory of the harmony of interests and the merely temporary character of the sacrifice which man makes in renouncing some immediate gain lest he endanger the existence of society. In their eyes there is an insoluble conflict between the individual's aims and those of society. They did not see that the individual must practice morality for his own, not for somebody else's or for the state's or society's welfare. The ethics of the German philosophers are heteronomous. Some mystical entity orders man to behave morally, that is to renounce his selfishness for the advantage of a higher, nobler, and more powerful being, society.

Whoever does not understand that the moral laws serve the interests of all and that there is no insoluble conflict between private and social interests is also incapable of understanding that there is no insoluble conflict between the different collective entities. The logical outcome of his philosophy is the belief in an irremediable antagonism between the interest of every nation and the whole of human society. Man must choose between allegiance to his nation and allegiance to humanity. Whatever best serves the great international society is detrimental to every nation, and vice versa. But, adds the nationalist philosopher, only the nations are true collective entities, while the concept of a great human society is illusory. The concept of humanity was a devilish brew concocted by the Jewish founders of Christianity and of Western and Jewish utilitarian philosophy in order to debilitate the Aryan master race. The first principle of morality is to serve one's own nation. Right is whatever best serves the German nation. This implies that right is whatever is detrimental to the races that stubbornly resist Germany's aspirations for world domination.

This is very fragile reasoning. It is not difficult to expose its fallacies. The Nazi philosophers are fully aware that they are unable logically to refute the teachings of liberal philosophy, economics, and sociology. And thus they resort to polylogism.

6. Polylogism

The Nazis did not invent polylogism. They only developed their own brand.

Until the middle of the nineteenth century no one ventured to dispute the fact that the logical structure of mind is unchangeable and common to all human beings. All human interrelations are based on this assumption of a uniform logical structure. We can speak to each other only because we can appeal to something common to all of us, namely, the logical structure of reason. Some men can think deeper and more refined thoughts than others. There are men who unfortunately cannot grasp a process of inference in long chains of deductive reasoning. But as far as a man is able to think and to follow a process of discursive thought, he always clings to the same ultimate principles of reasoning that are applied by all other men. There are people who cannot count further than three; but their counting, as far as it goes, does not differ from that of Gauss or Laplace. No historian or traveler has ever brought us any knowledge of people for whom *a* and non-*a* were identical, or who could not grasp the difference between affirmation and negation. Daily, it is true, people violate logical principles in reasoning. But whoever examines their inferences competently can uncover their errors.

Because everyone takes these facts to be unquestionable, men enter into discussions; they speak to each other; they write letters and books; they try to prove or to disprove. Social and intellectual coöperation between men would be impossible if this were not so. Our minds cannot even consistently imagine a world peopled by men of different logical structures or a logical structure different from our own.

Yet, in the course of the nineteenth century this undeniable fact has been contested. Marx and the Marxians, foremost among them the "proletarian philosopher" Dietzgen, taught that thought is determined by the thinker's class position. What thinking produces is not truth but "ideologies." This word means, in the context of Marxian philosophy, a disguise of the selfish interest of the social class to which the thinking individual is attached. It is therefore useless to discuss anything with people of another social class. Ideologies do not need to be refuted by discursive reasoning; they must be *unmasked* by denouncing the class position, the social background, of their authors. Thus Marxians do not discuss the merits of physical theories; they merely uncover the "bourgeois" origin of the physicists.

The Marxians have resorted to polylogism because they could not refute by logical methods the theories developed by "bourgeois" economics, or the inferences drawn from these theories demonstrating the impracticability of socialism. As they could not rationally demonstrate the soundness of their own ideas or the unsoundness of their adversaries' ideas, they have denounced the accepted logical methods. The success of this Marxian stratagem was unprecedented. It has rendered proof against any reasonable criticism all the absurdities of Marxian would-be economics and would-be sociology. Only by the logical tricks of polylogism could etatism gain a hold on the modern mind.

Polylogism is so inherently nonsensical that it cannot be carried consistently to its ultimate logical consequences. No Marxian was bold enough to draw all the conclusions that his own epistemological viewpoint would require. The principle of polylogism would lead to the inference that Marxian teachings also are not objectively true but are only "ideological" statements. But the Marxians deny it. They claim for their own doctrines the character of absolute truth. Thus Dietzgen teaches that "the ideas of proletarian logic are not party ideas but the outcome of logic pure and simple." * The proletarian logic is not "ideology" but absolute logic. Present-day Marxians, who label their teachings the *sociology of knowledge,* give proof of the same inconsistency. One of their champions, Professor Mannheim, tries to demonstrate that there exists a group of men, the "unattached intellectuals," who are equipped with the gift of grasping truth without falling prey to ideological errors.† Of course, Professor Mannheim is convinced that he is the foremost of these "unattached intellectuals." You simply cannot refute him. If you disagree with him, you only prove thereby that you yourself are not one of this elite of "unattached intellectuals" and that your utterances are ideological nonsense.

The German nationalists had to face precisely the same problem as the Marxians. They also could neither demonstrate the correctness of their own statements nor disprove the theories of economics and praxeology. Thus they took shelter under the roof of polylogism, prepared for them by the Marxians. Of course, they concocted their own brand of polylogism. The logical structure of mind, they say, is different with different nations and races. Every race or nation has its own logic and therefore its own economics, mathematics, physics, and so on. But, no less inconsistently than Professor Mannheim, Professor Tirala, his counterpart as champion of Aryan epistemology, declares that the only true, correct, and perennial logic and science are those of the Aryans.‡ In the eyes of the Marxians Ricardo, Freud, Bergson, and Einstein are wrong because they are bourgeois; in the eyes of the Nazis they are wrong because they are Jews. One of the foremost goals of the Nazis is to free the Aryan soul from the pollution of the Western philosophies of Descartes, Hume, and John Stuart Mill. They are in search of an *arteigen* § German science, that is, of a science adequate to the racial character of the Germans.

We may reasonably assume as a hypothesis that man's mental

---

* Dietzgen, *Briefe über Logik, speziell demokratisch-proletarische Logik* (2d ed. Stuttgart, 1903), p. 112.

† Mannheim, *Ideology and Utopia* (London, 1936), pp. 137 ff.

‡ Tirala, *Rasse, Geist und Seele* (Munich, 1935), pp. 190 ff.

§ The word *arteigen* is one of the many German terms coined by the Nazis. It is a main concept of their polylogism. Its counterpart is *artfremd,* or alien to the racial character. The criterion of science and truth is no longer correct or incorrect, but *arteigen* or *artfremd* abilities are the outcome of his bodily features. Of course, we cannot demonstrate the correctness of this hypothesis, but neither is it possible to demonstrate the correctness of the opposite view as expressed in the theological hypothesis. We are forced to recognize that we do not know how out of physiological processes thoughts result. We have some vague notions of the detrimental effects produced by traumatic or other damage inflicted on certain bodily organs; we know that such damage may restrict or completely destroy the mental abilities and functions of men. But that is all. It would be no less than insolent humbug to assert that the natural sciences provide us with any information concerning the alleged diversity of the logical structure of mind. Polylogism cannot be derived from physiology or anatomy or any other of the natural sciences.

Neither Marxian nor Nazi polylogism ever went further than to declare that the logical structure of mind is different with various classes or races. They never ventured to demonstrate precisely in what the logic of the proletarians differs from the logic of the bourgeois, or in what the logic of the Aryans differs from the logic of the Jews or the British. It is not enough to reject wholesale the Ricardian theory of comparative cost or the Einstein theory of relativity by unmasking the alleged racial background of their authors. What is wanted is first to develop a system of Aryan logic different from non-Aryan logic. Then it would be necessary to examine point by point these two contested theories and to show where in their reasoning inferences are made which—although correct from the viewpoint of non-Aryan logic—are invalid from the viewpoint of Aryan logic. And, finally, it should be explained what kind of conclusions the replacement of the non-Aryan inferences by the correct Aryan inferences must lead to. But all this never has been and never can be ventured by anybody. The garrulous champion of racism and Aryan polylogism, Professor Tirala, does not say a word about the difference between Aryan and non-Aryan logic. Polylogism, whether Marxian or Aryan, or whatever, has never entered into details.

Polylogism has a peculiar method of dealing with dissenting views. If its supporters fail to unmask the background of an opponent, they simply brand him a traitor. Both Marxians and Nazis know only two categories of adversaries. The aliens—whether members of a nonproletarian class or of a non-Aryan race—are wrong because they are aliens; the opponents of proletarian or Aryan origin are wrong because they are traitors. Thus they lightly dispose of the unpleasant fact that there is dissension among the members of what they call their own class or race.

The Nazis contrast German economics with Jewish and Anglo-Saxon economics. But what they call German economics differs not at all from some trends in foreign economics. It developed out of the teachings of the Genevese Sismondi and of the French and British socialists. Some of the older representatives of this alleged German economics merely imported foreign thought into Germany. Frederick List brought the ideas of Alexander Hamilton to Germany, Hildebrand and Brentano brought the ideas of early British socialism. Arteigen German economics is almost identical with contemporary trends in other countries, e.g., with American Institutionalism.

On the other hand, what the Nazis call Western economics and therefore artfremd is to a great extent an achievement of men to whom even the Nazis cannot deny the term German. Nazi economists wasted much time in searching the genealogical tree of Carl Menger for Jewish ancestors; they did not succeed. It is nonsensical to explain the conflict between economic theory, on the one hand, and Institutionalism and historical empiricism, on the other hand, as a racial or national conflict.

Polylogism is not a philosophy or an epistemological theory. It is an attitude of narrow-minded fanatics, who cannot imagine that anybody could be more reasonable or more clever than they themselves. Nor is polylogism scientific. It is rather the replacement of reasoning and science by superstitions. It is the characteristic mentality of an age of chaos.

7. *Pan-Germanism and Nazism*

The essential ideas of Nazism were developed by the Pan-Germans and the socialists of the chair in the last thirty years of the nineteenth century. The system was completed long before the outbreak of the first World War. Nothing was lacking and nothing but a new name was added later. The plans and policies of the Nazis differ from those of their predecessors in imperial Germany only in the fact that they are adapted to a different constellation of political conditions. The ultimate aim, German world hegemony, and the means for its attainment, conquest, have not changed.

One of the most curious facts of modern history is that the foreigners for whom this German nationalism was a menace did not sooner become aware of the danger. A few Englishmen saw through it. But they were laughed at. To Anglo-Saxon common sense the Nazi plans seemed too fantastic to be taken seriously. Englishmen, Americans, and Frenchmen seldom have a satisfactory command of the German language; they do not read German books and newspapers. English politicians who had visited Germany as tourists and had met German statesmen were regarded by their fellow countrymen as experts on German problems. Englishmen who had once attended a ball at the court in Berlin or dined in the officers' mess of a Potsdam regiment of the Royal Guards came home with the glad tidings that Germany is peace loving and a good friend of Great Britain. Proud of their knowledge acquired on the spot, they arrogantly dismissed the holders of dissenting views as "theorists and pedantic doctrinaires."

King Edward VII, himself the son of a German father and of a mother whose German family did not assimilate itself to British life, was highly suspicious of the challenging attitudes of his nephew, William II. It was to the King's credit that Great Britain, almost too late, turned toward a policy of defense and of coöperation with France and Russia. But even then the British did not realize that not the Kaiser alone but almost the whole German nation was eager for conquest. President Wilson labored under the same mistake. He too believed that the court and the Junkers were the instigators of the aggressive policy and that the people were peace loving.

Similar errors prevail today. Misled by Marxian prejudices, people cling to the opinion that the Nazis are a comparatively small group which has, through fraud and violence, imposed its yoke on the reluctant masses. They do not understand that the internal struggles which shook Germany were disputes among people who were unanimous in regard to the ultimate ends of German foreign policy. Rathenau, whom the Nazis assassinated, was one of the outstanding literary champions both of German socialism and of German nationalism. Stresemann, whom the Nazis disparaged as pro-Western, was in the years of the first World War one of the most radical advocates of the so-called German peace—i.e., the annexation of huge territories at both western and eastern borders of the Reich. His Locarno policy was a make-shift devised to give Germany a free hand in the East. If the communists had seized power in Germany, they would not have adopted a less aggressive policy than the Nazis did. Strasser, Rauschning, and Hugenberg were personal rivals of Hitler, not opponents of German nationalism.

VII. THE SOCIAL DEMOCRATS IN IMPERIAL GERMANY

1. The Legend

KNOWLEDGE concerning Germany and the evolution and present-day actions of Nazism is obscured by the legends about the German Social Democrats.

The older legend, developed before 1914, runs like this: The German bourgeoisie have betrayed freedom to German militarism. They have taken refuge with the imperial government in order to preserve, through the protection of the Prussian Army, their position as an exploiting class, which was menaced by the fair claims of labor. But the cause of democracy and freedom, which the bourgeois have deserted, has found new advocates in the proletarians. The Social Democrats are gallantly fighting Prussian militarism. The Emperor and his aristocratic officers are eager to preserve feudalism. The bankers and industrialists, who profit from armaments, have hired corrupt writers in order to spread a nationalist ideology and to make the world believe that Germany is united in nationalism. But the proletarians cannot be deceived by the nationalist hirelings of big business. Thanks to the education that they got from the Social Democrats they see through this fraud. Millions vote the socialist ticket and return to Parliament members fearlessly opposing militarism. The Kaiser and his generals arm for war, but they fail to take account of the people's strength and resolution. There are the 110 socialist members of Parliament.* Behind them are millions of workers organized in the trade-unions who vote for the Social Democrats, in addition to other voters, who —although not registered members of the party—also vote its ticket. They all combat nationalism. They stand with the (second) International Working Men's Association, and are firmly resolved to oppose war at all costs. These truly democratic and pacifist men can be relied upon without hesitation. They, the workers, are the deciding factor, not the exploiters and parasites, the industrialists and Junkers.

The personalities of the Social Democratic leaders were well known all over the world. The public listened whenever they addressed the Reichstag or party congresses. Their books were translated into nearly every language and read everywhere. Led by such men, mankind seemed to be marching toward a better future.

Legends die hard. They blind the eyes and close the mind

* Elected in 1912, the last election in the imperial Reich.

against criticism or experience. It was in vain that Robert Michels *
and Charles Andler † tried to give a more realistic picture of the
German Social Democrats. Not even the later events of the first
World War shattered these illusions. To the old legend, instead, a
new one was added.

This new legend goes: Before the outbreak of the first World
War the party's great old men, Bebel and Liebknecht, unfortunately died. Their successors, mainly intellectuals and other professional politicians of nonproletarian background, betrayed the
party's principles. They coöperated with the Kaiser's policy of
aggression. But the workers, who in their capacity as proletarians
naturally and necessarily were socialist, democratic, revolutionary,
and internationally minded, deserted these traitors and replaced
them by new leaders, old Liebknecht's son Karl and Rosa Luxemburg. The workers, not their old dishonest leaders, made the Revolution of 1918 and dethroned the Kaiser and other German princes.
But the capitalists and the Junkers did not give up the game. The
treacherous party leaders Noske, Ebert, and Scheidemann aided
them. For fourteen long years the workers fought a life-and-death
struggle for democracy and freedom. But, again and again betrayed
by their own leaders, they were doomed to fail. The capitalists
concocted a satanic scheme which finally brought them victory.
Their armed gangs seized power, and now Adolf Hitler, the puppet
of big business and finance, rules the country. But the masses despise this wretched hireling. They yield unwillingly to the terrorism which has overpowered them, and they gallantly prepare the
new decisive rebellion. The day of victory for genuine proletarian
communism, the day of liberation, is already dawning.

Every word of these legends distorts the truth.

2. *Marxism and the Labor Movement*

Karl Marx turned to socialism at a time when he did not yet
know economics and because he did not know it. Later, when the
failure of the Revolution of 1848 and 1849 forced him to flee Germany, he went to London. There, in the reading room of the British Museum, he discovered in the 'fifties not, as he boasted, the laws
of capitalist evolution, but the writings of British political economy, the reports published by the British Government, and the
pamphlets in which earlier British socialists used the theory of

* See the bibliography of Michels' writings in *Studi in Memoria di Roberto Michels,*
"Annali della Facoltà di Giurisprudenza delle R. Università di Perugia" (Padova,
1937), Vol. XLIX.

† Andler, *Le Socialisme impérialiste dans l'Allemagne contemporaine, Dossier d'une
polémique avec Jean Jaurès* (1912–13) (Paris, 1918).

value as expounded by classical economics for a moral justification of labor's claims. These were the materials out of which Marx built his "economic foundations" of socialism.

Before he moved to London Marx had quite naïvely advocated a program of interventionism. In the Communist Manifesto in 1847 he expounded ten measures for imminent action. These points, which are described as "pretty generally applicable in the most advanced countries," are defined as "despotic inroads on the rights of property and on the conditions of bourgeois methods of production." Marx and Engels characterize them as "measures, economically unsatisfactory and untenable, but which in the course of events outstrip themselves, necessitate further inroads upon the old social order and are indispensable as a means of entirely revolutionizing the whole mode of production." * Eight of these ten points have been executed by the German Nazis with a radicalism that would have delighted Marx. The two remaining suggestions (namely, expropriation of private property in land and dedication of all rents of land to public expenditure, and abolition of all right of inheritance) have not yet been fully adopted by the Nazis. However, their methods of taxation, their agricultural planning, and their policies concerning rent restriction are daily approaching the goals determined by Marx. The authors of the Communist Manifesto aimed at a step-by-step realization of socialism by measures of social reform. They were thus recommending procedures which Marx and the Marxians in later years branded as socio-reformist fraud.

In London, in the fifties, Marx learned very different ideas. The study of British political economy taught him that such acts of intervention in the operation of the market would not serve their purpose. From then on he dismissed such acts as "petty-bourgeois nonsense" which stemmed from ignorance of the laws of capitalist evolution. Class-conscious proletarians are not to base their hopes on such reforms. They are not to hinder the evolution of capitalism as the narrow-minded petty bourgeois want to. The proletarians, on the contrary, should hail every step of progress in the capitalist system of production. For socialism will not replace capitalism until capitalism has reached its full maturity, the highest stage of its own evolution. "No social system ever disappears before all the productive forces are developed for the development of which it is broad enough, and new higher methods of production never appear before the material conditions of their existence have been hatched

---

* Communist Manifesto, end of the second section. In their preface to a new edition of the Manifesto, dated June 24, 1872, Marx and Engels declare that because of changed circumstances "stress is no longer laid on the revolutionary measures proposed at the end of the second section."

out in the womb of the previous society." * Therefore there is but *one* road toward the collapse of capitalism—i.e., the progressive evolution of capitalism itself. Socialization through the expropriation of capitalists is a process "which executes itself through the operation of the inherent laws of capitalist production." Then "the knell of capitalistic private property sounds." † Socialism dawns and "ends . . . the primeval history of human society." ‡

From this viewpoint it is not only the endeavors of social reformers eager to restrain, to regulate, and to improve capitalism that must be deemed vain. No less contrary to purpose appear the plans of the workers themselves to raise wage rates and their standard of living, through unionization and through strikes, within the framework of capitalism. "The very development of modern industry must progressively turn the scales in favor of the capitalist against the workingman," and "consequently the general tendency of capitalist production is not to raise but to sink the average standard of wages." Such being the tendency of things within the capitalist system, the most that trade-unionism can attempt is to make "the best of the occasional chances for their temporary improvement." Trade-unions ought to understand that and to change their policies entirely. "Instead of the *conservative* motto: *A fair day's wages for a fair day's work,* they ought to inscribe on their banner the *revolutionary* watchword: *Abolition of the wages system!*" §

These Marxian ideas might impress some Hegelians steeped in dialectics. Such doctrinaires were prepared to believe that capitalist production begets "with the inexorability of a law of nature its own negation" as "negation of negation," ‖ and to wait until, "with the change of the economic basis," the "whole immense superstructure will have, more or less rapidly, accomplished its revolution." ¶ A political movement for the seizure of power, as Marx envisaged it, could not be built up on such beliefs. Workers could not be made supporters of them. It was hopeless to look for coöperation on the ground of such views from the labor movement, which did not have to be inaugurated but was already in existence. This labor movement was essentially a trade-union movement. Fully impregnated with ideas branded as petty bourgeois by Marx, unionized labor sought higher wage rates and fewer hours of work; it demanded labor legislation, price control of consumer's goods, and rent re-

* Marx, *Zur Kritik der politischen Oekonomie,* edited by Kautsky (Stuttgart, 1897), p. xii.
† Marx, *Das Kapital* (7th ed. Hamburg, 1914), I, 728.
‡ Marx, *Zur Kritik der politischen Oekonomie,* p. xii.
§ Marx, *Value, Price and Profit,* edited by Eleanor Marx Aveling (New York, 1901), pp. 72–74.
‖ Marx, *Das Kapital, op. cit.,* p. 729.
¶ Marx, *Zur Kritik der politischen Oekonomie,* p. xi.

striction. The workers sympathized not with Marxian teachings and the recipes derived from them but with the program of the interventionists and the social reformers. They were not prepared to renounce their plans and wait quietly for the far-distant day when capitalism was bound to turn into socialism. These workers were pleased when the Marxian propagandists explained to them that the inevitable laws of social evolution had destined them for greater things, that they were chosen to replace the rotten parasites of capitalist society, that the future was theirs. But they wanted to live for their own day, not for a distant future, and they asked for an immediate payment on account of their future inheritance.

The Marxians had to choose between a rigid uncompromising adherence to their master's teachings and an accommodating adaptation to the point of view of the workers, who could provide them with honors, power, influence and, last but not least, with a nice income. They could not resist the latter temptation, and yielded. They kept on discussing Marxian dialectics in the midst of their own circles; Marxism, moreover, had an esoteric character. But out in the open they talked and wrote in a different way. They headed the labor movement for which wage raises, labor legislation, and social insurance provisions were of greater importance than sophisticated discussions concerning "the riddle of the average rate of profit." They organized consumer's coöperatives and housing societies; they backed all the anticapitalist policies which they stigmatized in their Marxian writings as petty-bourgeois issues. They did everything that their Marxian theories denounced as nonsense, and they were prepared to sacrifice all their principles and convictions if some gain at the next election campaign could be expected from such a sacrifice. They were implacable doctrinaires in their esoteric books and unprincipled opportunists in their political activities.

The German Social Democrats developed this double-dealing into a perfect system. There was on the one side the very narrow circle of initiated Marxians, whose task it was to watch over the purity of the orthodox creed and to justify the party's political actions, incompatible with these creeds, by some paralogisms and fallacious inferences. After the death of Marx, Engels was the authentic interpreter of Marxian thought. With the death of Engels, Kautsky inherited this authority. He who deviated an inch from the correct dogma had to recant submissively or face pitiless exclusion from the party's ranks. For all those who did not live on their own funds such an exclusion meant the loss of the source of income. On the other hand, there was the huge, daily increasing body of party bureaucrats, busy with the political activities of the labor movement. For these men the Marxian phraseology was only an adornment to their propaganda. They did not care a whit for historical materialism or for the theory of value. They were interventionists and reformers. They did whatever would make them popular with the masses, their employers. This opportunism was extremely successful. Membership figures and contributions to the party, its trade unions, coöperatives, and other associations increased steadily. The party became a powerful body with a large budget and thousands of employees. It controlled newspapers, publishing houses, printing offices, assembly halls, boarding houses, coöperatives, and plants to supply the needs of the coöperatives. It ran a school for the education of the rising generation of party executives. It was the most important agency in the Reich's political structure, and was paramount in the Second International Working Men's Association.

It was a serious mistake not to perceive this dualism, which housed under the same roof two radically different principles and tendencies, incompatible and incapable of being welded together. For it was the most characteristic feature of the German Social Democratic party and of all parties formed abroad after its model. The very small groups of zealous Marxians—probably never more than a few hundred persons in the whole Reich—were completely segregated from the rest of the party membership. They communicated with their foreign friends, especially with the Austrian Marxians (the "Austro-Marxian doctrinaires"), the exiled Russian revolutionaries, and with some Italian groups. In the Anglo-Saxon countries Marxism in those days was practically unknown. With the daily political activities of the party these orthodox Marxians had little in common. Their points of view and their feelings were strange, even disgusting, not only to the masses but also to many party bureaucrats. The millions voting the Social Democratic ticket paid no attention to these endless theoretical discussions concerning the concentration of capital, the collapse of capitalism, finance capital and imperialism, and the relations between Marxian materialism and Kantian criticism. They tolerated this pedantic clan because they saw that they impressed and frightened the "bourgeois" world of statesmen, entrepreneurs, and clergymen, and that the government-appointed university professors, that German Brahmin caste, took them seriously and wrote voluminous works about Marxism. But they went their own way and let the learned doctors go theirs.

Much has been said concerning the alleged fundamental difference between the German labor movement and the British. But it is not recognized that a great many of these differences were of an accidental and external character only. Both labor parties desired socialism; both wanted to attain socialism gradually by reforms within the framework of capitalist society. Both labor movements were essentially trade-union movements. For German labor in the imperial Reich Marxism was only an ornament. The Marxians were a small group of literati.

The antagonism between the Marxian philosophy and that of labor organized in the Social Democratic party and its affiliated trade-unions became crucial the instant the party had to face new problems. The artificial compromise between Marxism and labor interventionism broke down when the conflict between doctrine and policies spread into fields which up to that moment had had no practical significance. The war put the party's alleged internationalism to the test, as the events of the postwar period did its alleged democratic tendencies and its program of socialization.

3. The German Workers and the German State

For an understanding of the role played by the Social Democratic labor movement within imperial Germany, a correct conception of the essential features of trade-unionism and its methods is indispensable. The problem is usually dealt with from the viewpoint of the right of workers to associate with one another. But this is not at all the question. No liberal government has ever denied anybody the right to form associations. Furthermore, it does not matter whether the laws grant or do not grant the employees and wage earners the right to break contracts *ad libitum*. For even if the workers are legally liable to indemnify the employer concerned, practical expediency renders the claims of the employer worthless.

The chief method which trade-unions can and do apply for the attainment of their aims—more favorable terms for labor—is the strike. At this point of our inquiry we do not need to discuss again whether trade-unions can ever succeed in raising wages, lastingly and for all workers, above the rates fixed by the unhampered market; we need merely mention the fact that economic theory—both the old classic theory, including its Marxian wing, and the modern, including its socialist wing—categorically answers this question in the negative.* We are here concerned only with the problem of what kind of weapon trade-unions employ in their dealings with employers. The fact is that all their collective bargaining is conducted under the threat of a suspension of labor. Union spokesmen argue that a yellow or company union is a spurious union, because it objects to recourse to strike. If the labor unions

* See above, pp. 64–65.

were not to threaten the employer with a strike, their collective bargaining would succeed no better than the individual bargaining of each worker. But a strike may be frustrated by the refusal of some of the workers to join it, or the entrepreneur's employing strikebreakers. The trade-unions use intimidation and coercion against everyone who tries to oppose the strikers. They resort to acts of violence against the persons and property of both strikebreakers and entrepreneurs or executives who try to employ strikebreakers. In the course of the nineteenth century the workers of all countries achieved this privilege, not so much by explicit legislative sanction as by the accommodating attitudes of the police and the courts. Public opinion has espoused the unions' cause. It has approved strikes, stigmatized strikebreakers as treacherous scoundrels, approved the punishment inflicted by organized labor on reluctant employers and on strikebreakers, and reacted strongly when the authorities tried to interfere to protect the assaulted. A man who ventures to oppose trade-unions has been practically an outlaw, to whom the protection of the government is denied. A law of custom has been firmly established that entitles trade-unions to resort to coercion and violence.

This resignation on the part of the governments has been less conspicuous in the Anglo-Saxon countries, where custom always allowed a wider field for the individual's redress of his private grievances, than in Prussia and the rest of Germany, where the police were almighty and accustomed to interfere in every sphere of life. Woe to anybody who in the realm of the Hohenzollerns was found guilty of the slightest infraction of one of the innumerable decrees and *"verboten!"* The police were busy interfering, and the courts pronounced draconic sentences. Only three kinds of infringements were tolerated. Dueling, although prohibited by the penal code, was practically free, within certain limits, to commissioned officers, university students, and men of that social rank. The police also connived when drunken members of smart university students' clubs kicked up a row, disturbed quiet people, and took their pleasures in other kinds of disorderly conduct. Of incomparably greater importance, however, was the indulgence granted to the excesses usually connected with strikes. Within a certain sphere the violent action of strikers was tolerated.

It is in the nature of every application of violence that it tends toward a transgression of the limit within which it is tolerated and viewed as legitimate. Even the best discipline cannot always prevent police officers from striking harder than circumstances require, or prison wardens from inflicting brutalities on inmates. Only formalists, cut off from reality, fall into the illusion that fighting soldiers can be induced to observe the rules of warfare strictly. Even if the field customarily assigned for the violent action of trade-unions had been limited in a more precise manner, transgressions would have occurred. The attempt to put boundaries around this special privilege has led again and again to conflicts between officials and strikers. And because the authorities time and again could not help interfering, sometimes even with the use of weapons, the illusions spread that the government was assisting the employers. For that reason the public's attention has been diverted from the fact that employers and strikebreakers were within broad limits at the mercy of the strikers. Wherever there was a strike, there was within certain limits no longer any government protection for the opponents of the trade-unions. Thus the unions became in effect a public agency entitled to use violence to enforce their ends, as were later the pogrom gangs in Czarist Russia and the Storm Troopers in Nazi Germany.

That the German Government granted these privileges to the trade-unions became of the highest importance in the course of German affairs. Thus from the 1870's on successful strikes became possible. There had been some strikes, it is true, before then in Prussia. But at that time conditions were different. The employers could not find strikebreakers in the neighborhood of plants located in small places; and the backward state of transportation facilities, the laws restricting freedom of migration within the country, and lack of information about labor market conditions in other districts prevented them from hiring workers from distant points. When these circumstances changed, strikes could only be successful when supported by threats, violence, and intimidation.

The imperial government never seriously considered altering its pro-union policy. In 1899, seemingly yielding to the demands of the employers and nonunionized workers, it brought up in the Reichstag a bill for the protection of nonstrikers. This was merely a deception. For the lack of protection of those ready to work was not due to the inadequacy or defectiveness of the existing penal code but to the purposeful neglect of the valid laws on the part of the police and other authorities. Neither the laws nor the rulings of the courts played any real role in this matter. As the police did not interfere and the state's attorneys did not prosecute, the laws were not enforced and the tribunals had no opportunity to pass judgment. Only when the trade-unions transgressed the actual limits drawn by the police could a case be brought to the tribunals. The government was firmly resolved not to change this state of affairs. It was not eager to induce Parliament to agree to the proposed bill; and Parliament in fact rejected it. If the government had taken the bill seriously, Parliament would have proceeded quite differently. The German Government knew very well how to make the Reichstag yield to its wishes.

The outstanding fact in modern German history was the imperial government's entering into a virtual alliance and factual political coöperation with all groups hostile to capitalism, free trade, and an unhampered market economy. Hohenzollern militarism tried to fight "bourgeois" liberalism and "plutocratic" parliamentarism by associating with the pressure groups of labor, farming, and small business. It aimed at substituting, for what it called a system of unfair exploitation, government interference with business and, at a later stage, all-round national planning.

The ideological and speculative foundations of this system were laid down by the socialists of the chair, a group of professors monopolizing the departments of the social sciences at the German universities. These men, whose tenets were almost identical with those later held by the British Fabians and the American Institutionalists, acted, as it were, as the brain trust of the government. The system itself was called by its supporters *Sozialpolitik,* or *das soziale Königtum der Hohenzollern.* Neither expression lends itself to a literal translation. Perhaps they should be translated as New Deal; for their main features—labor legislation, social security, endeavors to raise the price of agricultural products, encouragement of coöperatives, a sympathetic attitude toward tradeunionism, restrictions imposed on stock exchange transactions, heavy taxation of corporations—corresponded to the American policy inaugurated in 1933.*

The new policy was inaugurated at the end of the 'seventies and was solemnly advertised in an imperial message of November 17, 1881. It was Bismarck's aim to outdo the Social Democrats in measures beneficial to labor interests. His old-fashioned autocratic inclinations pushed him into a hopeless fight against the Social Democratic leaders. His successors dropped the antisocialist laws but unswervingly continued the Sozialpolitik. It was with regard to British policies that Sidney Webb said, as early as in 1889: "It may now fairly be claimed that the socialist philosophy of today is but the conscious and explicit assertion of principles of social organization which have been already in great part unconsciously adopted. The economic history of the century is an almost continuous record of the progress of socialism." † However, in those years German Sozialpolitik was far ahead of contemporary British reformism.

* Elmer Roberts used the term "monarchical socialism." See his book *Monarchical Socialism in Germany* (New York, 1913).

† Sidney Webb in *Fabian Essays in Socialism* (American ed. New York, 1891), p. 4.

The German socialists of the chair gloried in the achievements of their country's social progress. They prided themselves on the fact that Germany was paramount in pro-labor policies. It escaped their notice that Germany could eclipse Great Britain in matters of social legislation and trade-unionism only because its protective tariff and its cartels raised domestic prices above world market prices, while the English still clung to free trade. German real wages did not rise more than the productivity of labor. Neither the government's Sozialpolitik nor trade-union activities but the evolution of capitalist enterprise caused the improvement in the general standard of living. It was no merit of the government or of trade-unions that the entrepreneurs perfected the methods of production and filled the market with more and better goods. The German worker could consume more goods than his father and grandfather, because, thanks to the new methods of production, his work was more efficient and produced more and better commodities. But in the eyes of the professors the fall of mortality figures and the rise in per capita consumption were a proof of the blessings of the Hohenzollern system. They attributed the increase of exports to the fact that Germany was now one of the most powerful nations, and that the imperial navy and army made other nations tremble before it. Public opinion was fully convinced that but for the government's interference the workers would be no better off than they had been fifty or a hundred years earlier.

Of course, the workers were prepared to believe that the government was slow to act and that its pro-labor policy could proceed much more quickly. They found in every new measure only an incentive to ask for more. Yet while criticizing the government for its tardiness they did not disapprove of the attitude of the Social Democrat members of the Reichstag who voted against all bills proposed by the government and supported by the "bourgeois" members. The workers agreed both with the Social Democrats, who called every new pro-labor measure an insolent fraud imposed by the bourgeoisie on labor, and with the government-appointed professors, who lauded the same measures as the most beneficial achievements of German Kultur. They were delighted with the steady rise in their standard of living, which they too attributed not to the working of capitalism but to the activities both of trade-unions and of the government. They ventured no attempts at upheaval. They liked the revolutionary phraseology of the Social Democrats because it frightened the capitalists. But the glory and the splendor of the Reich fascinated them. They were loyal citizens of the Reich, his Majesty's loyal opposition.

This allegiance was so firm and unshakable that it stood the test of the laws against the Social Democrats. These laws were but one link in the long series of blunders committed by Bismarck in his domestic policies. Like Metternich, Bismarck was fully convinced that ideas could be successfully defeated by policemen. But the results obtained were contrary to his intentions. The Social Democrats emerged from the trial of these years no less invigorated than in the 'seventies the Center party and the Catholic Church had emerged from the *Kulturkampf*, the great anti-Catholic campaign. In the twelve years the antisocialist laws were in force (1878–90) the socialist votes increased considerably. The laws touched only those socialists who took an active part in politics. They did not seriously discommode the trade-unions and the masses voting for the socialists. Precisely in those years the government's pro-labor policy made its greatest steps forward; the government wanted to surpass the socialists. The workers realized that the state was becoming more and more their own state and that it was increasingly backing their fight against the employers; the government-appointed factory inspectors were the living personification of this coöperation. The workers had no reason to be hostile to this state merely because it annoyed the party leaders.* The individual party member in the years of the antisocialist laws punctually and regularly received newspapers and pamphlets smuggled in from Switzerland, and read the Reichstag speeches of the socialist deputies. He was a loyal "revolutionary" and a—somewhat critical and sophisticated—monarchist. Marx and the Kaiser both were mistaken in their belief that these quiet fellows thirsted for the princes' blood. But Lassalle had been right when he delineated the future coöperation of the Hohenzollern state and the socialist proletarians.

The unconditional loyalty of the proletarians made the army an accommodating tool in the hands of its commanders. Liberalism had shaken the foundations of Prussian absolutism. In the days of its supremacy the king and his aides no longer trusted the bulk of their army; they knew that this army could not be used against the domestic foe or for wars of undisguised aggression. Socialism and interventionism, the Kaiser's New Deal, had restored the loyalty of the armed forces; now they could be used for any purpose. The men responsible for the new trend in politics, the statesmen and professors, were fully aware of this. It was just because they strove toward this end that they supported the inauguration of the Sozialpolitik and asked for its intensification. The officers of the army were convinced that the Social Democratic soldiers were completely

---

* In those days in the happy 'eighties people used to speak of "persecutions." But compared with what the Bolsheviks and the Nazis have since done to their opponents, these persecutions were little more than a nuisance.

reliable men. The officers disapproved, therefore, of the Kaiser's contemptuous disparagement of the Social Democrats just as in earlier years they had disapproved of Bismarck's measures against them (as well as of his anti-Catholic policy). They detested the defiant speeches of the socialist deputies but trusted the Social Democratic soldier. They themselves hated the wealthy entrepreneurs no less than the workers did. In the days of the antisocialist campaign, in 1889, their lyrical spokesman, Detlev von Liliencron, admitted it frankly.* Junkers and officers were firmly welded into a virtual coalition with labor by the instrument that forges the most solid unions, deadly hatred. When the Social Democrats paraded in the streets, the officers—in plain clothes—looked upon the marching columns and smilingly commented: "We ourselves have taught these boys how to march properly; they will do a very good job under our orders when Mobilization day comes." Later events proved the correctness of these expectations.

On August 3, 1914, Reich's Chancellor Bethmann-Hollweg received the chairmen of all parliamentary party groups at a conference. Comrade Scheidemann reports: "The Chancellor shook hands with each of us. It seemed to me that he shook my hand in a surprising way, firmly and long, and when he then said, *How do you do, Mr. Scheidemann,* I felt as if he were giving me to understand: *Well, now I hope our traditional squabble is finished for some time.*" † Such were the views of the party's great popular leader on the fifty years of antagonism. Not a historical struggle of the class-conscious proletariat against exploiters and imperialistic warmongers, as the official speakers at party meetings used to declare, but merely a squabble that could be ended by a handshake.

4. The Social Democrats Within the German Caste System

Capitalism improved the social and economic position of hired labor. From year to year the number of hands employed in German industries increased. From year to year the incomes and living standard of labor went up. The workers were more or less contented. Of course, they envied the wealth of the upper middle classes (but not that of the princes and the aristocrats) and they were eager to get more. But looking back to the conditions under which their parents had lived and remembering the experiences of their own childhood, they had to confess that things were after

* See his letter of September 17, 1889, published in *Deutsche Rundschau*, XXI (Berlin, 1910), 663.
† Scheidemann, *Der Zusammenbruch* (Berlin, 1921), p. 9.

all not so bad. Germany was prosperous and the working masses shared its prosperity.

There was still much poverty left in Germany. It could hardly be otherwise in a country in which public opinion, government, and almost all political parties were eager to put obstacles in the way of capitalism. The standards of living were unsatisfactory in eastern agriculture, in coal mining, and in some branches of production which failed to adjust their methods to changed conditions. But those workers who were not themselves involved were not much concerned about the lot of their less fortunate fellow workers. The concept of class solidarity was one of the Marxian illusions.

Yet one thing vexed the more prosperous workers just because they were prosperous. In their capacity as wage earners they had no definite standing in German society. Their new caste lacked recognition by the old established castes. The petty bourgeois, the small traders, shopkeepers, and craftsmen, and the numerous class of people holding minor offices in the service of the Reich, of the individual states, and of the municipalities turned up their noses at them. The incomes of these petty bourgeois were no higher than the workers'; their jobs indeed were often more tedious than the average worker's; but they were haughty and priggish and disdained the wage earners. They were not prepared to admit workers to their bowling circles, to permit them to dance with their daughters, or to meet them socially. Worst of all, the burghers would not let the workers join their ex-warriors' associations.* On Sundays and on state occasions these ex-warriors, clad in correct black frock coats, with tall silk hats and black ties, paraded gravely through the main streets, strictly observing the rules of military marching. It distressed the workers very much that they could not participate. They felt ashamed and humiliated.

For such grievances the Social Democratic organization provided an efficacious remedy. The Social Democrats gave the workers bowling clubs, dances, and outdoor gatherings of their own. There were associations of class-conscious proletarian canary breeders, philatelists, chess-players, friends of Esperanto, and so on. There were independent workers' athletics, with labor championships. And there were proletarian parades with bands and flags. There were countless committees and conferences; there were chairmen and deputy chairmen, honorary secretaries, honorary treasurers, committee members, shop stewards, wardens, and other party officers. The workers lost their feeling of inferiority and sense of loneliness. They were no longer society's stepchildren; they were firmly in-

---

* The official name of these clubs was Warriors' Associations (*Kriegervereine*). The members were men who had served in the Reich's armed forces.

tegrated into a large community; they were important people burdened with responsibilities and duties. And their official speakers, spectacled scholars with academic degrees, convinced them that they were not only as good but better than the petty bourgeois, a class that was in any event doomed to disappear.

What the Social Democrats really achieved was not to implant a revolutionary spirit in the masses but on the contrary to reconcile them to the German caste system. The workers got a status within the established order of the German clan system; they became a caste by themselves, with all the narrow-mindedness and all the prejudices of a social set. They did not cease to fight for higher wages, shorter hours of work, and lower prices for cereals, but they were no less loyal citizens than the members of those other pressure groups, the farmers and the artisans.

It was one of the paradoxical phenomena of imperial Germany that the Social Democratic workers used to talk sedition in public while remaining in their hearts perfectly loyal, and that the upper middle class and the professions, although flamboyantly advertising their loyalty to king and fatherland, grumbled in private. One of the main objects of their worry was their relation to the army.

The Marxian legends, which have misrepresented every angle of German life, have distorted this too. The bourgeoisie, they say, surrendered to militarism because they were anxious to obtain commissions in the reserve of the armed forces. Not to be an officer in the reserve, it is true, was a serious blow to the honor and reputation of a man of the upper middle class. The civil servants, the professional men, the entrepreneurs, and the business executives who did not achieve this were seriously handicapped in their careers and business activities. But the attainment and maintenance of a commission in the reserve also brought their troubles. It was not the fact that an officer of the reserve was forbidden to be connected in any way with opposition parties that made them complain. The judges and the civil servants were in any case members of the parties backing the government; if they had not been they would never have received their appointments. The entrepreneurs and the business executives were, by the working of the interventionist system, forced to be politically neutral or to join one of the pro-government parties. But there were other difficulties.

Governed by Junker prejudices, the army required that in his private life and business an officer of the reserve should strictly comply with its own code of gentlemanly conduct. It was not officerlike for an entrepreneur or an executive to do any manual work in his plant, even merely to show a worker how he should perform his task. The son of an entrepreneur who worked for some time at a machine, in order to become familiar with the business, was not eligible for a commission. Neither was the owner of a big store who occasionally looked after a customer. A lieutenant of the reserve who happened to be an architect of world-wide fame was once reprimanded by his colonel because one day, when supervising the redecoration of the reception room in the town hall of a large city, he had taken off his jacket and personally hung an old painting on the wall. There were men who were distressed because they did not obtain commissions in the reserve, and there were officers who secretly boiled with rage because of the attitude of their superiors. It was, in brief, not a pleasure for a commoner to be an officer of the reserve in the Prussian Army.

The lower classes, of course, were not familiar with these tribulations of the officers of the reserve. They saw only the insolence with which these men overcompensated their feelings of inferiority. But they observed too that the officers—both commissioned and noncommissioned—were eager to harass the so-called one-year men, i.e., the high-school graduates who had only one year to serve. They exulted when the officers called the son of their boss names and shouted that in the ranks of the army neither education nor wealth nor one's father's big business made any difference.

The social life of the upper middle class was poisoned by the continuous friction between the pretensions of the noble officers and the bourgeoisie. But the civilians were helpless. They had been defeated in their struggle for a reorganization of Germany.

5. *The Social Democrats and War*

Marx was not a pacifist. He was a revolutionary. He scorned the wars of emperors and kings, but he worked for the great civil war, in which the united proletarians of the world should fight the exploiters. Like all other utopians of the same brand, he was convinced that this war would be the last one. When the proletarians had conquered and established their everlasting regime, nobody would be in a position to deprive them of the fruits of their victory. In this last war Engels assigned to himself the role of commander in chief. He studied strategy in order to be equal to his task when *the day* should dawn.

This idea of the coöperation of all proletarians in the last struggle for liberation led to the foundation of the First International Working Men's Association in 1864. This association was hardly more than a round table of doctrinaires. It never entered the field of political action. Its disappearance from the scene attracted as little notice as had its previous existence.

In 1870 two of the five Social Democratic members of the North German Parliament, Bebel and Liebknecht, opposed the war with France. Their attitudes, as the French socialist Hervé observed, were "personal gestures which had no consequences and did not meet with any response." The two nations, the Germans and the French, says Hervé, "were heart and soul on the battlefields. The Internationalists of Paris were the most fanatical supporters of the war to the knife. . . . The Franco-German War was the moral failure of the International." *

The Second International, founded in Paris in 1889, was an achievement of one of the many international congresses held in cities blessed by a world's fair. In the twenty-five years which had passed since the foundation of the First International the concept of a great world revolution had lost a good deal of its attraction. The new organization's purpose could no longer be presented as coördinating the military operations of the proletarian armies of various countries. Another object had to be found for its activities. This was rather difficult. The labor parties had begun to play a very important role in the domestic policies of their countries. They were dealing with innumerable problems of interventionism and economic nationalism, and were not prepared to submit their own political tactics to the supervision of foreigners. There were many serious problems in which the conflict of interests between the proletarians of different countries became apparent. It was not always feasible to evade discussion of such annoying matters. Sometimes even immigration barriers had to be discussed; the result was a violent clash of dissenting views and a scandalous exposure of the Marxian dogma that there is an unshakable solidarity among proletarian interests all over the world. The Marxian pundits had some difficulty in tolerably concealing the fissures that had become visible.

But one neutral and innocuous subject could be found for the agenda of the International's meetings: peace. The discussion soon made plain how vain the Marxian catchwords were. At the Paris congress Frederick Engels declared that it was the duty of the proletarians to prevent war at all costs until they themselves had seized power in the most important countries.† The International discussed various measures in the light of this principle: the general strike, general refusal of military service, railroad sabotage, and so on. But it was impossible not to touch on the problem of whether destroying one's own country's defense system would really serve the interests of the workers. The worker has no fatherland, says the

* Hervé, *L'Internationalisme* (Paris, 1910), pp. 129 ff.
† Kautsky, *Sozialisten und Krieg* (Prague, 1937), p. 300.

Marxian; he has nothing to lose but his chains. Very well. But it is really of no consequence to the German worker whether he exchanges his German chains for Russian ones? Should the French workingman let the republic fall prey to Prussian militarism? This Third Republic, said the German Social Democrats, is only a plutodemocracy and a counterfeit republic; it is not the French proletarian's business to fight for it. But the French could not be persuaded by such reasoning. They clung to their prejudice against the Hohenzollerns. The Germans took offense at what they called French stubbornness and petty bourgeois sentiments, although they themselves made it plain that the Social Democrats would unconditionally defend Germany against Russia. Even Bebel had boasted that in a war with Russia he himself, old fellow as he was, would shoulder a rifle.* Engels, in a contribution to the almanac of the French worker's party for 1892, declared: "If the French Republic aids his Majesty the Czar and Autocrat of all the Russias, the German Social Democrats will be sorry to fight them but they will fight them nevertheless." † The request which Engels put in these words to the French was in full agreement with the naïve demands of the German nationalists. They, too, considered it the duty of France to isolate itself diplomatically and either remain neutral in a war between the Triple Alliance and Russia or find itself without allies in a war against Germany.

The amount of delusion and insincerity in the dealings of the Second International was really amazing. It is still more astonishing that people followed these loquacious discussions with eager attention and were convinced that the speeches and resolutions were of the highest importance. Only the pro-socialist and pro-Marxian bias of public opinion can explain this phenomenon. Whoever was free from this could easily understand that it was mere idle talk. The oratory of these labor congresses meant no more than the toasts proposed by monarchs at their meetings. The Kaiser and the Czar too used to speak on such occasions of the comradeship and traditional friendship which linked them and to assure each other that their only concern was the maintenance of peace.

Within the Second International the German Social Democratic party was paramount. It was the best organized and largest of all socialist parties. Thus the congresses were an exact replica of conditions within the German party. The delegates were Marxians who interlarded their speeches with quotations from Marx. But the parties which they represented were parties of trade-unions, for which internationalism was an empty concept. They profited from

* Kautsky, *op. cit.*, p. 307.
† *Idem*, p. 352.

economic nationalism. The German workers were biased not only against Russia but also against France and Great Britain, the countries of Western capitalism. Like all other Germans they were convinced that Germany had a fair title to claim British and French colonies. They found no fault with the German Morocco policy but its lack of success.* They criticized the administration of military and naval affairs; but their concern was the armed forces' readiness for war. Like all other Germans they too viewed the sword as the main tool of foreign policy. And they too were sure that Great Britain and France envied Germany's prosperity and planned aggression.

It was a serious mistake not to recognize this militarist mentality of the German masses. On the other hand, too much attention has been paid to the writings of some socialists who, like Schippel, Hildebrand, and others, proposed that the Social Democrats should openly support the Kaiser's aggressive policy. After all, the Social Democrats were a party of opposition; it was not their job to vote for the government. Their accommodating attitude, however, was effective enough to encourage the nationalist trend of foreign policy.

The government was fully aware that the Social Democratic workers would back it in the event of war. About the few orthodox Marxians the administration leaders were less assured; but they knew very well that a wide gulf separated these doctrinaires from the masses, and they were convinced that the bulk of the party would condone precautionary measures against the Marxian extremists. They ventured, therefore, to imprison several party leaders at the outbreak of the war; later they realized that this was needless. But the party's executive committee, badly informed as it had always been, did not even learn that the authorities had changed their minds and that there was nothing to fear from them. Thus on August 3, 1914, the party chairman, Ebert, and the treasurer, Braun, fled to Switzerland with the party funds.†

It is nonsense to say that the socialist leaders in voting for war credits betrayed the masses. The masses unanimously approved the Kaiser's war. Even those few members of Parliament and editors who dissented were bound to respect the will of the voters. The Social Democratic soldiers were the most enthusiastic fighters in this war for conquest and hegemony.

Later, of course, things changed. The hoped-for victories did not come. Millions of Germans were sacrificed in unsuccessful attacks against the enemy's trenches. Women and children were starv-

* Andler, *op. cit.,* p. 107.
† Ziekursch, *op. cit.,* III, 385.

ing. Then even the trade-union members discovered they had been mistaken in considering the war a favorable opportunity to improve their standard of living. The nation became ripe for the propaganda of radicalism. But these radicals did not advocate peace; they wanted to substitute class war—civil war—for the war against the external foe.

VIII. ANTI-SEMITISM AND RACISM

1. The Role of Racism

NAZISM is frequently regarded as primarily a theory of racism.

German chauvinism claims for the Germans a lofty ancestry. They are the scions of the Nordic-Aryan master race, which includes all those who have contributed to the development of human civilization. The Nordic is tall, slim, with fair hair and blue eyes; he is wise, a gallant fighter, heroic, ready to sacrifice, and animated by "Faustic" ardor. The rest of mankind are trash, little better than apes. For, says Hitler, "the gulf which separates the lowest so-called human beings from our most noble races is broader than the gulf between the lowest men and the highest apes." * It is obvious that this noble race has a fair claim to world hegemony.

In this shape the Nordic myth serves the national vanity. But political nationalism has nothing in common with chauvinistic self-praise and conceit. The German nationalists do not strive for world domination because they are of noble descent. The German racists do not deny that what they are saying of the Germans could be said, with better justification, of the Swedes or Norwegians. Nevertheless, they would call these Scandinavians lunatics if they ventured to adopt the policies which they recommend for their own German nation. For the Scandinavians lack both of the conditions which underlie German aggressivism: high population figures and a strategically advantageous geographical position.

The idiomatic congeniality of the Indo-European languages was once explained on the hypothesis of a common descent of all these peoples. This Aryan hypothesis was scientifically disproved long ago. The Aryan race is an illusion. Scientific anthropology does not recognize this fable.†

The first Mosaic book tells us that Noah is the ancestor of all men living today. Noah had three sons. From one of them, Shem, stem the old Hebrews, the people whom Moses delivered from Egyptian slavery. Judaism teaches that all persons embracing the Jewish religion are the scions of this people. It is impossible to prove this statement; no attempt has ever been made to prove it.

* Speech at the party meeting at Nuremberg, September 3, 1933. *Frankfurter Zeitung,* September 4, 1933.

† Houzé, *L'Aryen et l'Anthroposociologie* (Brussels, 1906), pp. 3 ff.; Hertz, *Rasse und Kultur* (3d ed. Leipzig, 1925), pp. 102 ff.

There are no historical documents reporting the immigration of Jews from Palestine to Central or Eastern Europe; on the other hand, there are documents available concerning the conversion of European non-Jews to Judaism. Nevertheless, this ancestry hypothesis is widely accepted as an unshakable dogma. The Jews maintain it because it forms an essential teaching of their religion; others because it can justify a policy of discrimination against Jews. The Jews are called Asiatic strangers because, according to this hypothesis, they immigrated into Europe only some 1800 years ago. This explains also the use of the term Semites to signify people professing the Jewish religion and their offspring. The term Semitic languages is used in philology to signify the family of languages to which Hebrew, the idiom of the Old Testament, belongs. It is a fact, of course, that Hebrew is the religious language of Judaism, as Latin is of Catholicism and Arabic of Islam.

For more than a hundred years anthropologists have studied the bodily features of various races. The undisputed outcome of these scientific investigations is that the peoples of white skin, Europeans and non-European descendants of emigrated European ancestors, represent a mixture of various bodily characteristics. Men have tried to explain this fact as the result of intermarriage between the members of pure primitive stocks. Whatever the truth of this, it is certain that there are today no pure stocks within the class or race of white-skinned people.

Further efforts have been made to coördinate certain bodily features—racial characteristics—with certain mental and moral characteristics. All these endeavors have also failed.

Finally people have tried, especially in Germany, to discover the physical characteristics of an alleged Jewish or Semitic race as distinguished from the characteristics of European non-Jews. These quests, too, have failed completely. It has proved impossible to differentiate the Jewish Germans anthropologically from the non-Jewish ones. In the field of anthropology there is neither a Jewish race nor Jewish racial characteristics. The racial doctrine of the anti-Semites pretends to be natural science. But the material from which it is derived is not the result of the observation of natural phenomena. It is the genealogy of Genesis and the dogma of the rabbis' teaching that all members of their religious community are descended from the subjects of King David.

Men living under certain conditions often acquire in the second, sometimes even in the first generation, a special physical or mental conformation. This is, of course, a rule to which there are many exceptions. But very often poverty or wealth, urban or rural environment, indoor or outdoor life, mountain peaks or lowlands, sedentary habits or hard physical labor stamp their peculiar mark on a man's body. Butchers and watchmakers, tailors and lumbermen, actors and accountants can often be recognized as such by their expression or physical constitution. Racists intentionally ignore these facts. However, they alone can account for the origin of those types which are in everyday speech called aristocratic or plebeian, an officers' type, a scholarly type, or a Jewish type.

The laws promulgated by the Nazis for discrimination against Jews and the offspring of Jews have nothing at all to do with racial considerations proper. A law discriminating against people of a certain race would first have to enumerate with biological and physiological exactitude the characteristic features of the race concerned. It would then have to decree the legal procedure and proper formalities by which the presence or absence of these characteristics could be duly established for every individual. The validly executed final decisions of such procedures would then have to form the basis of the discrimination in each case. The Nazis have chosen a different way. They say, it is true, that they want to discriminate not against people professing the Jewish religion but against people belonging to the Jewish race. Yet they define the members of the Jewish race as people professing the Jewish religion or descended from people professing the Jewish religion. The characteristic legal feature of the Jewish race is, in the so-called racial legislation of Nuremberg, the membership of the individual concerned or of his ancestors in the religious community of Judaism. If a law pretends that it tends toward a discrimination against the shortsighted but defines shortsightedness as the quality of being bald, people using the generally accepted terminology would not call it a law to the disadvantage of the shortsighted but of the bald. If Americans want to discriminate against Negroes, they do not go to the archives in order to study the racial affiliation of the people concerned; they search the individual's body for traces of Negro descent. Negroes and whites differ in racial—i.e., bodily—features; but it is impossible to tell a Jewish German from a non-Jewish one by any racial characteristic.

The Nazis continually speak of race and racial purity. They call their policies an outcome of modern anthropology. But it is useless to search their policies for racial considerations. They consider— with the exception of Jews and the offspring of Jews—all white men speaking German as Aryans. They do not discriminate among them according to bodily features. German-speaking people are in their opinion Germans, even if it is beyond doubt that they are the scions of Slavonic, Romanic, or Mongol (Magyar or Finno-Ugric) ancestors. The Nazis have claimed that they were fighting the decisive war between the Nordic master race and the human under-dogs. Yet for this struggle they were allied with the Italians, whom their racial doctrines depicted as a mongrel race, and with the slit-eyed, yellow-skinned, dark-haired Japanese Mongols. On the other hand, they despise the Scandinavian Nordics who do not sympathize with their own plans for world supremacy. The Nazis call them-selves anti-Semites but they aid the Arab tribes in their fight against the British, whom they themselves consider as Nordic. The Arabs speak a Semitic idiom, and the Nazi scholars call them Semites. Who, in the Palestinian struggles, has the fairer claim to the ap-pellation "anti-Semites"?

Even the racial myth itself is not a product of Germany. It is of French origin. Its founders, especially Gobineau, wanted to justify the privileges of the French aristocracy by demonstrating the gentle Frankish birth of the nobility. Hence originated in Western Europe the mistaken belief that the Nazis too recognize the claims of princes and noblemen to political leadership and caste privileges. The German nationalists, however, consider the whole German people—with the exception of the Jews and the offspring of Jews —a homogeneous race of noblemen. Within this noble race they make no discriminations. No higher degree of nobility than Ger-manhood is conceivable. Under the laws of the Nazis all German-speaking people are comrades (*Volksgenossen*) and as such equal. The only discrimination which the Nazis make among Germans is according to the intensity of their zeal in the display of those qualities which are regarded as genuinely German. Every non-Jewish German—prince, nobleman, or commoner—has the same right to serve his nation and to distinguish himself in this service.

It is true that in the years preceding the first World War the nationalists too clung to the prejudice, once very popular in Ger-many, that the Prussian Junkers were extraordinarily gifted for military leadership. In this respect only did the old Prussian legend survive until 1918. The lessons taught by the failure of the Prussian officers in the campaign of 1806 were long since forgotten. Nobody cared about Bismarck's skepticism. Bismarck, himself the son of a nonaristocratic mother, observed that Prussia was breeding officers of lower ranks up to the position of regimental commanders of a quality unsurpassed by any other country; but that as far as the higher ranks were concerned, the native Prussian stock was no longer so fertile in producing able leaders as it had been in the days of Frederick II.* But the Prussian historians had extolled the deeds of the Prussian Army until all critics were silenced. Pan-Germans, Catholics, and Social Democrats were united in their

* Bismarck, *op. cit.*, I, 6.

dislike of the arrogant Junkers but fully convinced that these Junkers were especially fitted for military leadership and for commissions. People complained about the exclusion of nonaristocratic officers from the Royal Guards and from many regiments of the cavalry, and about the disdainful treatment they received in the rest of the army; but they never ventured to dispute the Junkers' paramount military qualifications. Even the Social Democrats had full confidence in the active officers of the Prussian Army. The firm conviction that the war would result in a smashing German victory, which all strata of the German nation held in 1914, was primarily founded on this overestimation of the military genius of the Junkers.

People did not notice that the German nobility, who had long since ceased to play a leading role in political life, were now on the point of losing the army's reins. They had never excelled in science, art, and literature. Their contributions in these fields cannot be compared with the achievements of British, French, and Italian aristocrats. Yet in no other modern country was the position of the aristocrats more favorable or that of the commoners less auspicious than in Germany. At the peak of his life and success Goethe wrote, full of bitterness: "I do not know how conditions are in foreign countries, but in Germany only the nobleman can attain a certain universal and personal perfection. A commoner may acquire merit, he may, at best, cultivate his mind; but his personality goes astray, whatever he tries." * But it was commoners and not noblemen who created the works which led Germany to be called the "nation of poets and thinkers."

In the ranks of the authors who formed the nation's political thought there were no noblemen. Even the Prussian conservatives got their ideologies from plebeians, from Stahl, Rodbertus, Wagener, Adolf Wagner. Among the men who developed German nationalism there was hardly a member of the aristocracy. Pan-Germanism and Nazism are in this sense "bourgeois" movements like socialism, Marxism, and interventionism. Within the ranks of the higher bureaucracy there was a steady penetration of nonaristocratic elements.

It was the same with the armed forces. The hard work in the offices of the General Staff, in the technical services, and in the navy did not suit the tastes and desires of the Junkers. Many important posts in the General Staff were occupied by commoners. The outstanding personality in German prewar militarism was Admiral Tirpitz, who attained nobility only in 1900. Ludendorff, Groener, and Hoffmann were also commoners.

* Goethe, *Wilhelm Meister's Lehrjahre*, Book V, chap. iii.

But it was the defeat in the first World War which finally destroyed the military prestige of the Junkers. In the present German Army there are still many aristocrats in higher ranks, because the officers who got their commissions in the last years preceding the first World War have now reached the top of the ladder. But there is no longer any preference given to aristocrats. Among the political leaders of Nazism there are few nobles—and the titles even of these are often questionable.

The German princes and nobles, who unswervingly disparaged liberalism and democracy and until 1933 stubbornly fought for the preservation of their privileges, have completely surrendered to Nazism and connive at its egalitarian principles. They are to be found in the ranks of the most fanatical admirers of the Führer. Princes of the blood take pride in serving as satellites of notorious racketeers who hold party offices. One may wonder whether they act out of sincere conviction or out of cowardice and fear. But there can be no doubt that the belief, common to many members of the British aristocracy, that a restoration of the German dynasties would change the German mentality and the temper of politics is entirely mistaken.*

2. *The Struggle against the Jewish Mind*

Nazism wants to combat the Jewish mind. But it has not succeeded so far in defining its characteristic features. The Jewish mind is no less mythical than the Jewish race.

The earlier German nationalists tried to oppose to the Jewish mind the "Christian-Teutonic" world-view. The combination of Christian and Teutonic is, however, untenable. No exegetical tricks can justify a German claim to a preferred position within the realm of Christianity. The Gospels do not mention the Germans. They consider all men equal under God. He who is anxious to discriminate not only against Jews but against the Christian descendants of Jews has no use for the Gospels. Consistent anti-Semites must reject Christianity.

We do not need to decide here whether or not Christianity itself can be called Jewish.† At any rate Christianity developed out of the Jewish creed. It recognizes the Ten Commandments as eternal law and the Old Testament as Holy Writ. The Apostles and the members of the primitive community were Jews. It could be ob-

* The last sovereign duke of Saxe-Coburg-Gotha, born and brought up in Great Britain as a grandson of Queen Victoria, was the first German prince who—long before 1933—took office in the Nazi party.

† Pope Pius XI is credited with the dictum: "Spiritually we are Semites." G. Seldes, *The Catholic Crisis* (New York, 1939), p. 45.

jected that Christ did not agree in his teachings with the rabbis. But the facts remain that God sent the Saviour to the Jews and not to the Vandals, and that the Holy Spirit inspired books in Hebrew and in Greek but not in German. If the Nazis were prepared to take their racial myths seriously and to see in them more than oratory for their party meetings, they would have to eradicate Christianity with the same brutality they use against liberalism and pacifism. They failed to embark upon such an enterprise, not because they regarded it as hopeless, but because their *politics* had nothing at all to do with racism.

It is strange indeed in a country in which the authorities officially outrage Jews and Judaism in filthy terms, which has outlawed the Jews on account of their Judaism, and in which mathematical theorems, physical hypotheses, and therapeutical procedures are boycotted, if their authors are suspected of being "non-Aryans," that priests continue in many thousands of churches of various creeds to praise the Ten Commandments, revealed to the Jew Moses, as the foundation of moral law. It is strange that in a country in which no word of a Jewish author must be printed or read, the Psalms and their German translations, adaptations, and imitations are sung. It is strange that the German armies, which exult in Eastern Europe in cowardly slaughtering thousands of defenseless Jewish women and children, are accompanied by army chaplains with Bibles in their hands. But the Third Reich is full of such contradictions.

Of course, the Nazis do not comply with the moral teachings of the Gospels. Neither do any other conquerors and warriors. Christianity is no more allowed to become an obstacle in the way of Nazi politics than it was in the way of other aggressors.

Nazism not only fails explicitly to reject Christianity; it solemnly declares itself a Christian party. The twenty-fourth point of the *"unalterable* Party Program" proclaims that the party stands for *positive Christianity*, without linking itself with one of the various Christian churches and denominations. The term "positive" in this connection means neutrality in respect to the antagonisms between the various churches and sects.*

Many Nazi writers, it is true, take pleasure in denouncing and deriding Christianity and in drafting plans for the establishment of a new German religion. The Nazi party as such, however, does not combat Christianity but the Christian churches as autonomous establishments and independent agencies. Its totalitarianism can-

* For another interpretation of the term "positiv" see *Die Grundlagen des Nationalsozialismus* (Leipzig, 1937, p. 59) by Bishop Alois Hudal, the outstanding Catholic champion of Nazism.

not tolerate the existence of any institution not completely subject to the Führer's sovereignty. No German is granted the privilege of defying an order issued by the state by referring to an independent authority. The separation of church and state is contrary to the principles of totalitarianism. Nazism must consequently aim at a return to the conditions prevailing in the German Lutheran churches and likewise in the Prussian Union Church before the Constitution of Weimar. Then the civil authority was supreme in the church too. The ruler of the country was the supreme bishop of the Lutheran Church of his territory. His was the *jus circa sacra.*

The conflict with the Catholic Church is of a similar character. The Nazis will not tolerate any link between German citizens and foreigners or foreign institutions. They dissolved even the German Rotary Clubs because they were tied up with the Rotary International, whose headquarters are located in Chicago. A German citizen owes allegiance to his Führer and nation only; any kind of internationalism is an evil. Hitler could tolerate Catholicism only if the Pope were a resident of Germany and a subordinate of the party machine.

Except for Christianity, the Nazis reject as Jewish everything which stems from Jewish authors. This condemnation includes the writings of those Jews who, like Stahl, Lassalle, Gumplowicz, and Rathenau, have contributed many essential ideas to the system of Nazism. But the Jewish mind is, as the Nazis say, not limited to the Jews and their offspring only. Many "Aryans" have been imbued with Jewish mentality—for instance the poet, writer, and critic Gotthold Ephraim Lessing, the socialist Frederick Engels, the composer Johannes Brahms, the writer Thomas Mann, and the theologian Karl Barth. They too are damned. Then there are whole schools of thought, art, and literature rejected as Jewish. Internationalism and pacifism are Jewish, but so is warmongering. So are liberalism and capitalism, as well as the "spurious" socialism of the Marxians and of the Bolsheviks. The epithets Jewish and Western are applied to the philosophies of Descartes and Hume, to positivism, materialism and empiro-criticism, to the economic theories both of the classics and of modern subjectivism. Atonal music, the Italian opera style, the operetta and the paintings of impressionism are also Jewish. In short, Jewish is what any Nazi dislikes. If one put together everything that various Nazis have stigmatized as Jewish, one would get the impression that our whole civilization has been the achievement only of Jews.

On the other hand, many champions of German racism have tried to demonstrate that all the eminent men of non-German nations were Aryan Nordics of German extraction. The ex-Marxian Woltmann, for example, has discovered features of Germanism in Petrarch, Dante, Ariosto, Raphael, and Michelangelo, who have their genius as an inheritance from their Teutonic ancestors. Woltmann is fully convinced that he has proved that "the entire European civilization, even in the Slavonic and Latin countries, is an achievement of the German race." *

It would be a waste of time to dwell upon such statements. It is enough to remark that the various representatives of German racism contradict one another both in establishing the racial characteristics of the noble race and in the racial classification of the same individuals. Very often they contradict even what they themselves have said elsewhere. The myth of the master race has been elaborated carelessly indeed.†

All Nazi champions insist again and again that Marxism and Bolshevism are the quintessence of the Jewish mind, and that it is the great historic mission of Nazism to root out this pest. It is true that this attitude did not prevent the German nationalists either from coöperating with the German communists in undermining the Weimar Republic, or from training their black guards in Russian artillery and aviation camps in the years 1923—1933, or—in the period from August, 1939, until June, 1941—from entering into a close political and military complicity with Soviet Russia. Nevertheless, public opinion supports the view that Nazism and Bolshevism are philosophies—Weltanschauungen—implacably opposed to each other. Actually there have been in these last years all over the world two main political parties: the anti-Fascists, i.e., the friends of Russia (communists, fellow travelers, self-styled liberals and progressives), and the anticommunists, i.e., the friends of Germany (parties of shirts of different colors, not very accurately called "Fascists" by their adversaries). There have been few genuine liberals and democrats in these years. Most of those who have called themselves such have been ready to support what are really totalitarian measures, and many have enthusiastically praised the Russian methods of dictatorship.

The mere fact that these two groups are fighting each other does not necessarily prove that they differ in their philosophies and first principles. There have always been wars between people who adhered to the same creeds and philosophies. The parties of the Left and of the Right are in conflict because they both aim at supreme power. Charles V used to say: "I and my cousin, the King

---

* See Woltmann's books: *Politische Anthropologie* (Eisenach, 1903); *Die Germanen und die Renaissance in Italien* (Leipzig, 1905); *Die Germanen in Frankreich* (Jena, 1907).
† Hertz, *op. cit.*, pp. 159 ff.

of France, are in perfect agreement; we are fighting each other because we both aim at the same end: Milan." Hitler and Stalin aim at the same end; they both want to rule in the Baltic States, in Poland, and in the Ukraine.

The Marxians are not prepared to admit that the Nazis are socialists too. In their eyes Nazism is the worst of all evils of capitalism. On the other hand, the Nazis describe the Russian system as the meanest of all types of capitalist exploitation and as a devilish machination of World Jewry for the domination of the gentiles. Yet it is clear that both systems, the German and the Russian, must be considered from an economic point of view as socialist. And it is only the economic point of view that matters in debating whether or not a party or system is socialist. Socialism is and has always been considered a system of economic organization of society. It is the system under which the government has full control of production and distribution. As far as socialism existing merely within individual countries can be called genuine, both Russia and Germany are right in calling their systems socialist.

Whether the Nazis and the Bolsheviks are right in styling themselves workers' parties is another question. The Communist Manifesto says, "The proletarian movement is the self-conscious independent movement of the immense majority," and it is in this sense that old Marxians used to define a workers' party. The proletarians, they explained, are the immense majority of the nation; they themselves, not a benevolent government or a well-intentioned minority, seize power and establish socialism. But the Bolsheviks have abandoned this scheme. A small minority proclaims itself the vanguard of the proletariat, seizes the dictatorship, forcibly dissolves the Parliament elected by universal franchise, and rules by its own right and might. Of course, this ruling minority claims that what it does serves best the interests of the many and indeed of the whole of society, but this has always been the pretension of oligarchic rulers.

The Bolshevists set the precedent. The success of the Lenin clique encouraged the Mussolini gang and the Hitler troops. Both Italian Fascism and German Nazism adopted the political methods of Soviet Russia.* The only difference between Nazism and Bol-

---

* Few people realize that the economic program of Italian Fascism, the *stato corporativo*, did not differ from the program of British Guild Socialism as propagated during the first World War and in the following years by the most eminent British and by some continental socialists. The most brilliant exposition of this doctrine is the book of Sidney and Beatrice Webb (Lord and Lady Passfield), *A Constitution for the Socialist Commonwealth of Great Britain*, published in 1920. Compared with this volume the speeches of Mussolini and the writings of the Italian professors of the *economia corporativa* appear clumsy. Of course, neither the British Left-wing socialists nor the Italian Fascists ever made any serious attempts to put this widely adver-

shevism is that the Nazis got a much bigger minority in the elections preceding their coup d'état than the Bolsheviks got in the Russian elections in the fall of 1917.

The Nazis have not only imitated the Bolshevist tactics of seizing power. They have copied much more. They have imported from Russia the one-party system and the privileged role of this party and its members in public life; the paramount position of the secret police; the organization of affiliated parties abroad which are employed in fighting their domestic governments and in sabotage and espionage, assisted by public funds and the protection of the diplomatic and consular service; the administrative execution and imprisonment of political adversaries; concentration camps; the punishment inflicted on the families of exiles; the methods of propaganda. They have borrowed from the Marxians even such absurdities as the mode of address, party comrade (*Parteigenosse*), derived from the Marxian comrade (*Genosse*), and the use of a military terminology for all items of civil and economic life.* The question is not in which respects both systems are alike but in which they differ.

It has already been shown wherein the socialist patterns of Russia and Germany differ.† These differences are not due to any disparity in basic philosophical views; they are the necessary consequence of the differences in the economic conditions of the two countries. The Russian pattern was inapplicable in Germany, whose population cannot live in a state of self-sufficiency. The German pattern seems very inefficient when compared with the incomparably more efficient capitalist system, but it is far more efficient than the Russian method. The Russians live at a very low economic level notwithstanding the inexhaustible richness of their natural resources.

There is inequality of incomes and of standards of living in both countries. It would be futile to try to determine whether the difference in the living standards of party comrade Goering and the average party comrade is greater or smaller than that in the standards of comrade Stalin and *his* comrades. The characteristic feature of socialism is not equality of income but the all-round control of business activities by the government, the government's exclusive power to use all means of production.

The Nazis do not reject Marxism because it aims at socialism

---

tised program into effect. Its realization would lead to complete chaos. The economic regime of Fascist Italy was actually an abortive imitation of German Zwangswirtschaft. See Mises' *Nationalökonomie* (Geneva, 1940), pp. 705–715.

  * For a comparison of the two systems see Max Eastman, *Stalin's Russia* (New York, 1940), pp. 83–94.

  † See above, pp. 57–58.

but because, as they say, it advocates internationalism.* Marx's internationalism was nothing but the acceptance of eighteenth-century ideas on the root causes of war: princes are eager to fight each other because they want aggrandizement through conquest, while free nations do not covet their neighbors' land. But it never occurred to Marx that this propensity to peace depends upon the existence of an unhampered market society. Neither Marx nor his school was ever able to grasp the meaning of international conflicts within a world of etatism and socialism. They contented themselves with the assertion that in the Promised Land of socialism there would no longer be any conflicts at all.

We have already seen what a questionable role the problem of the maintenance of peace played in the Second International. For Soviet Russia the Third International has been merely a tool in its unflagging warfare against all foreign governments. The Soviets are as eager for conquest as any conqueror of the past. They did not yield an inch of the previous conquests of the Czars except where they were forced to do so. They have used every opportunity to expand their empire. Of course they no longer use the old Czarist pretexts for conquest; they have developed a new terminology for this purpose. But this does not render the lot of the subdued any easier.

What the Nazis really have in mind when indicting the Jewish mind for internationalism is the liberal theory of free trade and the mutual advantages of international division of labor. The Jews, they say, want to corrupt the innate Aryan spirit of heroism by the fallacious doctrines of the advantages of peace. One could hardly overrate in a more inaccurate way the contribution of Jews to modern civilization. Peaceful coöperation between nations is certainly more than an outcome of Jewish machinations. Liberalism and democracy, capitalism and international trade are not Jewish inventions.

Finally, the Nazis call the business mentality Jewish. Tacitus informs us that the German tribes of his day considered it clumsy and shameful to acquire with sweat what could be won by bloodshed. This is also the first moral principle of the Nazis. They despise individuals and nations eager to profit by serving other people; in their eyes robbery is the noblest way to make a living. Werner Sombart has contrasted two specimens of human being: the peddlers (*Händler*) and heroes (*Helden*). The Britons are peddlers, the

* In a similar way many Christian authors reject Bolshevism only because it is anti-Christian. See Berdyaew, *The Origin of Russian Communism* (London, 1937), pp. 217–225.

Germans heroes. But more often the appellation peddlers is assigned to the Jews.

The Nazis simply call everything that is contrary to their own doctrines and tenets Jewish and communist. When executing hostages in the occupied countries they always declare that they have punished Jews and communists. They call the President of the United States a Jew and a communist. He who is not prepared to surrender to them is by that token unmistakably a Jew. In the Nazi dictionary the terms Jew and communist are synonymous with non-Nazi.

3. Interventionism and Legal Discrimination against Jews

In the days before the ascendancy of liberalism the individuals professing a certain religious creed formed an order, a caste, of their own. The creed determined the membership in a group which assigned to each member privileges and disqualifications (*privilegia odiosa*.) In only a few countries has liberalism abolished this state of affairs. In many European countries, in which in any other respect freedom of conscience and of the practice of religion and equality of all citizens under the law are granted, matrimonial law and the register of births, marriages, and deaths remain separate for each religious group. Membership within a church or religious community preserves a peculiar legal character. Every citizen is bound to belong to one of the religious groups, and he bestows this quality upon his children. The membership and procedure to be observed in cases of change of religious allegiance are regulated by public law. Special provisions are made for people who do not want to belong to any religious community. This state of things makes it possible to establish the religious allegiance of a man and of his ancestors with legal precision in the same unquestionable way in which kinship can be ascertained in inheritance cases.

The bearing of this fact can be elucidated by contrasting it with conditions concerning attachment to a linguistic group. Membership within a linguistic group never had a caste quality. It was and is a matter of fact but not a legal status.* It is as a rule impossible to establish the linguistic group to which a man's dead ancestors belonged. The only exceptions are those ancestors who were eminent personalities, writers, or political leaders of linguistic groups. It is further for the most part impossible to establish whether or not a man changed his linguistic allegiance at some

* We may disregard some occasional attempts, made in old Austria, to give legal status to a man's linguistic character.

time in his past. He who speaks German and declares himself to be a German need seldom fear that his statement could be disproved by documentary evidence that his parents or he himself in the past were not German. Even a foreign accent need not betray him. In countries with a linguistically mixed population the accent and inflection of each group influence the other. Among the leaders of German nationalism in the eastern parts of Germany, and in Austria, Czechoslovakia, and the other eastern countries there were numerous men who spoke German with a sharp Slavonic, Hungarian, or Italian accent, whose names sounded foreign, or who had only a short time before substituted German-sounding names for their native ones. There were even Nazi Storm Troopers whose still living parents understood no German. It happened often that brothers and sisters belonged to different linguistic groups. One could not attempt to discriminate legally against such neophytes, because it was impossible to determine the facts in a legally unquestionable way.

In an unhampered market society there is no legal discrimination against anybody. Everyone has the right to obtain the place within the social system in which he can successfully work and make a living. The consumer is free to discriminate, provided that he is ready to pay the cost. A Czech or a Pole may prefer to buy at higher cost in a shop owned by a Slav instead of buying cheaper and better in a shop owned by a German. An anti-Semite may forego being cured of an ugly disease by the employment of the "Jewish" drug Salvarsan and have recourse to a less efficacious remedy. In this arbitrary power consists what economists call consumer's sovereignty.

Interventionism means compulsory discrimination, which furthers the interests of a minority of citizens at the expense of the majority. Nevertheless discrimination can be applied in a democratic community too. Various minority groups form an alliance and thereby a majority group in order to obtain privileges for each. For instance, a country's wheat producers, cattle breeders, and wine growers form a farmers' party; they succeed in obtaining discrimination against foreign competitors and thus privileges for each of the three groups. The costs of the privilege granted to the wine growers burden the rest of the community—including the cattle breeders and wheat producers—and so on for each of the others.

Whoever sees the facts from this angle—and logically they cannot be viewed from any other—realizes that the arguments brought forward in favor of this so-called producer's policy are untenable. One minority group alone could not obtain any such privilege because the majority would not tolerate it. But if all minority groups or enough of them obtain a privilege, every group that did not get a more valuable privilege than the rest suffers. The political ascendancy of interventionism is due to the failure to recognize this obvious truth. People favor discrimination and privileges because they do not realize that they themselves are consumers and as such must foot the bill. In the case of protectionism, for example, they believe that only the foreigners against whom the import duties discriminate are hurt. It is true the foreigners are hurt, but not they alone: the consumers who must pay higher prices suffer with them.

Now wherever there are Jewish minorities—and in every country the Jews are only a minority—it is as easy to discriminate against them legally as against foreigners, because the quality of being a Jew can be established in a legally valid way. Discrimination against this helpless minority can be made to seem very plausible; it seems to further the interests of all non-Jews. People do not realize that it is certain to hurt the interests of the non-Jews as well. If Jews are barred from access to a medical career, the interests of non-Jewish doctors are favored, but the interests of the sick are hurt. Their freedom to choose the doctor whom they trust is restricted. Those who did not want to consult a Jewish doctor do not gain anything but those who wanted to do so are injured.

In most European countries it is technically feasible to discriminate legally against Jews and the offspring of Jews. It is furthermore politically feasible, because Jews are usually insignificant minorities whose votes do not count much in elections. And finally, it is considered economically sound in an age in which government interference for the protection of the less efficient producer against more efficient and cheaper competitors is regarded as a beneficial policy. The non-Jewish grocer asks, Why not protect me too? You protect the manufacturer and the farmer against the foreigners producing better and at lower cost; you protect the worker against the competition of immigrant labor; you should protect me against the competition of my neighbor, the Jewish grocer.

Discrimination need have nothing to do with hatred or repugnance toward those against whom it is applied. The Swiss and Italians do not hate the Americans or Swedes; nevertheless, they discriminate against American and Swedish products. People always dislike competitors. But for the consumer the foreigners who supply him with commodities are not competitors but purveyors. The non-Jewish doctor may hate his Jewish competitor. But he asks for the exclusion of Jews from the medical profession precisely because many non-Jewish patients not only do not hate Jewish doctors but prefer them to many non-Jewish doctors and patronize them. The fact that the Nazi racial laws impose heavy penalties for sexual intercourse between Jews and "Aryans" does not indicate the existence of hatred between these two groups. It would be needless to keep people who hate each other from sexual relations. However, in an investigation devoted to the political problems of nationalism and Nazism we need not deal with the issues of sex pathology involved. To study the inferiority complexes and sexual perversity responsible for the Nuremberg racial laws and for the sadistic bestialities exhibited in killing and torturing Jews is the task of psychiatry.

In a world in which people have grasped the meaning of a market society, and therefore advocate a consumer's policy, there is no legal discrimination against Jews. Whoever dislikes the Jews may in such a world avoid patronizing Jewish shopkeepers, doctors, and lawyers. On the other hand, in a world of interventionism only a miracle can in the long run hinder legal discrimination against Jews. The policy of protecting the less efficient domestic producer against the more efficient foreign producer, the artisan against the manufacturer, and the small shop against the department store and the chain stores would be incomplete if it did not protect the "Aryan" against the Jew.

Many decades of intensive anti-Semitic propaganda did not succeed in preventing German "Aryans" from buying in shops owned by Jews, from consulting Jewish doctors and lawyers, and from reading books by Jewish authors. They did not patronize the Jews unawares—"Aryan" competitors were careful to tell them again and again that these people were Jews. Whoever wanted to get rid of his Jewish competitors could not rely on an alleged hatred of Jews; he was under the necessity of asking for legal discrimination against them.

Such discrimination is not the result of nationalism or of racism. It is basically—like nationalism—a result of interventionism and the policy of favoring the less efficient producer to the disadvantage of the consumer.

Nearly all writers dealing with the problem of anti-Semitism have tried to demonstrate that the Jews have in some way or other, through their behavior or attitudes, excited anti-Semitism. Even Jewish authors and non-Jewish opponents of anti-Semitism share this opinion; they too search for Jewish faults driving non-Jews toward anti-Semitism. But if the cause of anti-Semitism were really to be found in distinctive features of the Jews, these properties would have to be extraordinary virtues and merits which would qualify the Jews as the elite of mankind. If the Jews themselves are to blame for the fact that those whose ideal is perpetual war and bloodshed, who worship violence and are eager to destroy freedom, consider them the most dangerous opponents of their endeavors, it must be because the Jews are foremost among the champions of freedom, justice, and peaceful coöperation among nations. If the Jews have incurred the Nazis' hatred through their own conduct, it is no doubt because what was great and noble in the German nation, all the immortal achievements of Germany's past, were either accomplished by the Jews or congenial to the Jewish mind. As the parties seeking to destroy modern civilization and return to barbarism have put anti-Semitism at the top of their programs, this civilization is apparently a creation of the Jews. Nothing more flattering could be said of an individual or of a group than that the deadly foes of civilization have well-founded reasons to persecute them.

The truth is that while the Jews are the objects of anti-Semitism, their conduct and qualities did not play a decisive role in inciting and spreading its modern version. That they form everywhere a minority which can be legally defined in a precise way makes it tempting, in an age of interventionism, to discriminate against them. Jews have, of course, contributed to the rise of modern civilization; but this civilization is neither completely nor predominantly their achievement. Peace and freedom, democracy and justice, reason and thought are not specifically Jewish. Many things, good and bad, happen on the earth without the participation of Jews. The anti-Semites grossly exaggerate when they see in the Jews the foremost representatives of modern culture and make them alone responsible for the fact that the world has changed since the centuries of the barbarian invasions.*

In the dark ages heathens, Christians, and Moslems persecuted the Jews on account of their religion. This motive has lost much of its strength and is still valid only for a comparatively few Catholics and Fundamentalists who make the Jews responsible for the spread of free thinking. And this too is a mistaken idea. Neither Hume nor Kant, neither Laplace nor Darwin were Jews. Higher criticism of the Bible was developed by Protestant theologians.† The Jewish rabbis opposed it bitterly for many years.

* We are dealing here with conditions in Central and Western Europe and in America. In many parts of Eastern Europe things were different. There modern civilization was really predominantly an achievement of Jews.

† Bishop Hudal calls David Friedrich Strauss, the outstanding figure in German higher criticism, a "non-Aryan." (*op. cit.,* p. 23). This is incorrect; Strauss had no Jewish ancestors (see his biography by Th. Ziegler, I, 4–6). On the other hand, Nazi anti-Catholics say that Ignatius of Loyola, the founder of the Jesuit order, was of Jewish origin (Seldes, *op. cit.,* p. 261). There is no proof of this statement.

Neither were liberalism, capitalism, or a market economy Jewish achievements. There are those who try to justify anti-Semitism by denouncing the Jews as capitalists and champions of laissez faire. Other anti-Semites—and often the same ones—blame the Jews for being communists. These contradictory charges cancel each other. But it is a fact that anticapitalist propaganda has contributed a good deal to the popularity of anti-Semitism. Simple minds do not grasp the meaning of the abstract terms capital and exploitation, capitalists and exploiters; they substitute for them the terms Jewry and Jews. However, even if the Jews were more unpopular with some people than is really the case, there would be no discrimination against them if they were not a minority clearly distinguishable legally from other people.

4. The "Stab in the Back"

The end of the first World War glaringly exposed the nucleus of German nationalism's dogma. Ludendorff, idol of the nationalists, himself had to confess that the war was lost, that the Reich had suffered a crushing defeat. The news of this failure was not anticipated by the nation. For more than four years the government had told the credulous people that Germany was victorious. It was beyond doubt that the German armies had occupied almost the whole territory of Belgium and several departments of France, while the Allied armies held only a few square miles of the Reich's territory. German armies had conquered Brussels, Warsaw, Belgrade, and Bucharest. Russia and Rumania had been forced to sign peace treaties dictated by Germany. Look at the map, said the German statesmen, if you want to see who is victorious. The British Navy, they boasted, had been swept from the North Sea and was creeping into port; the British Merchant Marine was an easy prey for German U-boats. The English were starving. The citizens of London could not sleep for fear of Zeppelins. America was not in a position to save the Allies; the Americans had no army, and if they had had, they would have lacked the ships to send it to Europe. The German generals had given proof of ingenuity: Hindenburg, Ludendorff, and Mackensen were equal to the most famous leaders of the past; and in the German armed forces everybody was a hero, above all the intrepid pilots and the unflinching crews of the submarines.

And now, the collapse! Something horrible and ghastly had happened, for which the only explanation could be treason. Once again a traitor had ambushed the victor from a safely hidden corner. Once again Hagen had murdered Siegfried. The victorious army had been stabbed in the back. While the German men were fighting the enemy, domestic foes had stirred up the people at home to rise in the November rebellion, that most infamous crime of the ages. Not the front but the hinterland had failed. The culprits were neither the soldiers nor the generals but the weaklings of the civil government and of the Reichstag who failed to curb the rebellion.

Shame and contrition for the events of November, 1918, were the greater with aristocrats, officers, and nationalist notables because they had behaved in those days in a way that they themselves very soon were bound to regard as scandalous. Several officers on battleships had tried to stop the mutineers, but almost all other officers had bowed to the revolution. Twenty-two German thrones were smashed without any attempt at resistance. Court dignitaries, adjutants, orderly officers, and bodyguards quietly acquiesced when the princes to whom they had sworn oaths of personal allegiance unto death were dethroned. The example once set by the Swiss Guards who died for Louis XVI and his consort was not imitated. There was not a trace of the Fatherland party and of the nationalists when the masses assaulted the castles of the various kings and dukes.

It was salvation for the self-esteem of all these disheartened souls when some generals and nationalist leaders found a justification and an excuse: it had been the work of the Jews. Germany was victorious by land and sea and air, but the Jews had stabbed the victorious forces in the back. Whoever ventured to refute this legend was himself denounced as a Jew or a bribed servant of the Jews. No rational argument could shake the legend. It has been picked to pieces; each of its points has been disproved by documentary evidence; an overwhelming mass of material has been brought to its refutation—in vain.

It must be realized that German nationalism managed to survive the defeat of the first World War only by means of the legend of the stab in the back. Without it the nationalists would have been forced to drop their program, which was founded wholly on the thesis of Germany's military superiority. In order to maintain this program it was indispensable to be able to tell the nation: "We have given new proof of our invincibility. But our victories did not bring us success because the Jews have sabotaged the country. If we eliminate the Jews, our victories will bring their due reward."

Up to that time anti-Semitism had played but a small role in the structure of the doctrines of German nationalism. It was mere byplay, not a political issue. The endeavors to discriminate against the Jews stemmed from interventionism, as did nationalism. But they had no vital part in the system of German political nationalism. Now anti-Semitism became the focal point of the nationalist creed, its main issue. That was its meaning in domestic politics. And very soon it acquired an equal importance in foreign affairs.

5. Anti-Semitism as a Factor in International Politics

It was a very strange constellation of political forces that turned anti-Semitism into an important factor in world affairs.

In the years after the first World War Marxism swept triumphantly over the Anglo-Saxon countries. Public opinion in Great Britain came under the spell of the neo-Marxian doctrines on imperialism, according to which wars are fought only for the sake of the selfish class interests of capital. The intellectuals and the parties of the Left felt rather ashamed of England's participation in the World War. They were convinced that it was both morally unfair and politically unwise to oblige Germany to pay reparations and to restrict its armaments. They were firmly resolved never again to let Great Britain fight a war. They purposely shut their eyes to every unpleasant fact that could weaken their naïve confidence in the omnipotence of the League of Nations. They overrated the efficacy of sanctions and of such measures as outlawing war by the Briand-Kellogg Pact. They favored for their country a policy of disarmament which rendered the British Empire almost defenseless within a world indefatigably preparing for new wars.

But at the same time the same people were asking the British government and the League to check the aspirations of the "dynamic" powers and to safeguard with every means—short of war —the independence of the weaker nations. They indulged in strong language against Japan and against Italy; but they practically encouraged, by their opposition to armaments and their unconditional pacifism, the imperialistic policies of these countries. They were instrumental in Great Britain's rejecting Secretary Stimson's proposals to stop Japan's expansion in China. They frustrated the Hoare-Laval plan, which would have left at least a part of Abyssinia independent; but they did not lift a finger when Italy occupied the whole country. They did not change their policy when Hitler seized power and immediately began to prepare for the wars which were meant to make Germany paramount first on the European continent and later in the whole world. Theirs was an ostrich policy in the face of the most serious situation that Britain ever had to encounter.*

The parties of the Right did not differ in principle from those

---

* An amazing manifestation of this mentality is Bertrand Russell's book, *Which Way to Peace?*, published in 1936. Devastating criticism of the British Labor party's foreign policy is provided in the editorial, "The Obscurantists," in *Nineteenth Century and After*, No. 769 (March, 1941), pp. 209–229.

of the Left. They were only more moderate in their utterances and eager to find a rational pretext for the policy of inactivity and indolence in which the Left acquiesced lightheartedly and without a thought of the future. They consoled themselves with the hope that Germany did not plan to attack France but only to fight Soviet Russia. It was all wishful thinking, refusing to take account of Hitler's schemes as exposed in *Mein Kampf*. The Left became furious. Our reactionaries, they shouted, are aiding Hitler because they are putting their class interests over the welfare of the nation. Yet the encouragement which Hitler got from England came not so much from the anti-Soviet feelings of some members of the upper classes as from the state of British armament, for which the Left was even more responsible than the Right. The only way to stop Hitler would have been to spend large sums for rearmament and to return to conscription. The whole British nation, not only the aristocracy, was strongly opposed to such measures. Under these conditions it was not unreasonable that a small group of lords and rich commoners should try to improve relations between the two countries. It was, of course, a plan without prospect of success. The Nazis could not be dissuaded from their aims by comforting speeches from socially prominent Englishmen. British popular repugnance to armaments and conscription was an important factor in the Nazi plans, but the sympathies of a dozen lords were not. It was no secret that Great Britain would be unable, right at the outbreak of a new war, to send an expeditionary force of seven divisions to France as it did in 1914; that the Royal Air Force was numerically much inferior to the German Air Force; or that even the British Navy was less formidable than in the years 1914–18. The Nazis knew very well that many politicians in South Africa opposed that dominion's participating in a new war, and they were in close touch with the anti-British parties in the East Indies, in Egypt, and the Arabian countries.

The problem which Great Britain had to face was simply this: Is it in the interest of the nation to permit Germany to conquer the whole European continent? It was Hitler's great plan to keep England neutral at all costs, until the conquest of France, Poland, Czechoslovakia, and the Ukraine should be completed. Should Great Britain render him this service? Whoever answered this question in the negative must not talk but act. But the British politicians buried their heads in the sand.

Given the state of British public opinion, France should have understood that it was isolated and must meet the Nazi danger by itself. The French know little about the German mentality and German political conditions. Yet when Hitler seized power every

French politician should have realized that the main point in his plans was the annihilation of France. Of course the French parties of the Left shared the prejudices, illusions, and errors of the British Left. But there was in France an influential nationalist group which had always mistrusted Germany and favored an energetic anti-German policy. If the French nationalists in 1933 and the years following had seriously advocated measures to prevent German rearmament, they would have had the support of the whole nation with the exception of the intransigent communists. Germany had already started to rearm under the Weimar Republic. Nevertheless in 1933 it was not ready for a war with France, nor for some years thereafter. It would have been forced either to yield to a French threat or to wage a war without prospect of success. At that time it was still possible to stop the Nazis with threats. And even had war resulted, France would have been strong enough to win.

But then something amazing and unexpected happened. Those nationalists who for more than sixty years had been fanatically anti-German, who had scorned everything German, and who had always demanded an energetic policy against the Weimar Republic changed their minds overnight. Those who had disparaged as Jewish all endeavors to improve Franco-German relations, who had attacked as Jewish machinations the Dawes and Young plans and the Locarno agreement, and who had held the League suspect as a Jewish institution suddenly began to sympathize with the Nazis. They refused to recognize the fact that Hitler was eager to destroy France once and for all. Hitler, they hinted, is less a foe of France than of the Jews; as an old warrior he sympathizes with his French fellow warriors. They belittled German rearmament. Besides, they said, Hitler rearms only in order to fight Jewish Bolshevism. Nazism is Europe's shield against the assault of World Jewry and its foremost representative, Bolshevism. The Jews are eager to push France into a war against the Nazis. But France is wise enough not to pull any chestnuts out of the fire for the Jews. France will not bleed for the Jews.

It was not the first time in French history that the nationalists put their anti-Semitism above their French patriotism. In the Dreyfus Affair they fought vigorously in order to let a treacherous officer quietly evade punishment while an innocent Jew languished in prison.

It has been said that the Nazis corrupted the French nationalists. Perhaps some French politicians really took bribes. But politically this was of little importance. The Reich would have wasted its funds. The anti-Semitic newspapers and periodicals had a wide circulation; they did not need German subsidies. Hitler left the League; he annulled the disarmament clauses of the Treaty of Versailles; he occupied the demilitarized zone on the Rhine; he stirred anti-French tendencies in North Africa. The French nationalists for the most part criticized these acts only in order to put all the blame on their political adversaries in France: it was they who were guilty, because they had adopted a hostile attitude toward Nazism.

Then Hitler invaded Austria. Seven years earlier France had vigorously opposed the plan of an Austro-German customs union. But now the French Government hurried to recognize the violent annexation of Austria. At Munich—in coöperation with Great Britain and Italy—it forced Czechoslovakia to yield to the German claims. All this met with the approval of the majority of the French nationalists. When Mussolini, instigated by Hitler, proclaimed the Italian aspirations for Savoy, Nice, Corsica, and Tunis, the nationalists' objections were ventured timidly. No Demosthenes rose to warn the nation against Philip. But if a new Demosthenes had presented himself the nationalists would have denounced him as the son of a rabbi or a nephew of Rothschild.

It is true that the French Left did not oppose the Nazis either, and in this respect they did not differ from their British friends. But that is no excuse for the nationalists. They were influential enough to induce an energetic anti-Nazi policy in France. But for them every proposal seriously to resist Hitler was a form of Jewish treachery.

It does credit to the French nation that it loved peace and was ready to avoid war even at the price of sacrifice. But that was not the question. Germany openly prepared a war for the total annihilation of France. There was no doubt about the intentions of the Nazis. Under such conditions the only policy appropriate would have been to frustrate Hitler's plans at all costs. Whoever dragged in the Jews in discussing Franco-German relations forsook the cause of his nation. Whether Hitler was a friend or foe of the Jews was irrelevant. The existence of France was at stake. This alone had to be considered, not the desire of French shopkeepers or doctors to get rid of their Jewish competitors.

That France did not block Hitler's endeavors in time, that it long neglected its military preparations, and that finally, when war could no longer be avoided, it was not ready to fight was the fault of anti-Semitism. The French anti-Semites served Hitler well. Without them the new war might have been avoided, or at least fought under much more favorable conditions.

When war came, it was stigmatized by the French Right as a

war for the sake of the Jews and by the French communists as a war for the sake of capitalism. The unpopularity of the war paralyzed the hands of the military chiefs. It slowed down work in the armament factories. From a military point of view matters in June, 1940, were not worse than in early September, 1914, and less unfavorable than in September, 1870. Gambetta, Clemenceau, or Briand would not have capitulated. Neither would Georges Mandel. But Mandel was a Jew and therefore not eligible for political leadership. Thus the unbelievable happened: France disavowed its past, branded the proudest memories of its history Jewish, and hailed the loss of its political independence as a national revolution and a regeneration of its true spirit.

Not alone in France but the world over anti-Semitism made propaganda for Nazism. Such was the detrimental effect of interventionism and its tendencies toward discrimination that a good many people became unable to appreciate problems of foreign policy from any viewpoint but that of their appetite for discrimination against successful competitors. The hope of being delivered from a Jewish competitor fascinated them while they forgot everything else, their nation's independence, freedom, religion, civilization. There were and are pro-Nazi parties all over the world. Every European country has its Quislings. Quislings commanded armies whose duty it was to defend their country. They capitulated ignominiously; they coöperated with invaders; they had the impudence to style their treachery true patriotism. The Nazis have an ally in every town or village where there is a man eager to get rid of a Jewish competitor. The secret weapon of Hitler is the anti-Jewish inclinations of many millions of shopkeepers and grocers, of doctors and lawyers, professors and writers.

The present war would never have originated but for anti-Semitism. Only anti-Semitism made it possible for the Nazis to restore the German people's faith in the invincibility of its armed forces, and thus to drive Germany again into the policy of aggression and the struggle for hegemony. Only the anti-Semitic entanglement of a good deal of French public opinion prevented France from stopping Hitler when he could still be stopped without war. And it was anti-Semitism that helped the German armies find in every European country men ready to open the doors to them.

Mankind has paid a high price indeed for anti-Semitism.

IX. THE WEIMAR REPUBLIC AND ITS COLLAPSE

1. The Weimar Constitution

THE main argument brought forward in favor of the Hohenzollern militarism was its alleged efficiency. Democracy, said the nationalist professors, may be a form of government adequate to small countries, whose independence is safeguarded by the mutual rivalries of the great powers, or to nations like England and the United States sheltered by their geographical situation; but it is different with Germany. Germany is surrounded by hostile nations; it stands alone in the world; its borders are not protected by natural barriers; its security is founded on its army, that unique achievement of the house of Hohenzollern. It would be foolish to hand over this invincible instrument to a parliament, to a body of talkative and incompetent civilians.

But now the first World War had resulted in a smashing defeat and had destroyed the old prestige of the royal family, of the Junkers, the officers, and the civil servants. The parliamentary system of the West had given evidence of its military superiority. The war to which President Wilson had assigned the aim of making the world safe for democracy appeared as an ordeal by fire for democracy. The Germans began to revise their political creeds. They turned toward democracy. The term democracy, almost forgotten for half a century, became popular again in the last weeks of the war. Democracy meant in the minds of the Germans the return to the civil liberties, the rights of man, suspended in the course of the war, and above all the substitution of parliamentary government for monarchical half-despotism. These points were, as every German knew, implied in the official program of the most numerous parliamentary party, the Social Democrats. Men expected that the Social Democrats would now realize the democratic principles of their program, and were ready to back this party in its endeavors for political reconstruction.

But from the ranks of the Marxians came an answer which nobody outside the small group of professional Marx experts could have foreseen. We class-conscious proletarians, the Marxians proclaimed, have nothing to do with your bourgeois concepts of freedom, parliamentarism, and democracy. We do not want democracy but the dictatorship of the proletariat, i.e., our dictatorship. We are not prepared to grant you bourgeois parasites the rights of men, to give you the franchise and parliamentary representation. Only Marxians and proletarians shall henceforth rule. If you misinterpreted our stand on democracy, that is your mistake. Had you studied the writings of Marx more carefully, you would have been better informed.

On the second day of the revolution the Social Democrats in Berlin appointed a new government for the Reich, the Mandataries of the People. This government was a dictatorship of the Social Democrats. It was formed by the delegates of that party only, and it was not planned to give the other parties a share in the government.*

At the end of the war the old Social Democratic party was split into three groups: the majority socialists, the independent socialists, and the communists. One half of the government members belonged to the majority socialists, the other half to the independent socialists. The most radical of the three groups did not participate in the establishment of the government. They abhorred coöperation with the moderate majority socialists, whom they denounced as social traitors. These radicals, the Spartacus group or Communist party, immediately demanded the extermination of the bourgeoisie. Their condensed program was: all power must be in the hands of the Soviets of workers and soldiers. They vigorously rejected every plan to grant political rights to people who were not members of their own party, and they fanatically opposed the parliamentary system. They wanted to organize Germany according to the Soviet pattern and to "liquidate" the bourgeoisie in the Russian manner. They were convinced that the whole world was on the eve of the great proletarian revolution which was to destroy capitalism and establish the everlasting communist paradise, and they were eager to contribute their share to this glorious undertaking. The independent socialists sympathized with the views of the communists but they were less outspoken. This very reserve made them dependent on the communists, whose radical expression struck the keynote. The majority socialists had neither opinions of their own nor a clear idea what policy they ought to adopt. Their irresolution was not due to a change of mind with regard to their socialist convictions but to a realization that a great part of the German socialist workers had taken seriously the democratic points in the Social Democratic program and were opposed to the abandonment of parliamentarism. They still believed that socialism

* It is important to realize that the Social Democrats, although the largest single group in the Reichstag of monarchical Germany, were far outnumbered by the other parties combined. They never got the support of the majority of the voters. Never during the Weimar Republic did all the Marxian parties together succeed in polling an absolute majority of votes or winning an absolute majority in the Reichstag.

and democracy are compatible, indeed that socialism can only be realized within a democratic community. They neither recognized the incompatibility of socialism and democracy nor understood why Germany should prefer the Russian method of dictatorship to the Western principle of democracy.

The communists were eager to seize power through violence. They trusted to Russian aid but they felt themselves strong enough to conquer even without this foreign assistance. For they were fully convinced that the overwhelming majority of the German nation backed them. They deemed it therefore needless to make special preparations for the extermination of the bourgeoisie. As long as the adversaries kept quiet, it was unnecessary to strike the first blow. If the bourgeoisie were to start something, it would be easy to beat them down. And the first events confirmed this view. At Christmas time, 1918, a conflict broke out in Berlin between the new government and a pugnacious communist troop, the people's sailors' division. The sailors resisted the government. The People's Mandataries, in a panic, called to their aid a not-yet-disbanded body of the old army garrisoned in the environs of Berlin, a troop of dismounted cavalrymen of the former Royal Guards, commanded by an aristocratic general. A skirmish took place; then the government ordered the guardsmen to retreat. They had gained a slight tactical success, but the government withdrew its forces because it lacked confidence in its own cause; it did not want to fight the "comrades." This unimportant combat convinced the independent socialists that the victorious advance of communism could not be stopped. In order not to lose their popularity and not to come too late to participate in the prospective communist government they withdrew their representatives from the body of the People's Mandataries. The majority socialists were now alone in the government, alone responsible for everything that happened in the Reich, for the growing anarchy, for the unsatisfactory supply of food and other necessities, for the rapid spread of unemployment. In the eyes of the radicals they were the defenders of reaction and injustice.

There could be no doubt about the plans of these radicals. They would occupy the government buildings and imprison, probably even kill, the members of the government. In vain Noske, whom the government had appointed commander in chief, tried to organize a troop of majority socialists. No Social Democrat was willing to fight against the communists. The government's situation seemed hopeless when on January 5, 1919, the communists and independent socialists opened the battle in the streets of Berlin and got control of the main part of the capital. But in this utmost danger unexpected aid appeared.

The Marxians report the events that followed in this way: The masses were unanimous in their support of the radical Marxian leaders and in their desire for the realization of socialism. But unfortunately they were trusting enough to believe that the government, composed solely of old Social Democratic chiefs, would not hinder them in these endeavors. Yet Ebert, Noske, and Scheidemann betrayed them. These traitors, eager to save capitalism, plotted with the remnants of the old army and with the gangs hired by the capitalists, the free corps. The troops of reaction rushed in upon the unsuspecting communist leaders, assassinated them, and dispersed the masses which had lost their leaders. Thus started a policy of reaction which finally culminated in the fall of the Weimar Republic and in the ascendancy of Nazism.

This statement of the facts ignores the radical change which took place in the last weeks of 1918 in the political mentality of the German nation. In October and early November, 1918, the great majority of the nation was sincerely prepared to back a democratic government. As the Social Democrats were considered a democratic party, as they were the most numerous parliamentary party, there was almost unanimity in the readiness to entrust to them the leading role in forming the future system of popular government. But then came the shock. Outstanding men of the Marxian party rejected democracy and declared themselves for the dictatorship of the proletariat. All that they had professed for fifty years, in short, consisted of lies. All this talk had had but one end in view, to put Rosa Luxemburg, a foreigner, in the place of the Hohenzollerns. The eyes of the Germans had been opened. How could they have let themselves be deluded by the slogans of the Democrats? Democracy, they learned, was evidently a term invented for the deception of fools. In fact, as the conservatives had always asserted, the advocates of democracy wished to establish the rule of the mob and the dictatorship of demagogues.

The communists had grossly underrated the intellectual capacity of the German nation. They did not realize that it was impossible to deal with the Germans by the same methods that had succeeded in Russia. When they boasted that in fifty years of pro-democratic agitation they had never been sincere in advocating democracy; when they told the Germans: "You dupes, how clever we were in gulling you! Now we have caught you!" it was too much not only for the rest of the nation but even for the majority of the old members of the Social Democratic party. Within a few weeks Marxism and Marxian socialism—not socialism as an economic system—had lost all their former prestige. The idea of democracy itself became hopelessly suspect. From that time on the term democracy was for many Germans synonymous with fraud. At the beginning of 1919 the communists were already much less numerous than their leaders believed. And the great majority of organized labor was also solidly against them.

The nationalists were quick to comprehend this change in mentality. They seized their opportunity. A few weeks before they had been in a state of desperation. Now they learned how to stage a comeback. The "stab in the back" legend had already restored their lost self-confidence. And now they saw what their future policy must be. First they must thwart the establishment of a red dictatorship and prevent the communists from exterminating the nonproletarians wholesale.

The former conservative party and some affiliated groups had in November changed their party name to German Nationalist People's Party (*Deutsch-nationale Volkspartei*). In their first manifesto, issued on November 24, they asked "for a return from the dictatorship of one class only to parliamentary government as the only appropriate system in the light of recent events." They asked further for freedom of the individual and of conscience, for freedom of speech and science, and for equality of franchise. For the second time in German history a party which was essentially antidemocratic presented to the electorate for purely tactical reasons a program of liberalism and democracy. The Marxian methods found adepts; the nationalists had profited from reading Lenin and Bukharin. They had now elaborated a precise plan for their future operations for the seizure of power. They decided to support the cause of parliamentary government, freedom, and democracy for the immediate future in order to be able to overthrow them at a later time. They were ready to coöperate for the execution of the first part of this program not only with the Catholics but also with the majority socialists and their old leaders, who sat trembling in the government palaces of the Wilhelmstrasse.

In order to keep out Bolshevism and to save parliamentarism and freedom for the intermediate period, it was necessary to defeat the armed forces of the communists and of the independent socialists. The available remnants of the old army, when lead by able commanders, were strong enough to intervene successfully against the communists.

But such commanders could not be found in the ranks of the generals. Hindenburg was an old man; his role in the war had consisted simply in giving a free hand to Ludendorff; now, without Ludendorff, he was helpless. The other generals were waiting for Hindenburg's orders; they lacked initiative. But the disintegration of army discipline had already progressed so far that this apathy of the generals could no longer hinder the army's actions. Younger officers, sometimes even lieutenants, filled the gap. Out of demobilized soldiers, who were not too eager to go back to honest jobs and preferred the adventurous life of troopers to regular work, some of these officers formed free corps, at the head of which they fought on their own account. Other officers pushed aside the more scrupulous officers of the General Staff and, sometimes without proper respect, forced the generals to take part in the civil war.

The People's Mandataries had already lost all hope of salvation when suddenly help appeared. Troops invaded Berlin and suppressed the communist revolt. Karl Liebknecht and Rosa Luxemburg were taken prisoner and then assassinated. This victory did not end the civil war. It continued for months in the provinces, and time and again broke out afresh in Berlin. However, the victory reported by the troops in January, 1919, in Berlin safeguarded the elections for the Constituent Assembly, the session of this Parliament, and the promulgation of the Weimar Constitution. William II used to say: "Where my guards set foot, there is no further question of democracy." The Weimar democracy was of a peculiar sort. The horsemen of the Kaiser's guards had fought for it and won it. The Constitution of Weimar could be deliberated and voted only because the nationalist adversaries of democracy preferred it to the dictatorship of the communists. The German nation obtained parliamentary government as a gift from the hands of deadly foes of freedom, who waited for an opportunity to take back their present.

It was in vain that the majority socialists and their affiliate, the Democratic party, invented one legend more, in order to obfuscate these sad facts. In the first months following the November Revolution, they said, the Marxians discussed in their party circles the question of what form of government would serve best the interests of German labor. The disputations were sometimes very violent, because some radicals tried to disturb them. But finally, after careful deliberation, the workers resolved that parliamentary democracy would be the most appropriate form of government. This magnanimous renunciation of dictatorship was the outcome of a voluntary decision and gave new evidence of the political maturity of German labor.

This interpretation of events cautiously evades dealing with the main problem. In early January, 1919, there was but one political problem in Germany: the choice between Bolshevist totalitarianism under the joint dictatorship of Rosa Luxemburg and Karl Liebknecht, on the one hand, and parliamentarism on the other. This struggle could not be decided by the peaceful methods of democracy. The communists were not prepared to yield to the majority. They were an armed troop; they had gained control of the greater part of the capital and of a good many other places. But for the nationalist gangs and troops and for the remnants of the old army, they could have seized power throughout the Reich and established Bolshevism in Germany. There was but one factor that could stop their assault and that really did stop it: the armed forces of the Right.

The moderate Marxians are correct in asserting that not only the bourgeoisie and the farmers but also the greater part of organized labor was opposed to dictatorship and preferred parliamentary government. But at that time it was no longer a question of whether a man was ready to vote for a party ticket but of whether he was ready to stake his life for his conviction. The communists were only a small minority, but there was just one means left to combat them: by deadly weapons. Whoever wanted democracy—whether from the point of view of his Weltanschauung or simply as the lesser evil—had to attack the strongholds of communism, to rout its armed bands, and to put the government in control of the capital and of the rest of the country. Everyone knew that this was the state of affairs. Every member of the majority socialists was fully aware that not to fight the communists by force of arms was equivalent to yielding to communism. But only a few functionaries of the government made even a lame attempt to organize resistance; and their endeavors failed as all their political friends refused coöperation.

It is very important to understand the ideas which in those fateful days shaped the attitudes of the majority socialists. For these ideas sprang out of the very essence of Marxian thought. They reappear whenever and wherever in the world people imbued with Marxian doctrines have to face similar situations. We encounter in them one of the main reasons why Marxism—leaving its economic failure out of the question—even in the field of political action was and is the most conspicuous failure of history.

The German Marxians—remember, not the communists, but those sincerely rejecting dictatorship—argued this way: It is indispensable to smash the communists in order to pave the way for democratic socialism. (In those days of December, 1918, and January, 1919, the German noncommunist Marxians were still wrapped in the illusion that the majority of the people backed *their* socialist program.) It is necessary to defeat the communist revolt by armed resistance. But that is not our business. Nobody can expect us, Marxians and proletarians as we are, to rise in arms against our class and party comrades. A dirty job has to be done but it is not our task to do it. Our tenets are contrary to such a policy. We must cling to the principle of class and party solidarity. Besides, it would hurt our popularity and imperil our success at the impending election. We are, indeed, in a very unfortunate position. For the communists do not feel themselves bound by the same idea. They can fight us, because they have the enormous advantage of denouncing us as social traitors and reactionaries. We cannot pay them back in their own coin. They are revolutionaries in fighting us, but we would appear as reactionaries in fighting them. In the realm of Marxian thought the more radical are always right in despising and attacking the more prudent party members. Nobody would believe us if we were to call them traitors and renegades. As Marxians, in this situation we cannot help adopting an attitude of nonresistance.

These oversophisticated Marxians did not see what the German people—among them millions of old party members—realized very well: that this policy meant the abdication of German Marxism. If a ruling party has to admit: This has to be done now; this is the necessity of the hour; but we cannot do it because it does not comply with our creed; somebody else has to fill the gap—it renounces once and for all its claims to political leadership.

The noncommunist Marxians severely blame Ebert, Noske, and others of their leaders for their coöperation with the nationalist vanquishers of the communist forces. But this coöperation consisted in nothing more than some consultations. It is likely that the frightened Mandataries of the People and their aides did not conceal in these talks with the nationalist commanders that they were frightened and powerless and would be glad to be saved. But in the eyes of the adamant supporters of the principle of class solidarity this already meant treason.

The outstanding fact in all this is that German communism was defeated by the Right alone, while the noncommunist Marxians were eager to stay neutral. But for the nationalist armed intervention, Germany would have turned to Bolshevism in 1919. The outcome of the events of January, 1919, was an enormous increase in the prestige of the nationalists; theirs was the glory of having saved the nation, while the Social Democrats became despicable. Every new communist upheaval repeated the same experience. The nationalists fought the communists single-handed, while the Social Democrats hesitated to oppose their "communist comrades." The Social Democrats ruled Prussia, the paramount state, and some of the smaller states of the Reich; but they ruled only thanks to the support they got from the nationalists of the Reichswehr and of the free corps. From that time on the Social Democrats were at the mercy of the Right.

The Weimar Republic was regarded both by the nationalists and by the communists only as a battleground in their struggle for dictatorship. Both armed for civil war; both tried several times to open the attack and had to be beaten back by force. But the nationalists daily grew more powerful, while the communists gradually became paralyzed. It was not a question of votes and number of members in Parliament. The centers of gravity of these parties lay outside parliamentary affairs. The nationalists could act freely. They were supported by the majority of the intellectuals, salaried people, entrepreneurs, farmers, and by a part of skilled labor. They were familiar with the problems of German life. They could adjust their actions to the changing political and economic conditions of the nation and of each of its provinces. The communists, on the other hand, had to obey orders issued by ignorant Russian chiefs who were not familiar with Germany, and they were forced to change their policies over night whenever the central committee of Moscow ordered them to do so. No intelligent or honest man could endure such slavery. The intellectual and moral quality of the German communist leaders was consequently far below the average level of German politicians. They were no match for the nationalists. The communists played the role in German politics only of saboteurs and conspirators. After January, 1919, they no longer had any chance of success. Of course, the ten years of Nazi misrule have revived German communism; on the day of Hitler's collapse they will be the strongest party in Germany.

The Germans would have decided in 1918 in favor of democracy, if they had had the choice. But as things were, they had only the choice between the two dictatorships, of the communists and of the nationalists. Between these two dictatorial parties there was no third group ready to support capitalism and its political corollary, democracy. Neither the majority socialists and their affiliates, the Democratic party, nor the Catholic Center party was fitted for the adoption of "plutocratic" democracy and of "bourgeois" republicanism. Their past and their ideologies were strongly opposed to such an attitude. The Hohenzollerns lost their throne because they rejected British parliamentarism. The Weimar Republic failed because it rejected French republicanism as realized from 1875 to 1930 in the Third Republic. The Weimar Republic had no program but to steer a middle course between two groups aiming at dictatorship. For the supporters of the government parliamentarism was not the best system of government. It was only an emergency measure, an expedient. The majority socialists wanted to be moderate Marxians and moderate nationalists, nationalist Marxians and Marxian nationalists. The Catholics wanted to combine nationalism and socialism with Catholicism and yet to maintain democracy. Such eclecticism is doomed. It does not appeal to youth. It succumbs in every conflict with resolute adversaries.

There was only one alternative to nationalism left: the adoption of unrestricted free trade. Nobody in Germany considered such a reversion. It would have required an abandonment of all measures of Sozialpolitik, government control and trade-union pressure. Those parties that believed they were fighting radical nationalism —the Social Democrats and their satellites, then the communists, the Center, and some farmer groups—were, on the contrary, fanatical supporters of etatism and hyper-protectionism. But they were too narrow-minded to see that these policies presented Germany with the tremendous problem of autarky. They simply shut their eyes. We should not overrate the intellectual capacities of the German masses. But they were not too dull to see that autarky was the focal problem of Germany and that only the nationalist parties had an idea (although a spurious one) of how to deal with it. While the other parties shunned a discussion of its dangers, the nationalists offered a plan for a solution. As this plan of world conquest was the only one offered to the Germans, they endorsed it. No one told them that there was another way out. The Marxians and the Catholics were not even keen enough to point out that the Nazi plan of world domination was doomed to military failure; they were anxious not to hurt the vanity of the people, firmly assured of their own invincibility. But even if the adversaries of aggression had adequately exposed the dangers and the risks of a new war, the plain citizen would still have given preference to the Nazis. For the more cautious and subtle Nazis said: We have a precise plan for the salvation of Germany; it is a very risky plan and we cannot guarantee success. But anyhow it gives us a chance, while no one else has any idea how to deal with our serious condition. If you drift your fate is sealed; if you follow us there is at least a prospect of success.

The conduct of the German Left was no less an ostrich policy than that of the Left in Great Britain and in France. On the one hand, the Left advocated state omnipotence and consequently hyper-protectionism; on the other hand, it gave no thought to the fact that within a world of autarky Germany was doomed to starvation. The German Marxian refugees boast that their parties made some—very lame and timid, indeed—endeavors to prevent German rearmament. But this was only a proof of their inconsistency and their inability to see reality as it was. Whoever wanted to maintain peace had to fight etatism. Yet the Left was no less fanatical in its support of etatism than the Right. The whole German nation favored a policy of government interference with business which must result in Zwangswirtschaft. But only the Nazis grasped the fact that while Russia could live in autarky Germany could not. Therefore the Nazis succeeded, for they did not encounter any party advocating laissez faire, i.e., a market economy.

2. The Abortive Socialization

The Social Democrats had put at the top of their party programs the demand for the socialization (*Vergesellschaftung*) of the means of production. This would have been clear and unambiguous if people had been ready to interpret it as forcible expropriation of the means of production by the state, and consequently as government management of all branches of economic activity. But the Social Democrats emphatically asserted that this was not at all the meaning of their basic claim. Nationalization (*Verstaatlichung*) and socialization, they insisted, were two entirely different things. The measures of nationalization and municipalization (*Verstadtlichung*) of various plants and enterprises, which the Reich and its member states had considered since the 'eighties of the past century an essential part of their socio-economic policies, were, they maintained, neither socialization nor the first steps toward it. They were on the contrary the outcome of a capitalist policy extremely detrimental to the interests of labor. The unfavorable experience with these nationalized and municipalized concerns, therefore, had no bearing on the socialist demand for socialization. However, the Marxians did not explain what socialization really means and how it differs from nationalization. They made some clumsy attempts but very soon they retired from the discussion of this awkward problem. The subject was tabooed. No decent German was rash enough to break this ban by raising the question.

The first World War brought about a trend toward war socialism. One branch of business after the other was centralized, i.e., forcibly placed under the management of a committee whose members— the entrepreneurs of the branch concerned—were nothing but an advisory board of the government's commissary. Thus the government obtained full control of all vital branches of business. The Hindenburg program advocated an all-round application of this system for all branches of German trade and production. Its execution would have transformed Germany into a purely socialist commonwealth of the Zwangswirtschaft pattern. But the Hindenburg program was not yet completely realized when the German Empire collapsed.

War socialism was extremely unpopular in Germany. People even blamed it for what was not its fault. It was not exclusively to blame for German starvation. The blockade, the absence of millions of workers serving in the armed forces, and the fact that a good deal of the productive effort had to be directed to the production of armament and munitions contributed to the distress even more than the inadequacy of socialist methods of production. The Social Democrats should have pointed out these things as well. But they did not want to miss any opportunity which could be exploited for demagogic distortion of facts. They attacked the Zwangswirtschaft as such. The Zwangswirtschaft was the worst kind of capitalist exploitation and abuse, they contended; and it had demonstrated the urgent need for the substitution of socialism for capitalism.

The end of the war brought military defeat, revolution, civil war, famine, and desolation. Millions of demobilized soldiers, many of whom had retained their arms, flowed back to their homes. They robbed the military magazines. They stopped trains to search them for food. In company with workers, dismissed by plants which had been forced overnight to discontinue the production of munitions, they raided the open country for bread and potatoes. The villagers organized armed resistance. Conditions were chaotic. The inexperienced and ignorant socialists who had seized the government were helpless. They had no idea how to cope with the situation. Their orders and counterorders disintegrated the apparatus of administration. The starving masses called for food and were fed bombastic speeches.

In this emergency capitalism gave proof of its adaptability and efficiency. The entrepreneurs, at last defying the innumerable laws and decrees of the Zwangswirtschaft, tried to make their plants run again. The most urgent need was to resume production for export in order to buy food and raw materials in the neutral countries and in the Balkans. Without such imports Germany would have been doomed. The entrepreneurs succeeded in their efforts and thus saved Germany. People called them profiteers but scrambled for the goods brought to the market and were happy to acquire these badly needed necessities. The unemployed found jobs again. Germany began to return to normal.

The socialists did not worry much about the slackening of the Zwangswirtschaft. In their opinion this system, far from being socialist, was a capitalist evil that had to be abolished as soon as possible. Now real socialization had to start.

But what did socialization mean? It was, said the Marxians,

neither the kind of thing represented by the nationalization of state railroads, state mines, and so on, nor the war socialism of Zwangs-wirtschaft. But what else could it be? Marxians of all groups had to admit that they did not know. For more than fifty years they had advocated socialization as the focal point of their party program. Now that they had seized power they must start to execute their program. Now they had to socialize. But at once it became apparent that they did not know what socialization meant. It was really rather awkward.

Fortunately the socialist leaders remembered that there is a class of men whose business it is to know everything—the omniscient professors. The government appointed a socialization committee. The majority of its members were Social Democrats; yet it was not from these that the solution of the riddle was expected but from the professors. The professors whom the government nominated were not Social Democrats. They were advocates of that Sozialpolitik which in earlier years had favored the nationalization and municipalization of various enterprises, and in recent years had supported the planned economy, the Zwangswirtschaft. They had always backed precisely the reformism that the orthodox Marxians denounced as capitalist humbug, detrimental to the interests of the proletarians.

The socialization committee deliberated many years, splitting hairs, distilling oversophisticated definitions, drafting spurious plans, and selling very bad economics. Its minutes and reports, collected in shelves of thick volumes, rest in the libraries for the edification of future generations. They are a token of the intellectual decay brought about by Marxism and etatism. But they failed to answer the question of what else socialization could mean besides nationalization (Verstaatlichung) or planning (Zwangswirtschaft).

There are only two methods of socialization, both of which had been applied by the German Imperial Government. There is on the one hand outright nationalization, today the method of Soviet Russia; and there is on the other hand central planning, the Zwangswirtschaft of the Hindenburg program and the method of the Nazis. The German Marxians had barred both ways to themselves through their hypocritical demagogy. The Marxians of the Weimar Republic not only did not further the trend toward socialization; they tolerated the virtual abandonment of the most effective socialization measures inaugurated by the imperial government. Their adversaries, foremost among them the regime of the Catholic Chancellor Bruening, later resumed the policy of planning, and the Nazis perfected these endeavors by establishing all-round planning, the German socialism of the Zwangswirtschaft type.

The German workers, both Social Democrats and communists, were not much concerned about socialization. For them, as Kautsky remarked, the revolution meant only an opportunity to raise wages. Higher wages, higher unemployment doles, and shorter hours of work meant more to them than socialization.

This situation was not the result of treason on the part of the socialist leaders but of the inherent contradictions in the Social Democratic creed. The Marxians advocated a program whose realization was bound to render the state omnipotent and totalitarian; but they also talked indefatigably about shaking off "this state rubbish in its entirety," about "the withering away of the state." They advocated socialization but rejected the only two methods available for its achievement. They talked of the frustration of trade-unionism as a means of improving the conditions of the workers; but they made trade-union policies the focal point of their political action. They taught that socialism could not be attained before capitalism had reached its full maturity, and disparaged as petty bourgeois all measures designed to check or delay the evolution of capitalism. But they themselves vehemently and fanatically demanded such measures. These contradictions and inconsistencies, not machinations of capitalists or entrepreneurs, caused the downfall of German Marxism.

True, the leaders of the Social Democrats were incompetent; some were corrupt and insincere. But this was no accident. No intelligent man could fail to see the essential shortcomings of Marxian doctrine. Corruption is an evil inherent in every government not controlled by a watchful public opinion. Those who were prepared to take the demand for socialization seriously deserted the ranks of Marxism for those of Nazism. For the Nazis, although still more corrupt morally, aimed unambiguously at the realization of central planning.

3. The Armed Parties

The November Revolution brought a resurgence of a phenomenon that had long before disappeared from German history. Military adventurers formed armed bands or *Freikorps* and acted on their own behalf. The communist revolutionaries had inaugurated this method, but soon the nationalists adopted and perfected it. Dismissed officers of the old army called together demobilized soldiers and maladjusted boys and offered their protection to the peasants menaced by raids of starving townsfolk and to the population of the eastern frontiers suffering from Polish and Lithuanian guerrilla invasions. The landlords and the farmers provided them in return for their services with food and shelter. When the condition which had made their interference appear useful changed these gangs began to blackmail and to extort money from landowners, businessmen, and other wealthy people. They became a public calamity.

The government did not dare to dissolve them. Some of the bands had fought bravely against the communists. Others had successfully defended the eastern provinces against the Poles and Lithuanians. They boasted of these achievements, and the nationalist youth did not conceal their sympathy for them. The old leaders of the nationalist party were profoundly hostile to these unmanageable gang leaders, who defied their advice and whose heedless actions came into collision with their considered plans. The extortions of the free corps were a heavy burden for the landowners and peasants. The bands were no longer needed as a safeguard against communist uprisings. The Reichswehr, the new army reorganized according to the provisions of the Treaty of Versailles, was now strong enough for this task. The nationalist champions were quite right in suspecting that the young men who formed these corps hoped to displace them in the leadership of the nationalist movement. They devised a clever scheme for their suppression. The Reichswehr was to incorporate them and thus render them innocuous. As it became more difficult from day to day for the captains of the free corps to provide funds for the sustenance of their men, they were ready to accept this offer and to obey the orders of the army officers.

This solution, however, was a breach of the Treaty of Versailles, which had limited the size of the Reichswehr to a hundred thousand men. Hence conflicts arose with the French and the British representatives. The Allied Powers demanded the total disbandment of the so-called black Reichswehr. When the government, complying, decided to dissolve the most important black troop, the sailors' Ehrhardt brigade, it hastened the outbreak of the Kapp insurrection.

War and civil war, and the revolutionary mentality of the Marxians and of the nationalists, had created such a spirit of brutality that the political parties gave their organizations a military character. Both the nationalist Right and the Marxian Left had their armed forces. These party troops were, of course, entirely different from the free corps formed by nationalist hotspurs and by communist radicals. Their members were people who had their regular jobs and were busy from Monday to Saturday noon. On week ends they would don their uniforms and parade with brass bands, flags, and often with their firearms. They were proud of their membership in these associations but they were not eager to fight; they were not animated by a spirit of aggression. Their existence, their parades, their boasting, and the challenging speeches of their chiefs were a nuisance but not a serious menace to domestic peace.

After the failure of the revolutionary attempts of Kapp in March, 1920, that of Hitler and Ludendorff in November, 1923, and of various communist uprisings, of which the most important was the Holz riot in March, 1921, Germany was on the way back to normal conditions. The free corps and the communist gangs began slowly to disappear from the political stage. They still waged some guerrilla warfare with each other and against the police. But these fights degenerated more and more into gangsterism and rowdyism. Such riots and the plots of a few adventurers could not endanger the stability of the social order.

But the Social Democratic party and press made the blunder of repeatedly denouncing the few still operating nationalist free corps and vehemently insisting on their dissolution. This attitude was a challenge to the nationalist parties who disliked the adventurers no less than the Social Democrats did but did not dare to abandon them openly. They retorted by calling for the dissolution of the communist formations as well. But the Social Democrats were in a similar position with regard to the communist bands. They hated and feared them yet did not want to combat them openly.

As in the Bismarck Reich, so in the Weimar Republic, the main powers of civil administration were not assigned to the government of the Reich but to the governments of the member states. Prussia was the largest and richest member state; its population was the most numerous; it was the Reich's center of gravity, or, properly speaking, the Reich. The fact that the conservative party had dominated Prussia had given the conservatives hegemony over imperial Germany. The fact that the Social Democrats ruled Prussia under the Weimar Republic made them paramount in the republican Reich. When Chancellor Papen's coup d'état of July 20, 1932, overthrew the socialist regime in Prussia, the struggle for the Reich was virtually decided.

The Bavarian Government was reluctant to disband the nationalist bands on its territory. It was not sympathy with the nationalists but provincial particularism that determined this attitude. To disobey the central authority was for it a matter of principle. The Government of the Reich was helpless because it had but one means to impose its will on a disobedient member state, namely, civil war. In this plight the Social Democratic Prussian Government took recourse to a fateful measure. On February 22, 1924, in Magdeburg, it founded the *Reichsbanner Schwarz-Rot-Gold*. This was not a private troop like the other armed party forces. It was an army of Prussia's ruling party and had the full support of the Prussian Government. An outstanding Prussian functionary, the governor of the province of Saxony, was appointed its chief. The Reichsbanner was to be a nonpartisan association of all men loyal to the republican system of government and the Constitution of Weimar. Virtually, however, it was a Social Democratic institution. Its leaders insisted that members of other loyal parties were welcome in its ranks. But the immense majority of the members were Social Democrats who up to that time had been members of the various local and provincial Social Democratic armed party forces. Thus the foundation of the Reichsbanner did not strengthen the military forces of the Social Democrats; it only gave them a new, more centralized organization and the sanction of the Prussian state. Members of the Catholic Center party were never very numerous in the Reichsbanner and soon disappeared completely from its ranks. The third loyal party, the Democrats, were merely an insignificant affiliate of the Social Democrats.

The Social Democrats have tried to justify the foundation of the Reichsbanner by referring to the nationalist bias of the Reichswehr, the one hundred thousand soldiers who formed the Reich's army. But the Kapp revolt had demonstrated that the socialists had a very efficacious weapon available to defeat the nationalists in the general strike. The only serious menace for the Weimar Republic was the nationalist sympathies within the ranks of organized labor. The Social Democratic chiefs were unable to work successfully against these tendencies; many secretly sympathized with them.

The ominous import of the foundation of the Reichsbanner was that it provided Hitler with a good start. His Munich putsch of November, 1923, had resulted in complete failure. When he left prison in December, 1924, his political prospects looked black. The foundation of the Reichsbanner was just what he wanted. All the non-Marxians, i.e., the majority of the population, were terrified by the defiant speeches of its chiefs and the fact that at the end of the first year of its existence its membership was three millions—more than the membership of all the *Wehrverbände* of the Right together.* Like the Social Democrats, they overrated the strength of the Reichsbanner and its readiness to fight. Thus a good many people were prepared to aid the Nazi Storm Troopers.

But these Storm Troopers were very different from the other

* Stampfer, *Die vierzehn Jahre der ersten Deutschen Republik* (Karlsbad, 1936), p. 365.

armed party forces both of the Left and of the Right. Their mem·
bers were not elderly men who had fought in the first World War
and who now were eager to hold their jobs in order to support their
families. The Nazi Storm Troopers were, as the free corps had been,
jobless boys who made a living from their fighting. They were available at every hour of every day, not merely on week ends and holidays. It was doubtful whether the party forces—either of the Left
or the Right—would be ready to fight when seriously attacked.
It was certain that they would never be ready to wage a campaign
of aggression. But Hitler's troops were pugnacious; they were professional brawlers. They would have fought for their Führer in a
bloody civil war if the opponents of Nazism had not yielded without resistance in 1933.

Hitler got subsidies from big business in the first period of his
career. He extorted much greater sums from it in the second period
of his struggle for supremacy. Thyssen and the rest paid him but
they did not bribe him. Hitler took their money as a king takes the
tribute of his subjects. If they had refused to give him what he
asked, he would have sabotaged their plants or even murdered
them. Such drastic measures were needless. The entrepreneurs preferred to be reduced by Nazism to the status of shop managers than
to be liquidated by communism in the Russian way. As conditions
were in Germany, there was no third course open to them.

Both force and money are impotent against ideas. The Nazis
did not owe their conquest of Germany either to their getting a
few million Reichsmarks from big business or to their being ruthless fighters. The great majority of the German nation had been
both socialist and nationalist for many years. The Social Democratic trade-union members sympathized as much with nationalist
radicalism as did the peasants, the Catholics, and the shopkeepers.
The communists owed their votes in great part to the idea that
communism was the best means to establish German hegemony in
Europe and defeat Western capitalism. The German entrepreneurs
and businessmen contributed their share to the triumph of Nazism,
but so did all other strata of the nation. Even the churches, both
Catholic and Protestant, were no exception.

Great ideological changes are scarcely explained by saying that
somebody's money was spent in their behalf. The popularity of
communism in present-day America, whatever else it may be, is not
the result either of the lavish subventions of the Russian Government or of the fact that some millionaires subsidize the newspapers
and periodicals of the Left. And though it is true that some Jewish
bankers, frightened by Nazi anti-Semitism, contributed to socialist
party funds, and that far the richest endowment ever made for the

study of the social sciences in Germany was that of a Jewish grain dealer for the foundation of a Marxian institute at the University of Frankfort, German Marxism nevertheless was not, as the Nazis contend, the product of Jewish jobbers.

The slogan "national solidarity" (*Volksgemeinschaft*) had got such a hold on the German mentality that nobody dared to resist the Nazis when they struck their final blow. The Nazis crushed the hopes of many groups who once supported them. Big business, the landowners and the farmers, the artisans and the shopkeepers, the churches, all were disappointed. But the prestige of the main items of the Nazi creed—nationalism and socialism—was so overwhelming that this dissatisfaction had no important consequences.

Only one thing could put an end to Nazi rule: a military defeat. The blockade and the bombing of German cities by British and American planes will finally convince the Germans that Nazism is not the best means to make their nation prosperous.

4. The Treaty of Versailles

The four peace treaties of Versailles, Saint Germain, Trianon, and Sèvres together form the most clumsy diplomatic settlement ever carried out. They will be remembered as outstanding examples of political failure. Their aim was to bring lasting peace; the result was a series of minor wars and finally a new and more terrible World War. They were intended to safeguard the independence of small states; the results were the disappearance of Austria, Abyssinia, Albania, Czchoslovakia. They were designed to make the world safe for democracy; the results were Stalin, Hitler, Mussolini, Franco, Horthy.

However, one reproach generally cast upon the Treaty of Versailles is entirely unfounded. German propaganda succeeded in convincing public opinion in the Anglo-Saxon countries that the terms of the treaty were extremely unfair to Germany, that the hardships they inflicted upon the Germans drove them to despair, and that Nazism and the present war are the outcome of the mistreatment of Germany. This is wholly untrue. The political order given to Europe by the four treaties was very unsatisfactory. The settlement of East European problems was done with such disregard of the real conditions that chaos resulted. But the Treaty of Versailles was not unfair to Germany and it did not plunge the German people into misery. If the provisions of the treaty had been enforced, it would have been impossible for Germany to rearm and to attack again. The mischief was not that the treaty was bad so far as Germany was concerned, but that the victorious powers permitted Germany to defy some of its most important clauses.

The treaty obliged Germany to cede non-German territories that Prussia had conquered, and whose mainly non-German-speaking population was decidedly opposed to German rule. Germany's only title to these countries was previous conquest. It was not—as the German propagandists used to say—the most scandalous robbery ever committed that the Reich was forced to give back what the Hohenzollerns had seized in earlier years. The favorite subject of German propaganda was the Polish Corridor. What, shouted the Nazi speakers and their foreign friends, would the British or the French have said if a piece of land had been cut out from their country, dividing it into two disconnected parts, in order to give a passage way to some other nation? Such utterances impressed public opinion all over the world. The Poles themselves threw little light upon this subject. In all those years they were ruled by an incompetent and corrupt oligarchy, and this ruling clique lacked the intellectual power to combat the German propaganda.

The true facts are these. In the Middle Ages the Teutonic Knights conquered the country which is today known as the Prussian province of East Prussia. But they did not succeed in their attempts to conquer the territory which in 1914 was the Prussian province of West Prussia. Thus East Prussia did not adjoin the German Empire. Between the western boundaries of East Prussia and the eastern borders of the Holy Empire there lay a piece of land ruled by the Kings of Poland, forming a part of Poland, and inhabited by Poles. This piece of land, namely, West Prussia, was in 1772 annexed by Prussia at the first partition of Poland. It is important to realize that West Prussia (and the same is true for the Prussian province of Posen) was annexed by Prussia, not by the German Empire. These provinces belonged neither to the Holy Empire, which disintegrated in 1806, nor to the German Confederation, which from 1815 to 1866 was the political organization of the German nation. They were the "private property," as it were, of the kings of Prussia. The fact that the King of Prussia in his capacity as Elector-marquis of Brandenburg and as Duke of Pomerania was a member of the Holy Empire and of the German Confederation had legally and constitutionally no more significance for these eastern provinces than the fact once had for Great Britain that the King of England was in his capacity as Elector (and later as King) of Hanover a prince of the Holy Empire and later a member of the German Confederation. Until 1866 the relation of these provinces to Germany was like the relation of Virginia or Massachusetts to Germany between 1714 and 1776 and of Scotland from 1714 to 1837. They were foreign countries ruled by a prince who happened at the same time to rule a German country.

It was only in 1866 that the King of Prussia incorporated these provinces by his own sovereign decision into the Norddeutscher Bund and in 1871 into the Deutsches Reich. The people living in these countries were not asked whether they agreed or not. In fact they did not agree. They returned Polish members to the German Reichstag and they were anxious to preserve their Polish idiom and their allegiance to Polish traditions. For fifty years they resisted every endeavor of the Prussian Government to germanize them.

When the Treaty of Versailles renewed Poland's independence and restored the provinces of Posen and of West Prussia to Poland, it did not give a *corridor* to Poland. It simply undid the effects of earlier Prussian (not German) conquests. It was not the fault of the peacemakers or of the Poles that the Teutonic Knights had conquered a country not adjoining the Reich.

The Treaty of Versailles returned Alsace-Lorraine to France and northern Schleswig to Denmark. It did not rob Germany in these cases either. The population of these countries violently opposed German rule and longed to be freed from its yoke. Germany had but one title to oppress these people—conquest. The logical outcome of defeat was ceding the spoils of earlier conquest.

The second provision of the treaty which used to be criticized severely concerned reparations. The Germans had devastated a great part of Belgium and of northeastern France. Who was to pay for the reconstruction of these areas? France and Belgium, the assailed, or Germany, the aggressor? The victorious or the defeated? The treaty decided that Germany ought to pay.

We need not enter into a detailed discussion of the reparations problem. It is sufficient here to determine whether the reparations really meant misery and starvation for Germany. Let us see what Germany's income and reparation payments were in the period from 1925 to 1930.

Year	Income per capita in Reichsmarks	Reparation payments per capita in Reichsmarks	Reparation payments as a percentage of income
1925	961	16.25	1.69
1926	997	18.30	1.84
1927	1,118	24.37	2.18
1928	1,185	30.75	2.60
1929	1,187	38.47	3.24
1930	1,092	26.10*	2.39

* Income per capita: *Statistiches Jahrbuch für das Deutsche Reich*. Reparations per capita: figures obtained by dividing reparation payments by 65,000,000. As the population of Germany was increasing slightly during that period, the real proportion should be slightly lower than that given above.

It is a grotesque misrepresentation of the facts to assert that these payments made Germany poor and condemned the Germans to starvation. They would not have seriously affected the German standard of living even if the Germans had paid these sums out of their own pockets and not, as they did in fact, out of money borrowed from abroad.

For the years 1925–29 there are figures available concerning the increase of German capital. These increases are, in millions of Reichsmarks: *

1925	5,770
1926	10,123
1927	7,125
1928	7,469
1929	6,815

From September, 1924, until July, 1931, Germany paid as reparations under the Dawes and Young plans 10,821 million Reichsmarks. Then the payments stopped altogether. Against this outflow Germany's private and public indebtedness abroad, most of which originated in the same period, amounted to something over 20,500 million Reichsmarks. To this may be added approximately 5,000 million Reichsmarks of direct foreign investments in Germany. It is obvious that Germany did not suffer from lack of capital. If any more proof were needed it may be found in the fact that Germany invested in the same period approximately 10,000 million Reichsmarks abroad.†

The reparations were not responsible for Germany's economic distress. But if the Allies had insisted on their payment, they would have seriously hampered Germany's rearmament.

The antireparations campaign resulted in a complete fiasco for the Allies and in the full success of Germany's refusal to pay. What the Germans did pay they paid out of foreign borrowings which they later repudiated. Thus the whole burden in fact fell on foreigners.

With regard to possible future reparations it is extremely important to know the basic causes of this previous failure. The Allies were from the very beginning of the negotiations handicapped by their adherence to the spurious monetary doctrines of present-day etatist economics. They were convinced that the payments represented a danger to the maintenance of monetary stability in Germany, and that Germany could not pay unless its balance of

---

* "Zuwachs an bereitgestelltem Geldkapital," *Vierteljahrshefte fuer Konjunkturforschung,* Special number 22 (Berlin, 1931), p. 29.
† Stolper, *German Economy 1870–1940* (New York, 1940), p. 179.

trade were "favorable." They were concerned by a spurious "transfer" problem. They were disposed to accept the German thesis that "political" payments have effects radically different from payments originating from commercial transactions. This entanglement in mercantilist fallacies led them not to fix the total amount due in the Peace Treaty itself but to defer the decision to later negotiations. In addition it induced them to stipulate deliveries in kind, to insert the "transfer protection" clause, and finally to agree to the Hoover moratorium of July, 1931, and the cancellation of all reparation payments.

The truth is that the maintenance of monetary stability and of a sound currency system has nothing whatever to do with the balance of payments or of trade. There is only one thing that endangers monetary stability—inflation. If a country neither issues additional quantities of paper money nor expands credit, it will not have any monetary troubles. An excess of exports is not a prerequisite for the payment of reparations. The causation, rather, is the other way round. The fact that a nation makes such payments has the tendency to create such an excess of exports. There is no such thing as a "transfer" problem. If the German Government collects the amount needed for the payments (in Reichmarks) by taxing its citizens, every German taxpayer must correspondingly reduce his consumption either of German or of imported products. In the second case the amount of foreign exchange which otherwise would have been used for the purchase of these imported goods becomes available. In the first case the prices of domestic products drop, and this tends to increase exports and thereby the amount of foreign exchange available. Thus collecting at home the amount of Reichmarks required for the payment automatically provides the quantity of foreign exchange needed for the transfer. None of this, of course, depends in any way on whether the payments are "political" or commercial.

The payment of reparations, it is true, would have hurt the German taxpayer. It would have forced him to restrict his consumption. Under any circumstances, somebody had to pay for the damage inflicted. What the aggressors did not pay had to be paid by the victims of the aggression. But nobody pitied the victims, while hundreds of writers and politicians all over the world wept both crocodile and real tears over the Germans.

Perhaps it would have been politically wiser to choose another method for fixing the amount to be paid every year by Germany. For instance, the annual payment could have been brought into some fixed relation to the sums spent in future for Germany's armed forces. For every Reichmark spent on the German Army and Navy a multiple might have had to be paid as an installment. But all schemes would have proved ineffective as long as the Allies were under the spell of mercantilist fallacies.

The inflow of Germany's payments necessarily rendered the receiving countries' balance of trade "unfavorable." Their imports exceeded their exports *because* they collected the reparations. From the viewpoint of mercantilist fallacies this effect seemed alarming. The Allies were at once eager to make Germany pay and not to get the payments. They simply did not know what they wanted. But the Germans knew very well what *they* wanted. They did not want to pay.

Germany complained that the trade barriers of the other nations rendered its payments more burdensome. This grievance was well founded. The Germans would have been right, if they had really attempted to provide the means required for cash payments by an increase of exports. But what they paid in cash was provided for them by foreign loans.

The Allies were mistaken to the extent that they blamed the Germans for the failure of the treaty's reparation clauses. They should rather have indicted their own mercantilist prejudices. These clauses would not have failed if there had been in the Allied countries a sufficient number of influential spokesmen who knew how to refute the objections raised by the German nationalists.

Foreign observers have entirely misunderstood the role played by the Treaty of Versailles in the agitation of the Nazis. The nucleus of their propaganda was not the unfairness of the treaty; it was the "stab in the back" legend. We are, they used to say, the most powerful nation in Europe, even in the world. The war has evidenced anew our invincibility. We can, if we want to, put to rout all other nations. But the Jews have stabbed us in the back. The Nazis mentioned the treaty only in order to demonstrate the full villainy of the Jews.

"We, the victorious nation," they said, "have been forced to surrender by the November crime. Our government pays reparations, although nobody is strong enough to force us to do that. Our Jewish and Marxian rulers abide by the disarmament clauses of the treaty, because they want us to pay this money to World Jewry." Hitler did not fight the treaty. He fought those Germans who had voted in the German Parliament for its acceptance and who objected to its unilateral breach. For that Germany was powerful enough to annul the treaty the nationalists considered already proved by the "stab in the back" legend.

Many Allied and neutral critics of the Treaty of Versailles used to assert that it was a mistake to leave Germany any cause for grievance. This view was erroneous. Even if the treaty had left Germany's European territory untouched, if it had not forced it to cede its colonies, if it had not imposed reparation payments and limitation of armaments, a new war would not have been averted. The German nationalists were determined to conquer more dwelling space. They were eager to obtain autarky. They were convinced that their military prospects for victory were excellent. Their aggressive nationalism was not a consequence of the Treaty of Versailles. The grievances of the Nazis had little to do with the treaty. They concerned Lebensraum.

There have been frequent comparisons of the Treaty of Versailles with the settlements of 1814 and 1815. The system of Vienna succeeded in safeguarding European peace for many years. Its generous treatment of the vanquished French allegedly prevented France from planning wars of revenge. If the Allies had treated Germany in a similar way, it is contended, they would have had better results.

A century and a half ago France was the paramount power in continental Europe. Its population, its wealth, its civilization, and its military efficiency eclipsed those of the other nations. If the French of those days had been nationalists in the modern sense, they would have had the opportunity to attain and hold hegemony on the continent for some time. But nationalism was foreign to the French of the revolutionary period. They were, it is true, chauvinists. They considered themselves (perhaps on better grounds than some other peoples) the flower of mankind. They were proud of their newly acquired liberty. They believed that it was their duty to assist other nations in their struggle against tyranny. They were chauvinists, patriots, and revolutionaries. But they were not nationalists. They were not eager for conquest. They did not start the war; foreign monarchs attacked them. They defeated the invaders. It was then that ambitious generals, foremost among them Napoleon, pushed them toward territorial expansion. The French certainly connived at the beginning; but they grew more and more reluctant as they began to realize that they were bleeding for the sake of the Bonaparte family. After Waterloo they were relieved. Now they no longer had to worry about the fate of their sons. Few Frenchmen complained about the loss of the Rhineland, the Netherlands, or Italy. No Frenchman wept because Joseph was no longer King of Spain or Jerome no longer King of Westphalia. Austerlitz and Jena became historical reminiscences; the citizen's conceit derived edification from the poetry praising the late Emperor and his battles, but no one was now eager to subdue Europe.

Again, later, the events of June, 1848, directed attention to the

Emperor's nephew. Many expected him to overcome the new domestic troubles in the same way his uncle had dealt with the first revolution. There is no doubt that the third Napoleon owed his popularity solely to the glory of his uncle. Nobody knew him in France, and he knew nobody; he had seen the country only through prison bars and he spoke French with a German accent. He was only the nephew, the heir of a great name; nothing more. Certainly the French did not choose him because they wanted new wars. He brought them to his side by persuading them that his rule would safeguard peace. The empire means peace, was the slogan of his propaganda. Sevastopol and Solferino did not advance his popularity; they rather injured it. Victor Hugo, the literary champion of the first Napoleon's glory, unswervingly vilified his successor.

The work of the Congress of Vienna could endure, in short, because Europe was peaceloving and considered war an evil. The work of Versailles was doomed to fail in this age of aggressive nationalism.

What the Treaty of Versailles really tried to achieve was contained in its military clauses. The restriction of German armaments and the demilitarization of the Rhineland did not harm Germany, because no nation ventured to attack it. But they would have enabled France and Great Britain to prevent a new German aggression if they had been earnestly resolved to prevent it. It is not the fault of the treaty that the victorious nations did not attempt to enforce its provisions.

5. *The Economic Depression*

The great German inflation was the result of the monetary doctrines of the socialists of the chair. It had little to do with the course of military and political events. The present writer forecast it in 1912. The American economist B. M. Anderson confirmed this forecast in 1917. But most of those men who between 1914 and 1923 were in a position to influence Germany's monetary and banking policies and all journalists, writers, and politicians who dealt with these problems labored under the delusion that an increase in the quantity of bank notes does not affect commodity prices and foreign exchange rates. They blamed the blockade or profiteering for the rise of commodity prices, and the unfavorable balance of payments for the rise of foreign exchange rates. They did not lift a finger to stop inflation. Like all pro-inflation parties, they wanted to combat merely the undesirable but inevitable conse-

quences of inflation, i.e., the rise of commodity prices. Their
ignorance of economic problems pushed them toward price control
and foreign exchange restrictions. They could never understand
why these attempts were doomed to fail. The inflation was neither
an act of God nor a consequence of the Treaty of Versailles. It was
the practical application of the same etatist ideas that had begotten
nationalism. All the German political parties shared responsibility
for the inflation. They all clung to the error that it was not the
increase of bank credits but the unfavorable balance of payments
that was devaluing the currency.

The inflation had pauperized the middle classes. The victims
joined Hitler. But they did not do so because they had suffered
but because they believed that Nazism would relieve them. That
a man suffers from bad digestion does not explain why he consults
a quack. He consults the quack because he thinks that the man will
cure him. If he had other opinions, he would consult a doctor. That
there was economic distress in Germany does not account for
Nazism's success. Other parties also, e.g., the Social Democrats and
the communists, recommended their patent medicines.

Germany was struck by the great depression from 1929 on, but not
to a greater extent than other nations. On the contrary. In the years
of this depression the prices of foodstuffs and raw materials that
Germany imports decreased more than the prices of manufactures
that it exports.

The depression would have resulted in a fall in wage rates. But
as the trade-unions would not permit wage cuts, unemployment
increased. Both the Social Democrats and the communists were
confident that the increase of unemployment would strengthen
their forces. But it worked for Nazism.

The great depression was international. Only in Germany, however, did it result in the victory of a party recommending armaments and war as a panacea.

6. Nazism and German Labor

A riddle that has puzzled nearly all writers dealing with the
problems of Nazism is this: There were in Germany many millions
organized in the parties of the Social Democrats, of the communists, and of the Catholic Center; they were members of the
trade-unions affiliated with these parties. How could the Nazis
succeed in overthrowing these masses of resolute adversaries and in
establishing their totalitarian system? Did these millions change
their minds overnight? Or were they cowards, yielding to the terror

of the Storm Troopers and waiting for the day of redemption? Are the German workers still Marxians? Or are they sincere supporters of the Nazi system?

There is a fundamental error in posing the problem in this way. People take it for granted that the members of the various party clubs and trade-unions were convinced Social Democrats, communists, or Catholics, and that they fully endorsed the creeds and programs of their leaders. It is not generally realized that party allegiance and trade-union membership were virtually obligatory. Although the closed shop system was not carried to the extreme in Weimar Germany that it is today in Nazi Germany and in some branches of foreign industry, it had gone far enough. In the greater part of Germany and in most of the branches of German production it was practically impossible for a worker to stay outside of all the big trade-union groups. If he wanted a job or did not want to be dismissed, or if he wanted the unemployment dole, he had to join one of these unions. They exercised an economic and political pressure to which every individual had to yield. To join the union became practically a matter of routine for the worker. He did so because everybody did and because it was risky not to. It was not for him to inquire into the Weltanschauung of his union. Nor did the union bureaucrats trouble themselves about the tenets or feelings of the members. Their first aim was to herd as many workers as possible into the ranks of their unions.

These millions of organized workers were forced to pay lip service to the creeds of their parties, to vote for their candidates at the elections for Parliament and for union offices, to subscribe to the party newspapers, and to avoid open criticism of the party's policy. But daily experience nonetheless brought them the evidence that something was wrong with their parties. Every day they learned about new trade barriers established by foreign nations against German manufactures—that is, against the products of their own toil and trouble. As the trade-unions, with few exceptions, were not prepared to agree to wage cuts, every new trade barrier immediately resulted in increased unemployment. The workers lost confidence in the Marxians and in the Center. They became aware that these men did not know how to deal with their problems and that all they did was to indict capitalism. German labor was radically hostile to capitalism, but it found denunciation of capitalism unsatisfactory in this instance. The workers could not expect production to keep up if export sales dropped. They therefore became interested in the Nazi arguments. Such happenings, said the Nazis, are the drawbacks of our unfortunate dependence on foreign markets and the whims of foreign governments. Germany is doomed if it does not succeed in conquering more space and in attaining self-sufficiency. All endeavors to improve the conditions of labor are vain as long as we are compelled to serve as wage slaves for foreign capitalists. Such words impressed the workers. They did not abandon either the trade-unions or the party clubs since this would have had very serious consequences for them. They still voted the Social Democrat, the communist, or the Catholic ticket out of fear and inertia. But they became indifferent both to Marxian and to Catholic socialism and began to sympathize with national socialism. Years before 1933 the ranks of German trade-unions were already full of people secretly sympathizing with Nazism. Thus German labor was not greatly disturbed when the Nazis finally forcibly incorporated all trade-union members into their Labor Front. They turned toward Nazism because the Nazis had a program dealing with their most urgent problem—foreign trade barriers. The other parties lacked such a program.

The removal of the unpopular trade-union bureaucrats pleased the workers no less than the humiliations inflicted by the Nazis on the entrepreneurs and executives. The bosses were reduced to the rank of shop managers. They had to bow to the almighty party chiefs. The workers exulted over the misfortunes of their employers. It was their triumph when their boss, foaming with rage, was forced to march in their ranks on state holiday parades. It was balm for their hearts.

Then came the rearmament boom. There were no more unemployed. Very soon there was a shortage of labor. The Nazis succeeded in solving a problem that the Social Democrats had been unable to master. Labor became enthusiastic.

It is highly probable that the workers are now fully aware of the dark side of the picture. They are disillusioned.* The Nazis have not led them into the land of milk and honey. In the desert of the ration cards the seeds of communism are thriving. On the day of the defeat the Labor Front will collapse as the Marxian and the Catholic trade-unions did in 1933.

7. The Foreign Critics of Nazism

Hitler and his clique conquered Germany by brutal violence, by murder and crime. But the doctrines of Nazism had got hold of the German mind long before then. Persuasion, not violence, had

---

* However, the London *Times* as late as October 6, 1942, reported from Moscow that interrogation of German prisoners of war by the Russian authorities showed that a majority of the skilled workers were still strong supporters of the Nazis; particularly men in the age groups between 25 and 35, and those from the Ruhr and other older industrial centers.

converted the immense majority of the nation to the tenets of militant nationalism. If Hitler had not succeeded in winning the race for dictatorship, somebody else would have won it. There were plenty of candidates whom he had to eclipse: Kapp, General Ludendorff, Captain Ehrhardt, Major Papst, Forstrat Escherich, Strasser, and many more. Hitler had no inhibitions and thus he defeated his better instructed or more scrupulous competitors.

Nazism conquered Germany because it never encountered any adequate intellectual resistance. It would have conquered the whole world if, after the fall of France, Great Britain and the United States had not begun to fight it seriously.

The contemporary criticism of the Nazi program failed to serve the purpose. People were busy dealing with the mere accessories of the Nazi doctrine. They never entered into a full discussion of the essence of National Socialist teachings. The reason is obvious. *The fundamental tenets of the Nazi ideology do not differ from the generally accepted social and economic ideologies.* The difference concerns only the application of these ideologies to the special problems of Germany.

These are the dogmas of present-day "unorthodox" orthodoxy:

1. Capitalism is an unfair system of exploitation. It injures the immense majority for the benefit of a small minority. Private ownership of the means of production hinders the full utilization of natural resources and of technical improvements. Profits and interest are tributes which the masses are forced to pay to a class of idle parasites. Capitalism is the cause of poverty and must result in war.

2. It is therefore the foremost duty of popular government to substitute government control of business for the management of capitalists and entrepreneurs.

3. Price ceilings and minimum wage rates, whether directly enforced by the administration or indirectly by giving a free hand to trade-unions, are an adequate means for improving the lot of the consumers and permanently raising the standard of living of all wage earners. They are steps on the way toward entirely emancipating the masses (by the final establishment of socialism) from the yoke of capital. (We may note incidentally that Marx in his later years violently opposed these propositions. Present-day Marxism, however, endorses them fully.)

4. Easy money policy, i.e., credit expansion, is a useful method of lightening the burdens imposed by capital upon the masses and making a country more prosperous. It has nothing to do with the periodical recurrence of economic depression. Economic crises are an evil inherent in unhampered capitalism.

5. All those who deny the foregoing statements and assert that capitalism best serves the masses and that the only effective method of permanently improving the economic conditions of all strata of society is progressive accumulation of new capital are ill-intentioned and narrow-minded apologists of the selfish class interests of the exploiters. A return to laissez faire, free trade, the gold standard, and economic freedom is out of the question. Mankind will fortunately never go back to the ideas and policies of the nineteenth century and the Victorian age. (Let us note incidentally that both Marxism and trade-unionism have the fairest claim to the epithets "nineteenth-century" and "Victorian.")

6. The advantage derived from foreign trade lies exclusively in exporting. Imports are bad and should be prevented as much as possible. The happiest situation in which a nation can find itself is where it need not depend on any imports from abroad. (The "progressives," it is true, are not enthusiastic about this dogma and sometimes even reject it as a nationalist error; however, their political acts are thoroughly dictated by it.)

With regard to these dogmas there is no difference between present-day British liberals and the British labor party on the one hand and the Nazis on the other. It does not matter that the British call these principles an outgrowth of liberalism and economic democracy while the Germans, on better grounds, call them antiliberal and antidemocratic. It is not much more important that in Germany nobody is free to utter dissenting views, while in Great Britain a dissenter is only laughed at as a fool and slighted.

We do not need to deal here with the refutation of the fallacies in these six dogmas. This is the task of treatises expounding the basic problems of economic theory. It is a task that has already been fulfilled. We need only emphasize that whoever lacks the courage or the insight to attack these premises is not in a position to find fault with the conclusions drawn from them by the Nazis. The Nazis also desire government control of business. They also seek autarky for their own nation. The distinctive mark of their policies is that they refuse to acquiesce in the disadvantages which the acceptance of the same system by other nations would impose upon them. They are not prepared to be forever "imprisoned," as they say, within a comparatively overpopulated area in which the productivity of labor is lower than in other countries.

Both the German and foreign adversaries of Nazism were defeated in the intellectual battle against it because they were enmeshed in the same intransigent and intolerant dogmatism. The British Left and the American progressives want all-round control of business for their own countries. They admire the Soviet methods of economic management. In rejecting German totalitarianism they contradict themselves. The German intellectuals saw in Great Britain's abandonment of free trade and of the gold standard a proof of the superiority of German doctrines and methods. Now they see that the Anglo-Saxons imitate their own system of economic management in nearly every respect. They hear eminent citizens of these countries declare that their nations will cling to these policies in the postwar period. Why should not the Nazis be convinced, in the face of all this, that they were the pioneers of a new and better economic and social order?

The chiefs of the Nazi party and their Storm Troopers are sadistic gangsters. But the German intellectuals and German labor tolerated their rule because they agreed with the basic social, economic, and political doctrines of Nazism. Whoever wanted to fight Nazism as such, before the outbreak of the present war and in order to avoid it (and not merely to oust the scum which happens to hold office in present-day Germany), would have had to change the minds of the German people. This was beyond the power of the supporters of etatism.

It is useless to search the Nazi doctrines for contradictions and inconsistencies. They are indeed self-contradictory and inconsistent; but their basic faults are those common to all brands of present-day etatism.

One of the most common objections raised against the Nazis concerned the alleged inconsistency of their population policy. It is contradictory, people used to say, to complain, on the one hand, of the comparative overpopulation of Germany and ask for more Lebensraum and to try, on the other hand, to increase the birth rate. Yet there was in the eyes of the Nazis no inconsistency in these attitudes. The only remedy for the evil of overpopulation that they knew was provided by the fact that the Germans were numerous enough to wage a war for more space, while the small nations laboring under the same evil of comparative overpopulation were too weak to save themselves. The more soldiers Germany could levy, the easier it would be to free the nation from the curse of overpopulation. The underlying doctrine was faulty; but one who did not attack the whole doctrine could not convincingly find fault with the endeavors to rear as much cannon fodder as possible.

One reason why the objections raised to the despotism of the Nazis and the atrocities they committed had so little effect is that many of the critics themselves were inclined to excuse the Soviet methods. Hence the German nationalists could claim that their adversaries—both German and foreign—were being unfair to the Nazis in denouncing them for practices which they judged more mildly in the Russians. And they called it cant and hypocrisy when the Anglo-Saxons attacked their racial doctrines. Do the British and the Americans themselves, they retorted, observe the principle of equality of all races?

The foreign critics condemn the Nazi system as capitalist. In this age of fanatical anticapitalism and enthusiastic support of socialism no reproach seems to discredit a government more thoroughly in the eyes of fashionable opinion than the qualification pro-capitalistic. But this is one charge against the Nazis that is unfounded. We have seen in a previous chapter that the Zwangswirtschaft is a socialist system of all-round government control of business.

It is true that there are still profits in Germany. Some enterprises even make much higher profits than in the last years of the Weimar regime. But the significance of this fact is quite different from what the critics believe. There is strict control of private spending. No German capitalist or entrepreneur (shop manager) or any one else is free to spend more money on his consumption than the government considers adequate to his rank and position in the service of the nation. The surplus must be deposited with the banks or invested in domestic bonds or in the stock of German corporations wholly controlled by the government. Hoarding of money or banknotes is strictly forbidden and punished as high treason. Even before the war there were no imports of luxury goods from abroad, and their domestic production has long since been discontinued. Nobody is free to buy more food and clothing than the allotted ration. Rents are frozen; furniture and all other goods are unattainable. Travel abroad is permitted only on government errands. Until a short time ago a limited amount of foreign exchange was allotted to tourists who wanted to spend a holiday in Switzerland or Italy. The Nazi government was anxious not to arouse the anger of its then Italian friends by preventing its citizens from visiting Italy. The case with Switzerland was different. The Swiss Government, yielding to the demands of one of the most important branches of its economic system, insisted that a part of the payment for German exports to Switzerland should be balanced by the outlays of German tourists. As the total amount of German exports to Switzerland and of Swiss exports to Germany was fixed by a bilateral exchange agreement, it was of no concern to Germany how the Swiss distributed the surplus. The sum allotted to German tourists traveling in Switzerland was deducted from that destined for the repayment of German debts to Swiss banks. Thus the stockholders of the Swiss banks paid the expenses incurred by German tourists.

German corporations are not free to distribute their profits to the shareholders. The amount of the dividends is strictly limited according to a highly complicated legal technique. It has been asserted that this does not constitute a serious check, as the corporations are free to water the stock. This is an error. They are free to increase their nominal stock only out of profits made and declared and taxed as such in previous years but not distributed to the shareholders.

As all private consumption is strictly limited and controlled by the government, and as all unconsumed income must be invested, which means virtually lent to the government, high profits are nothing but a subtle method of taxation. The consumer has to pay high prices and business is nominally profitable. But the greater the profits are, the more the government funds are swelled. The government gets the money either as taxes or as loans. And everybody must be aware that these loans will one day be repudiated. For many years German business has not been in a position to replace its equipment. At the end of the war the assets of corporations and private firms will consist mainly of worn-out machinery and various doubtful claims against the government. Warring Germany lives on its capital stock, i.e., on the capital nominally and seemingly owned by its capitalists.

The Nazis interpret the attitudes of other nations with regard to the problem of raw materials as an acknowledgment of the fairness of their own claims. The League of Nations has established that the present state of affairs is unsatisfactory and hurts the interests of those nations calling themselves have-nots. The fourth point of the Atlantic Declaration of August 14, 1941, in which the chiefs of the governments of the United Kingdom and of the United States made known "certain common principles in the national policies of their respective countries on which they base their hope for a better future of the world," reads as follows: "They will endeavor, with due respect for their existing obligations, to further the enjoyment by all States, great or small, victor or vanquished, of access, on equal terms, to the trade and to the raw materials of the world which are needed for their economic prosperity."

The Roman Catholic Church is, in a world war, above the fighting parties. There are Catholics in both camps. The Pope is in a position to view the conflict with impartiality. It was, therefore, in the eyes of the Nazis very significant when the Pope discovered the root causes of the war in "that cold and calculating egoism which tends to hoard the economic resources and materials destined for the use of all to such an extent that the nations less favored by nature are not permitted access to them," and further declared that he saw "admitted the necessity of a participation of all in the natural riches of the earth even on the part of those nations which in the fulfillment of this principle belong to the category of *givers* and not to that of *receivers*." *

Well, say the Nazis, everybody admits that our grievances are reasonable. And, they add, in this world which seeks autarky of totalitarian nations, the only way to redress them is to redistribute territorial sovereignty.

It was often contended that the dangers of autarky which the Nazis feared were still far away, that Germany could still expand its export trade, and that its per capita income continued to increase. Such objections did not impress the Germans. They wanted to realize economic equality, i.e., a productivity of German labor as high as that of any other nation. The wage earners of the Anglo-Saxon countries too, they objected, enjoy today a much higher standard of living than in the past. Nevertheless, the "progressives" do not consider this fact a justification of capitalism, but approve of labor's claims for higher wages and the abolition of the wages system. It is unfair, said the Nazis, to object to the German claims when nobody objects to those of Anglo-Saxon labor.

The weakest argument brought forward against the Nazi doctrine was the pacifist slogan: War does not settle anything. For it cannot be denied that the present state of territorial sovereignty and political organization is the outcome of wars fought in the past. The sword freed France from the rule of the English kings and made it an independent nation, converted America and Australia into white men's countries, and secured the autonomy of the American republics. Bloody battles made France and Belgium predominantly Catholic and Northern Germany and the Netherlands predominantly Protestant. Civil wars safeguarded the unity of the United States and of Switzerland.

Two efficacious and irrefutable objections could well have been raised against the plans of German aggression. One is that the Germans themselves had contributed as much as they could to the state of affairs that they considered so deplorable. The other is that war is incompatible with the international division of labor. But "progressives" and nationalists were not in a position to challenge Nazism on these grounds. They were not themselves concerned with the maintenance of the international division of labor; they advocated government control of business which must necessarily lead toward protectionism and finally toward autarky.

The fallacious doctrines of Nazism cannot withstand the criticism of sound economics, today disparaged as orthodox. But whoever clings to the dogmas of popular neo-Mercantilism and advocates,

* Christmas Eve broadcast. *New York Times*, December 25, 1941.

government control of business is impotent to refute them. Fabian and Keynesian "unorthodoxy" resulted in a confused acceptance of the tenets of Nazism. Its application in practical policies frustrated all endeavors to form a common front of all nations menaced by the aspirations of Nazism.

X. NAZISM AS A WORLD PROBLEM

1. The Scope and Limitations of History

IT is the function of historical research to trace historical events back to their sources. The historian has to demonstrate how any historical situation developed out of previously existing—natural and social—conditions and how the actions of men and occurrences beyond human control transformed any previous state of affairs into the subsequent state of affairs. This analytical retrospection cannot be carried out indefinitely. Soon or late history reaches a point at which its methods of interpretation are of no further use. Then the historian can do nothing more than establish that a factor was operative which brought to pass what resulted. The usual way of putting this into words is to speak of individuality or uniqueness.

The same is essentially true of the natural sciences. They too inevitably sooner or later reach a point which they must simply take as a datum of experience, as the "given." Their scope is to interpret (or, as people once preferred to say, to explain) occurring changes as the outcome of forces working throughout the universe. They trace one fact back to previous facts; they show us that the *a,* the *b,* and the *n* are the outcome of the *x.* But there are *x's* which, at least in our day, cannot be traced back to other sources. Coming generations may succeed in pushing the limits of our knowledge further back. But there cannot be any doubt that there will always remain some items which cannot be traced back to others.

The human mind is not even capable of consistently grasping the meaning of such a concept as the ultimate cause of all things. Natural science will never go further than the establishment of some ultimate factors which cannot be analyzed and traced back to their sources, springs, or causes.

The term individuality as used by the historians means: here we are confronted with a factor which cannot be traced back to other factors. It does not provide an interpretation or explanation. It establishes, on the contrary, that we have to deal with an inexplicable datum of historical experience. Why did Caesar cross the Rubicon? The historians can provide us with various motives which might have influenced Caesar's decision, but they cannot deny that another decision would have been possible. Perhaps Cicero or Brutus, faced with a similar situation, would have behaved differently. The only correct answer is: he crossed the Rubicon because he was Caesar.

It is misleading to explain a man's or a group's behavior by referring to their character. The concept of character is tantamount to the concept of individuality. What we call a man's or a group's character is the totality of our knowledge about their conduct. If they had behaved otherwise than as they actually did, our notions of their character would be different. It is a mistake to explain the fact that Napoleon made himself emperor and tried in a rather foolish way to break into the circle of the old European dynasties as a result of his character. If he had *not* substituted emperorship for his lifelong consular dignity, and had *not* married an arch-duchess, we would, in the same way, have had to say that this was a peculiar mark of his character. The reference to character explains no more than does the famous explanation of the soporific effect of opium by its *virtus dormitiva qui facit sensus assupire.*

Therefore it is vain to expect any help from psychology, whether individual or mass psychology. Psychology does not lead us beyond the limits fixed in the concept of individuality. It does not *explain* why being crossed in love turns some people toward dipsomania, others to suicide, others to writing clumsy verses, while it inspired Petrarch and Goethe to immortal poems and Beethoven to divine music. The classification of men into various character types is not a very profitable expedient. Men are classified according to their conduct, and then people believe they have provided an explanation in deducing conduct from their classification. Moreover, every individual or group has traits which do not fit into the Procrustean bed of classification.

Neither can physiology solve the problem. Physiology cannot explain how external facts and circumstances bring about definite ideas and actions within human consciousness. Even if we were to know everything about the operation of brain cells and nerves, we should be at a loss to explain—otherwise than by referring to individuality—why identical environmental facts result with different individuals, and with the same individuals at various times, in diverse ideas and actions. The sight of a falling apple led Newton to the laws of gravitation; why not other people before him? Why does one man succeed in the correct solution of an equation whereas other people do not? In what does the physiological process resulting in the mathematically correct solution of a problem differ from that leading to an incorrect solution? Why did the same problems of locomotion in snow-covered mountains lead the Norwegians to the invention of skiing, while the inhabitants of the Alps did not have this inspiration?

No historical research can avoid reference to the concept of individuality. Neither biography, dealing with the life of only one personality, nor the history of peoples and nations can push its analysis further than a point where the last statement is: individuality.

2. *The Fallacy of the Concept of "National Character"*

The main deficiency of the character concept when applied as an explanation is in the permanency attributed to it. The individual or the group is conceived as equipped with a stable character of which all its ideas and actions are the outcome. The criminal is not a criminal because he has committed a crime; he commits the crime because he is a criminal. Therefore, the fact that a man has once committed a crime is the proof that he is a criminal and makes it plausible that he is guilty of any other crime ascribed to him. This doctrine has deeply influenced penal procedure in continental Europe. The state is eager to prove that the defendant has already committed other crimes in his previous career; the defense in the same way is eager to whitewash the defendant by demonstrating that his past life was free from fault.* Yet a man who has already committed several murders may be guiltless of the murder for which he is standing trial, whereas a man after sixty years of impeccable behavior may have committed an abominable crime.

The concept of a nation's character is a generalization of features discovered in various individuals. It is mainly the result of precipitate and ill-considered induction from an insufficient number of ill-assorted samples. In the old days the German citizens of Bohemia met few Czechs other than cooks and maids. Hence they concluded that the Czechs are servile, submissive, and cringing. A student of Czech political and religious history may rather qualify them as rebellious and lovers of freedom. But what entitles us to search for common characteristics of the various individuals of an aggregate which includes, on the one hand, John Huss and Žižka of Trocnov and, on the other, footmen and chambermaids? The criterion applied in the formation of the class concept "Czechs" is the use of the Czech language. To assume that all members of a linguistic group must have some other marks in common is a *petitio principii.*

The most popular interpretation of the ascendancy of Nazism explains it as an outcome of the German national character. The holders of this theory search German literature and history for texts, quotations, and deeds indicating aggressiveness, rapacity, and

* These statements do not apply to American penal procedure.

lust for conquest. From these scraps of knowledge they deduce the German national character, and from the character so established the rise of Nazism.

It is very easy indeed to assemble many facts of German history and many quotations from German authors that can be used to demonstrate an inherent German propensity toward aggression. But it is no less easy to discover the same characteristics in the history and literature of other linguistic groups, e.g., Italian, French, and English. Germany has never had more excellent and eloquent panegyrists of military heroism and war than Carlyle and Ruskin were, never a chauvinist poet and writer more eminent than Kipling, never more ruthless and Machiavellian conquerors than Warren Hastings and Lord Clive, never a more brutal soldier than Hodson of Hodson's Horse.

Very often the quotations are taken out of context and thus entirely distorted. In the first World War British propagandists used to cite over and over again a few lines from Goethe's *Faust*. But they omitted to mention that the character into whose mouth these words are put, Euphorion, is a counterpart of Lord Byron, whom Goethe admired more than any other contemporary poet (except for Schiller), although Byron's romanticism did not appeal to his own classicism. These verses do not at all express Goethe's own tenets. *Faust* concludes with a glorification of productive work; its guiding idea is that only the self-satisfaction received from rendering useful services to his fellow men can make a man happy; it is a panegyric upon peace, freedom, and—as the Nazis scornfully call it, "bourgeois"—security. Euphorion-Byron represents a different ideal: the restless craving for ends inaccessible to human beings, the yearning for adventure, combat, and glory which results in failure and in premature death. It is nonsensical to quote as proof of Germany's innate militarism the verses in which Euphorion answers his parents' commendation of peace with passionate praise of war and victory.

There have been in Germany, as in all other nations, eulogists of aggression, war, and conquest. But there have been other Germans too. The greatest are not to be found in the ranks of those glorifying tyranny and German world hegemony. Are Heinrich von Kleist, Richard Wagner, and Detlev von Liliencron more representative of the national character than Kant, Goethe, Schiller, Mozart, and Beethoven?

The idea of a nation's character is obviously arbitrary. It is derived from a judgment which omits all unpleasant facts contradicting the preconceived dogma.

It is not permissible to apply statistical procedures in the establishment of a nation's character. The question is not to find out how the Germans would have voted in the past if they had had to decide by plebiscites what course their country's policy should follow. Even if such an investigation could be successfully undertaken, its results would not provide us with any information helpful in our case. The political situation of each period has its unique form, its individuality. We are not justified in drawing from past events conclusions applicable to the present day. It would not clear up our problems if we knew whether the majority of the Goths approved of the invasion of the Roman Empire or whether the majority of the twelfth-century Germans favored Barbarossa's treatment of the Milanese. The present situation has too little in common with those of the past.

The usual method applied is to pick out some famous personalities of a nation's past and present and to take their opinions and actions as representative of the whole nation. This would be a faulty method even if people were conscientious enough to confront these arbitrarily chosen men with others who held contrary ideas and behaved in a different way. It is not permissible to attach the same representative importance to the tenets of Kant and to those of a dull professor of philosophy.

It is contradictory, on the one hand, to consider only *famous* men as representative while ignoring the rest, and, on the other hand, to treat even these, arbitrarily selected as famous, as constituting an undifferentiated group of equals. One man of this group may stand out as much from the rest as the whole group does from the entire nation. Hundreds of poetasters and rhymesters do not outweigh the unique Goethe.

It is correct to speak of a nation's mentality at a certain historical epoch if we conceive by this term the mentality of the majority. But it is subject to change. The German mentality has not been the same in the age of medieval feudalism, in the age of the Reformation, in that of the Enlightenment, in the days of liberalism, and in our time.

It is probable that today about 80 per cent of all German-speaking Europeans are Nazis. If we leave out the Jews, the Austrians, and the German-speaking Swiss, we might say that more than 90 per cent of the Germans support Hitler's fight for world hegemony. But this cannot be explained by referring to the characterization of the contemporary Germans given by Tacitus. Such an explanation is no better than the Nazis' method of proving the alleged barbarism of the present-day Anglo-Saxons by citing the execution of Jeanne d'Arc, the wholesale extermination of the aborigines of Tasmania by the British settlers, and the cruelties described in *Uncle Tom's Cabin*.

There is no such thing as a stable national character. It is a vicious circle to explain Nazism by alleging that the Germans have an inherent tendency to adopt the tenets of Nazism.

3. Germany's Rubicon

This book has tried to clarify the rise of Nazism; to show how, out of the conditions of modern industrialism and of present-day socio-economic doctrines and policies, there developed a situation in which the immense majority of the German people saw no means to avoid disaster and to improve their lot but those indicated by the program of the Nazi party. On the one hand they saw in an age rapidly moving toward economic autarky a dark future for a nation which can neither feed nor clothe its citizens out of its domestic natural resources. On the other hand they believed that they were powerful enough to avoid this calamity by conquering a sufficient amount of Lebensraum.

This explanation of the ascendancy of Nazism goes as far as any historical investigation can possibly go. It must stop at the points which limit our endeavors to study historical events. It has to take recourse to the concepts of individuality and nonrepeatable uniqueness.

For Nazism was not the only conceivable means of dealing with the problems that concern present-day Germany. There was and there is another solution: free trade. Of course, the adoption of free-trade principles would require the abandonment of interventionism and socialism and the establishment of an unhampered market economy. But why should this be brushed aside as out of the question? Why did the Germans fail to realize the futility of interventionism and the impracticability of socialism?

It is neither a sufficient explanation nor a valid excuse to say that all other nations also cling to etatism and to economic nationalism. Germany was threatened sooner, and in a worse way, by the effects of the trend toward autarky. The problem was first and for some time a German one, although it later concerned other great nations. Germany was forced to find a solution. Why did it choose Nazism and not liberalism, war and not peace?

If forty to sixty years ago Germany had adopted unconditional free trade, Great Britain, its crown colonies, British India, and some smaller European nations would not have abandoned free trade either. The cause of free trade would have received a mighty propulsion. The course of world affairs would have been different. The further progress of protectionism, monetary particularism, and discrimination against foreign labor and foreign capital would have been checked. The tide would have been stemmed. It is not unlikely that other countries would have imitated the example set by Germany. At any rate, Germany's prosperity would not have been menaced by the further advance of other nations toward autarky.

But the Germans did not even consider this alternative. The handful of men advocating unconditional freedom both in foreign and in domestic trade were laughed at as fools, despised as reactionaries, silenced by threats. In the 'nineties of the past century Germany was already almost unanimous in its support of policies which were designed as the preparation for the impending war for more space, the war for world hegemony.

The Nazis defeated all the other socialist, nationalist, and interventionist parties within Germany because they were not afraid to follow their program to its ultimate logical conclusion. People were confident that they meant it seriously. They offered a radical solution for the problem of foreign trade; and they outdid by this radicalism the other parties which advocated essentially the same solution but with moderation and in a vacillating and half-way manner. It was the same with other problems. There were, for instance, the territorial clauses of the Treaty of Versailles. All German parties, without exception, deplored these provisions as the most infamous inflicted on Germany, and as one of the main causes of its economic distress. The communists did not mention these clauses especially, but their disparagement of the whole treaty, this most shameful product of capitalist imperialism, as they said, included those clauses. It was no different with the pacifists. But only the Nazis were sincere and consistent enough to proclaim that there was no hope of reacquiring the lost provinces except by a victorious war. Thus they alone seemed to offer a remedy for an alleged evil that everyone decried.

But it is impossible to explain why, in all these critical years, the Germans never seriously considered the other alternative to nationalism: liberalism and free trade. The fateful decision against free trade and peace and in favor of nationalism and war is not open to explanation. In a unique, nonrepeatable historical situation the German nation chose war and rejected the peaceful solution. This was an individual historical event, which cannot be further analyzed or explained. They crossed their Rubicon.

We may say they acted in this way because they were Germans of the age of nationalism. But that explains nothing.

The American Civil War would have been avoided if the Northerners had acquiesced in the secession. The American Revolution would not have occurred if the colonists had not been ready to wage a risky war for their independence. These characteristics of the Americans of 1776 and 1861 are ultimate facts, individual cases of historical events.

We cannot explain why some people, faced with an alternative, choose *a* and not *b*.

Of course, the method chosen by Germany hurts not only every other people but the Germans as well. The Germans will not attain the ends sought. The Lebensraum wars will prove disastrous for them. But we do not know why the Americans in the two cases mentioned above made of their option a use which later events proved to be beneficial to them and to Western civilization, while the Germans chose the road to catastrophe.

The same thing can be said about the conduct of the nations menaced by the German plans for aggression. The present state of world affairs is due not only to the malicious aspirations of German nationalists but no less to the failure of the rest of the world to thwart them by appropriate measures. If the victims had substituted a close political and military coöperation for their mutual rivalries, Germany would have been forced to abandon its plans. Everybody knew that there was but one means to stop the aggressors and to prevent war: collective security. Why did those menaced not adopt this scheme? Why did they prefer to cling to their policies of economic nationalism, which rendered vain all plans for the formation of a united front of all the peaceful nations? Why did they not abandon etatism in order to be able to abolish trade barriers? Why did they fail, like the Germans, to consider a return to laissez faire?

Etatism not only brought about a situation from which the German nationalists saw no way out but conquest, but also rendered futile all attempts to stop Germany in time. While the Germans were busy rearming for the "day," Great Britain's main concern was to injure the interests of the French and of all other nations by barring their exports to Great Britain. Every nation was eager to use its sovereignty for the establishment of government control of business. This attitude necessarily implied a policy of insulation and economic nationalism. Every nation was waging a continuous economic war against every other nation. Every citizen glowed when the latest statistical report showed an increase in exports or a drop in imports. The Belgians were jubilant when the imports from the Netherlands diminished; the Dutch rejoiced when they succeeded in reducing the number of Dutch tourists visiting Belgium. The Swiss Government subsidized French tourists traveling in Switzerland; the French Government subsidized Swiss tourists traveling in France. The Polish Government penalized its citizens for visiting foreign countries. If a Pole, a Czech, a Hungarian, or a Rumanian wanted to consult a Viennese doctor or to send his son to a Swiss school, he had to apply for a special permit from the office of foreign exchange control.

Everybody was convinced that this was lunacy—unless it was an act of his own government. Every day the newspapers reported examples of especially paradoxical measures of economic nationalism and criticized them severely. But no political party was prepared to demolish its own country's trade walls. Everybody was in favor of free trade for all other nations and of hyper-protectionism for his own. It did not seem to occur to anyone that free trade begins at home. For nearly everyone favored government control of business within his own country.

For this attitude too history cannot provide any better explanation than recourse to the notion of individuality or uniqueness. Faced with a serious problem, the nations chose the way to disaster.

4. The Alternative

The reality of Nazism faces everybody else with an alternative: They must smash Nazism or renounce their self-determination, i.e., their freedom and their very existence as human beings. If they yield, they will be slaves in a Nazi-dominated world. Their civilizations will perish; they will no longer have the freedom to choose, to act, and to live as they wish; they will simply have to obey. The Führer, the vicar of the "German God," will become their Supreme Lord. If they do not acquiesce in such a state of affairs, they must fight desperately until the Nazi power is completely broken. There is no escape from this alternative; no third solution is available. A negotiated peace, the outcome of a stalemate, would not mean more than a temporary armistice. The Nazis will not abandon their plans for world hegemony. They will renew their assault. Nothing can stop these wars but the decisive victory or the final defeat of Nazism.

It is a fatal mistake to look at this war as if it were one of the many wars fought in the last centuries between the countries of Western civilization. This is total war. It is not merely the destiny of a dynasty or a province or a country that is at stake, but the destiny of all nations and civilizations. Europe has not had to encounter a similar danger since the Tartar invasions in the thirteenth century. The lot of the defeated would be worse than that of the Greeks and the Serbs under the Turkish yoke. The Turks did not attempt to wipe out the vanquished Greeks and Serbs, or to eradicate their language and their Christian creed. But the Nazis have other things in store for the conquered: extermination of those stubbornly resisting the master race, enslavement for those spontaneously yielding.

In such a war there cannot be any question of neutrality. The neutrals know very well what their fate will be if the Nazis conquer the United Nations. Their boasts that they are ready to fight for their independence if the Nazis attack them are vain. In the event of a defeat of the United Nations, military action on the part of Switzerland or Sweden would not be more than a symbolic gesture. Under present conditions neutrality is equal to a virtual support of Nazism.

The same holds true for German-speaking men and women whether they are citizens of the Reich or not. There are citizens of the Reich who want to save face by asserting that they are not Nazis but that they cannot help fighting in the ranks of their fellow citizens. It is a man's duty, they say, to be unconditionally loyal to his own linguistic group whether its cause is right or wrong. It was this idea that turned some citizens of Austria, Switzerland, and various American countries either toward Nazism or toward what they believed to be an attitude of neutrality.

But this doctrine of the unlimited solidarity of all members of a linguistic group is one of the main vices of nationalism. Nobody would be prepared to maintain such a principle of solidarity with regard to other groups. If the majority of the inhabitants of a town or a province decided to fight against the rest of the country, few would admit that the minority had a moral obligation to stand with the majority and to support its action. The issue in the struggle between Nazism and the rest of mankind is whether the community of people speaking the same language is the only legitimate social collectivity, or whether the supremacy must be assigned to the great society embracing all human beings. It is the fight of humanity against the claims of the intransigent particularism of a group. On better grounds than those on which the Nazis deny to the Austrians and the Swiss the rights of moral and political autonomy and of unrestricted sovereignty, the members of the human society must deny these rights to the various linguistic groups. No human coöperation and no lasting peace are conceivable if men put loyalty to any particular group above loyalty to humanity, moral law, and the principle of every individual's moral responsibility and autonomy. Renan was right in asserting that the problem is whether a man belongs to any particular group or to himself.*

The Nazis themselves realize clearly that under the conditions brought about by the international division of labor and the present state of industrialism, the isolation of nations or countries has become impossible. They do not want to withdraw from the world and to live on their own soil in splendid isolation. They do not want to destroy the great world-embracing society. They intend to organize it as an oligarchy. They alone are to rule in this oligarchy; the others are to obey and be their slaves. In such a struggle whoever does not take the part of those fighting against the Nazis furthers the cause of Nazism.

This is true today of many pacifists and conscientious objectors. We may admire their noble motives and their candid intentions. But there is no doubt that their attitudes result in complicity with Nazism. Nonresistance and passive obedience are precisely what the Nazis need for the realization of their plans. Kant was right in asserting that the proof of a principle's moral value is whether or not it could be accepted (the pragmatists would say, whether or not it would "work") as a universal rule of conduct. The general acceptance of the principle of nonresistance and of passive obedience by the non-Nazis would destroy our civilization and reduce all non-Germans to slavery.

There is but one means to save our civilization and to preserve the human dignity of man. It is to wipe out Nazism radically and pitilessly. Only after the total destruction of Nazism will the world be able to resume its endeavors to improve social organization and to build up the good society.

The alternative is humanity or bestiality, peaceful human co-operation or totalitarian despotism. All plans for a third solution are illusory.

* See above, p. 90.

PART IV

THE FUTURE OF WESTERN CIVILIZATION

XI. THE DELUSIONS OF WORLD PLANNING

1. The Term "Planning"

IT is obvious that in this age of international division of labor, on the one hand, and of government interference with business on the other, unrestricted sovereignty for each nation must lead to economic nationalism and through it to conflict. No one ventures to deny that economic nationalism and peace are incompatible. Therefore all projects for the establishment of a more satisfactory state of world affairs include proposals for the substitution of some kind of international coöperation for the permanent antagonisms of economic nationalism. The most popular of these suggestions are labeled World Planning or International Planning. Planning is the patent medicine of our day. People are convinced that it will cure all the evils of domestic and foreign affairs. The prestige of the catchword "planning" is so great that the mere mention of it is considered a solution of all economic problems.

In dealing with domestic affairs planning is used as a synonym for socialism. Sometimes only the German pattern of socialism—Zwangswirtschaft—is called planning, while the term socialism proper is reserved for the Russian pattern. At any rate planning always means planning by government authorities and execution of these plans by order of the government enforced by the police power. Planning is the antithesis of free enterprise and private ownership of the means of production. Planning and capitalism are utterly incompatible. Within a system of planning production is conducted according to the government's orders, not according to the plans of capitalist enterpreneurs eager to profit by best serving the wants of consumers.

It is a delusion to believe that planning and free enterprise can be reconciled. No compromise is possible between the two methods. Where the various enterprises are free to decide what to produce and how, there is capitalism. Where, on the other hand, the government authorities do the directing, there is socialist planning. Then the various firms are no longer capitalist enterprises; they are subordinate state organs bound to obey orders. The former entrepreneur becomes a shop manager like the Betriebsführer in Nazi Germany.

The idea of planning by the organized groups of the various branches of production is very popular with some businessmen. This would amount to a substitution of compulsory cartels for free enterprise and competition. It would set aside capitalism and put entrepreneur syndicalism in its place, something like a replica of the medieval guild system. It would not bring socialism, but all-round monopoly with all its detrimental consequences. It would impair supply and put serious obstacles in the way of technical improvements. It would not preserve free enterprise but give a privileged position to those who *now* own and operate plants, protecting them against the competition of efficient newcomers. It would mean a partial abdication of the state for the benefit of small groups of wealthy men.

In reference to international affairs the word planning sometimes means world socialism with a unitary world management. More often, however, it means the substitution of coöperative interventionism of all or many governments for the independent interventionism of every national government. We will have to deal with both of these conceptions.

But before beginning an economic examination of the problems involved it is desirable to make a few observations concerning the psychological roots of the popularity of the idea of planning.

2. The Dictatorship Complex

Man is born an asocial and antisocial being. The newborn child is a savage. Egoism is his nature. Only the experience of life and the teachings of his parents, his brothers, sisters, playmates, and later of other people force him to acknowledge the advantages of social coöperation and accordingly to change his behavior. The savage thus turns toward civilization and citizenship. He learns that his will is not almighty, that he has to accommodate himself to others and adjust his actions to his social environment, and that the aims and the actions of other people are facts with which he must reckon.

The neurotic lacks this ability to adapt himself to his environment. He is asocial; he never arrives at an adjustment with the facts. But whether he likes it or not, reality has its own way. It is beyond the neurotic's power to eliminate the will and the actions of his fellowmen and to sweep everything before him. Thus he escapes into daydreams. The weakling, lacking the strength to get on with life and reality, indulges in reveries on dictatorship and on the power to subdue everybody else. The land of his dreams is the land in which his will alone decides; it is the realm in which he alone gives orders and all others obey. In this paradise only that happens which he wants to happen. Everything is sound and reasonable, i.e., everything corresponds exactly to his ideas and wishes, is reasonable from the viewpoint of his reason.

In the secrecy of these daydreams the neurotic assigns to himself the role of the dictator; he himself is Caesar. When addressing his fellow citizens he must be more modest. He depicts a dictatorship operated by somebody else. But this dictator is only his substitute and handyman; he acts only as the neurotic wants him to act. A daydreamer who refrained from this cautious restriction and proposed himself for the post of the dictator, would risk being considered and treated as a lunatic. The psychiatrists would call his insanity megalomania.

Nobody ever recommended a dictatorship aiming at ends other than those he himself approved. He who advocates dictatorship always advocates the unrestricted rule of his own will, although operated by an intermediary, an amanuensis. He wants a dictator made in his own image.

Now we may grasp the causes of the popularity of planning. Everything that men do has to be planned, is the realization of plans. In this sense all economic activity means planning. But those disparaging *anarchic production* and advocating *planned economy* are eager to eliminate the plans of everybody else. *One* will alone should have the right to will, *one* plan alone should be realized, namely, the plan which the neurotic approves, the reasonable plan, the only plan. All obstacles should be removed, all other people's power should be broken, nothing should prevent the wretched neurotic from arranging the world according to his whims. Every means is right if it helps to raise the daydreamer's reason to the throne.

The unanimous approval of planning by our contemporaries is only apparent. The supporters of planning disagree with regard to their plans. They agree only in the refutation of the plans brought forward by other people.

Many popular fallacies concerning socialism are due to the mistaken belief that all friends of socialism advocate the same system. On the contrary, every socialist wants his own socialism, not the other fellow's. He disputes the other socialists' right to call themselves socialists. In the eyes of Stalin the Mensheviks and the Trotskyists are not socialists but traitors, and vice versa. The Marxians call the Nazis supporters of capitalism; the Nazis call the Marxians supporters of Jewish capital. If a man says socialism, or planning, he always has in view his own brand of socialism, his own plan. Thus planning does not in fact mean preparedness to coöperate peacefully. It means conflict.

3. A World Government

The establishment of a supernational world government is an old idea of pacifists.

Such a world government is not needed for the maintenance of peace, however, if democracy and an unhampered market economy prevail everywhere. Under free capitalism and free trade no special provisions or international institutions are required to safeguard peace. Where there is no discrimination against foreigners, when everyone is free to live and to work where he likes, there are no longer causes for war.

We may grant to the socialists that the same holds true for a socialist world state, provided the rulers of this state do not discriminate against any races, linguistic groups, or religions. But if, on the contrary, discrimination is applied, nothing can hinder the outbreak of wars if those who are injured by it believe that they are strong enough to sweep it away.

All talk about the establishment of a world authority to prevent armed conflicts by the aid of a world police force is vain if favored groups or nations are not prepared to renounce their special privileges. If these privileges are to be maintained, a world state can be conceived only as the despotic rule of the privileged nations over the underprivileged. A democratic commonwealth of free nations is incompatible with any discrimination against large groups.

A world parliament elected by the universal and equal suffrage of all adults would obviously never acquiesce in migration and trade barriers. It is absurd to assume that the peoples of Asia would be prepared to tolerate the immigration laws of Australia and New Zealand, or that the predominantly industrial nations of Europe would agree to a policy of protectionism for the countries producing raw materials and foodstuffs,

One should not allow oneself to be misled by the fact that within individual countries minority groups have succeeded in obtaining privileges beneficial to themselves and detrimental to the majority of the nation. We have dealt sufficiently with this phenomenon. Suppose we assume that the intricacy of the problem of the economic consequences of protectionism should so confuse the minds of the international lawmakers that the representatives of those injured by trade barriers were temporarily deluded into withdrawing their opposition. It is not very likely, but it could happen. But it is certain that a world parliament, in which the representatives of those injured by the working of immigration barriers would form a compact majority, would never consent to their permanent preservation. Such are the hard facts which render the ambitious plans for a democratic world state or world federation illusory. Under present conditions it is utopian to indulge in such projects.

We have already pointed out that the maintenance of migration barriers against totalitarian nations aiming at world conquest is indispensable to political and military defense. It would undoubtedly be wrong to assert that under present conditions all kinds of migration barriers are the outcome of the misguided selfish class interests of labor. However, as against the Marxian doctrine of imperialism, almost generally accepted today, it is necessary to emphasize that the capitalists and entrepreneurs in their capacity as employers are not at all interested in the establishment of immigration barriers. Even if we were to agree to the fallacious doctrine that profits and interest come into existence because the entrepreneurs and capitalists withhold from the worker a part of what should rightly be paid to him, it is obvious that neither their short-run nor their long-run interests push the capitalists and entrepreneurs toward measures which raise domestic wage rates. Capital does not favor immigration barriers any more than it does Sozialpolitik, whose inextricable outcome is protectionism. If the selfish class interests of big business were supreme in the world, as the Marxians tell us, there would be no trade barriers. The owners of the most efficient plants are—under domestic economic freedom—not interested in protection. They would not ask for import duties were it not to compensate for the rise in costs caused by prolabor policies.

As long as there are migration barriers, wage rates fixed on the domestic labor market remain at a higher level in those countries in which physical conditions for production are more favorable—as, for instance, in the United States—than in countries offering less favorable conditions. Tendencies toward an equalization of wage rates are absent when the migration of workers is prevented. Under free trade combined with migration barriers there would prevail in the United States a tendency toward an expansion of those branches of production in which wages form a comparatively small part of the total costs of production. Those branches which require comparatively more labor (for instance, the garment trade) would shrink. The resulting imports would bring about neither bad business nor unemployment. They would be compensated by an increase in the export of goods which can be produced to the greatest advantage in this country. They would raise the standard of living both in America and abroad. While some enterprises are menaced by free trade, the interests of the bulk of industry and of the whole nation are not. The main argument advanced in favor of American protectionism, namely, that protection is needed to maintain the nation's high standard of living, is fallacious. American wage rates are protected by the immigration laws.

Pro-labor legislation and union tactics result in raising wage rates above the level secured by the immigration laws. The social gains brought about by such methods are only apparent. If there is no tariff, they result either in a drop in wage rates or in unemployment, because the competitive power of domestic industries is weakened and because their sales drop concomitantly. If there is a protective tariff, they raise the prices of those commodities which on account of the increase in domestic production costs require protection. Thus the workers are hurt in their capacity as consumers.

Investors would not suffer if protection were denied to domestic industries. They are free to invest in those countries in which conditions seem to offer the best chances of profit. Only the interests of the capital already invested in some branches of industry are favored by protection.

The best evidence that big business does not derive an advantage from protection is provided by the fact that the biggest firms are operating plants in various countries. This is precisely the characteristic feature of large-scale enterprises in this age of hyperprotectionism.* However, it would be more profitable for them (and, of course, at the same time more advantageous for consumers) if they were able to concentrate their entire production in plants located where conditions are most favorable.

The real barrier to a full use of the productive forces is not, as the Marxians say, capital or capitalism, but those policies designed to reform and to check capitalism which Marx branded as petty bourgeois. At the same time these policies beget economic nationalism and substitute international conflict for peaceful coöperation under the international division of labor.

* For instance, the American motor-car manufacturers or the big oil, margarine, and soap concerns. The American automobile manufacturers do not advocate protection. In Germany the Association of Manufacturers of Machinery was the only organization which (up to 1933) had the courage to fight openly the protectionist program of the nationalist parties.

4. Planned Production

The more realistic suggestions for world planning do not imply the establishment of a world state with a world parliament. They propose international agreements and regulations concerning production, foreign trade, currency and credit, and finally foreign loans and investments.

Planners sometimes describe their proposals as measures to combat poverty and want. The description is ambiguous. All economic policies are designed as remedies for poverty. Laissez faire too is a method of abolishing poverty. Both history and economic theory have demonstrated that it has been more successful than any other policy. When the Japanese tried to expand their exports by underselling, they too sought to improve the lot of the Japanese masses. If economic nationalism in other countries had not hindered their endeavors, they would not only have attained this end but would at the same time have raised the standards of living in the importing countries by providing their peoples with cheaper goods.

It is necessary to emphasize that we are not dealing here with plans for international charity. It would relieve much suffering if some nations were prepared to aid the starving masses in the poor countries by gratuitously distributing food and clothing. But such actions are outside the scope of strictly economic considerations. They are modes of consumption, not of production of goods.

We may first examine the proposals for regulating—by international agreements of various governments or by the order of an international authority established for that task—the production of various commodities.

In the unhampered market the prices are the guides and regulators of production. Goods are produced whenever they can be produced at a profit and are not produced when production involves a loss. A profitable industry tends to expand and an unprofitable one to shrink. An industry is unprofitable if the prices which the producer can obtain for the products do not cover the cost of the materials and labor required for their production. The consumers therefore determine by their buying or nonbuying how much should be produced in every branch of industry. The amount of wheat produced is determined by the price which the consumers are ready to pay. An expansion of production beyond these limits would mean that factors of production (labor and capital), which in accordance with the demands of the consumers are needed for the production of other commodities, would be diverted to the satisfaction of needs which the consumers consider less urgent. There prevails under unhampered capitalism a tendency to fix the amount of production in every field at a level at which the marginal producer or producers i.e., those working under the least favorable conditions, neither make a profit nor incur a loss.

Conditions being such, a regulation providing for the expansion of production of a commodity would be to no purpose if the government or international authority did not subsidize the submarginal producers in order to indemnify them for the losses incurred. But this would result in a corresponding restriction of the output of other commodities. Factors of production would be withdrawn from other branches to be used to expand the industry subsidized. The consumers, who as taxpayers provide the means needed for the subsidies, must restrict their consumption. They get smaller amounts of commodities of which they want to get more, and have the opportunity to get more of other commodities for which their demand is less intense. The intervention of the government does not comply with their individual wishes. At bottom they cannot consider its result an improvement of their condition.

It is not in the power of governments to increase the supply of one commodity without a corresponding restriction in the supply of other commodities more urgently demanded by consumers. The authority may reduce the price of one commodity only by raising the prices of others.

There are of course hundreds of millions of people who would be ready to consume more wheat, sugar, rubber, or tin if the prices were lower. The sales of every commodity increase with falling prices. But no government interference could make these commodities cheaper without raising the prices of other commodities, e.g., meat, wool, or pulp. A general increase of production can be obtained only by the improvement of technical methods, by the accumulation of additional capital, and by a more efficient use of all factors of production. No planning—whether national or international—can effect a general lowering of real prices and redress the grievances of those for whom prices are too high.

But most supporters of international planning have not the least intention of making raw materials and foodstuffs cheaper. On the contrary. What they really have in mind is raising prices and restricting supply. They see the best promise in the policies by which various governments—mainly in the last twenty years—have tried to put into effect restrictions and price increases for the benefit of special groups of producers and to the disadvantage of consumers. True, some of these schemes worked only for a short time and then collapsed, while many did not work at all. But this, according to the planners, was due to faults in technical execution. It is the essence of all their projects for postwar economic planning that they will so improve the methods applied as to make them succeed in the future.

The dangerous fact is that while government is hampered in endeavors to make a commodity cheaper by intervention, it certainly has the power to make it more expensive. Governments have the power to create monopolies; they can force the consumers to pay monopoly prices; and they use this power lavishly.

Nothing more disastrous could happen in the field of international economic relations than the realization of such plans. It would divide the nations into two groups—the exploiting and the exploited; those restricting output and charging monopoly prices, and those forced to pay monopoly prices. It would engender insoluble conflicts of interests and inevitably result in new wars.

The advocates of these schemes try to justify their suggestions by pointing out that conditions are very unsatisfactory for the producers of raw materials and foodstuffs. There is overproduction, in these lines, they insist, and prices are so low that the producers lose money. The aim of their plans, they say, is to restore the profitability of production.

It is true that a good deal of the production of these commodities does not pay. The trend toward autarky makes it harder for the industrial nations to sell their manufactures abroad; consequently they have to restrict their buying of food and raw materials. Hence it is necessary to retrench production of food and raw materials; the submarginal producers must go out of business. It is very unfortunate for them, but they can blame only the politicians of their own countries who have been responsible for the hyper-protectionist policies. The only way to increase the sales of coffee and to make prices go up on a nonmonopolized market is to buy more products from those countries in which coffee consumption would expand if their exports increased. But the pressure groups of the producers reject this solution and work for monopoly prices. They want to substitute monopolistic schemes for the operation of an unhampered market. On an unhampered market the restriction in the output of raw materials and foodstuffs, made unavoidable by the protectionist policies of the producing countries, would take place automatically by the elimination of the submarginal producers— i.e., those for whom production does not pay at the market price. But the governments want to put into effect a much greater restriction for the sake of establishing monopoly prices.

It is often said that the mechanism of the capitalist market no longer works under present conditions. The submarginal producers, the argument runs, do not go out of business; they continue production; thus prices go down to a level at which production no longer pays any producer. Therefore government intervention is needed.

The fact is true; but its interpretation and the conclusions drawn from the interpretation are entirely wrong. The reason the submarginal producers do not stop producing is that they are confident that government intervention will render their business profitable again. Their continued production gluts the market so that prices no longer cover the costs even of the other producers. In this as in so many other instances the unsatisfactory effects of a previous government intervention are put forward as arguments for further intervention. Export sales drop because imports have been checked; thus the prices of export goods also drop; and then a demand arises for measures to make prices go up.

Let us look once again at conditions in American agriculture. From its early colonial beginnings there has been a continuous shifting of farming from less fertile to more fertile soil. There have always been submarginal farms on which production had to be discontinued because the competition of farmers producing at lower costs rendered them unprofitable. But with the New Deal things took a new turn. The government interfered to the advantage of the submarginal farmers. All farmers had to submit to a proportional restriction of output. The government embarked upon a vast scheme for restricting output, raising prices, and subsidizing the farmers. In interfering for the special benefit of the submarginal farmer it did so to the disadvantage of everyone consuming food and cotton and to the disadvantage of the taxpayer. It burdened the rest of the nation in order to pay bounties to some groups. Thus it split the nation into conflicting classes—a class of bounty receivers and a more numerous class of bounty payers. This is the inevitable outcome of interventionism. The government can give to one group only what it takes from another.

The domestic conflicts engendered by such policies are very serious indeed. But in the sphere of international relations they are incomparably more disastrous. To the extent that monopoly prices are charged for food and raw materials the grievances of the have-nots are justified.

Such are the prospects of international or world planning in the sphere of production of raw materials and foodstuffs. It would be difficult to imagine any program whose realization would contribute more to engendering future conflicts and wars.

5. Foreign Trade Agreements

In the age of laissez faire commercial treaties were considered a means of abolishing, step by step, trade barriers and all other measures of discrimination against foreigners. In those days the most-favored-nation clause was a requisite of such treaties.

Then the tide turned. With the ascendancy of interventionism imports were deemed disastrous to a nation's economic prosperity. Discrimination against foreigners then came to be regarded as a good means for promoting the well-being of a country. The meaning of commercial treaties changed radically. Governments became eager to overreach one another in negotiations. A treaty was valued in proportion as it hindered the other nation's export trade and seemed to encourage one's own. Most-favored-nation treatment gave way to hostile discrimination.

In the long run there cannot be such a thing as "moderate" protectionism. If people regard imports as an injury, they will not stop anywhere on the way toward autarky. Why tolerate an evil if there seems to be a way to get rid of it? Protectionism was bound to evolve into the license and quota system and into foreign exchange control. The ultimate goal of nearly every nation's foreign-trade policy today is to prevent all imports. This means autarky.

It is vain to expect anything from purely technical changes in the methods applied in international negotiations concerning foreign-trade matters. If Atlantis is resolved to bar access to cloth manufactured abroad, it is of no importance whether its delegates must negotiate directly with the delegates of Thule, or whether the subject can be dealt with by an international board in which other nations are represented. If Atlantis is prepared to admit a limited amount—a quota—of cloth from Thule only because it wants to sell a corresponding quota of wheat to Thule, it is not likely to yield to a suggestion that it allot a part of this quota to other nations. If pressure or violence is applied in order to force Atlantis to change its import regulations so that greater quantities of cloth can be imported, it will take recourse to other methods of interventionism. Under a regime of government interference with business a government has innumerable means at hand to penalize imports. They may be less easy to handle but they can be made no less efficacious than tariffs, quotas, or the total prohibition of imports.

Under present conditions an international body for foreign-trade planning would be an assembly of the delegates of governments attached to the ideas of hyper-protectionism. It is an illusion to assume that such an authority would be in a position to contribute anything genuine or lasting to the promotion of foreign trade.

Some people cling to the belief that while universal free trade and a world-embracing division of labor are quite wrong, at least neighboring countries should enter into closer economic coöperation. Their economies could complement each other, it is argued, if they were prepared to form regional economic blocs. This doctrine, first developed by German nationalism, is fallacious.

As a rule neighboring countries offer similar natural conditions for production, especially in agriculture. Their economic systems are less likely to complement each other than to make them competitors on the world market. A customs union between Spain and Portugal, or between Bulgaria and Yugoslavia, or between Germany and Belgium would mean little. The main problems of foreign trade are not regional. The conditions for Spanish wine export could not be improved through free trade with Portugal, or vice versa. The same holds true for the production of machines in Germany and Belgium, or for agricultural production in Bulgaria and Yugoslavia.

6. Monetary Planning

The gold standard was an international standard. It safeguarded the stability of foreign exchange rates. It was a corollary of free trade and of the international division of labor. Therefore those who favored etatism and radical protectionism disparaged it and advocated its abolition. Their campaign was successful.

Even at the height of liberalism governments did not give up trying to put easy money schemes into effect. Public opinion is not prepared to realize that interest is a market phenomenon which cannot be abolished by government interference. Everybody values a loaf of bread available for today's consumption higher than a loaf which will be available only ten or a hundred years hence. As long as this is true, every economic activity must take it into account. Even a socialist management would be forced to pay full regard to it.

In a market economy the rate of interest has a tendency to correspond to the amount of this difference in the valuation of future goods and present goods. True, governments can reduce the rate of interest in the short run. They can issue additional paper money. They can open the way to credit expansion by the banks. They can thus create an artificial boom and the appearance of prosperity. But such a boom is bound to collapse soon or late and to bring about a depression.

The gold standard put a check on governmental plans for easy money. It was impossible to indulge in credit expansion and yet cling to the gold parity permanently fixed by law. Governments had to choose between the gold standard and their—in the long run disastrous—policy of credit expansion. The gold standard did not collapse. The governments destroyed it. It was as incompatible with etatism as was free trade. The various governments went off the gold standard because they were eager to make domestic prices and wages rise above the world market level, and because they wanted to stimulate exports and to hinder imports. Stability of foreign exchange rates was in their eyes a mischief, not a blessing.*

No international agreements or international planning is needed if a government wants to return to the gold standard. Every nation, whether rich or poor, powerful or feeble, can at any hour once again adopt the gold standard. The only condition required is the abandonment of an easy money policy and of the endeavors to combat imports by devaluation.

The question involved here is not whether a nation should return to the particular gold parity that it had once established and has long since abandoned. Such a policy would of course now mean deflation. But every government is free to stabilize the existing exchange ratio between its national currency unit and gold, and to keep this ratio stable. If there is no further credit expansion and no further inflation, the mechanism of the gold standard or of the gold exchange standard will work again.

All governments, however, are firmly resolved not to relinquish inflation and credit expansion. They have all sold their souls to the devil of easy money. It is a great comfort to every administration to be able to make its citizens happy by spending. For public opinion will then attribute the resulting boom to its current rulers. The inevitable slump will occur later and burden their successors. It is the typical policy of *après nous le déluge*. Lord Keynes, the champion of this policy, says: "In the long run we are all dead." † But unfortunately nearly all of us outlive the short run. We are destined to spend decades paying for the easy money orgy of a few years.

Inflation is essentially antidemocratic. Democratic control is budgetary control. The government has but one source of revenue —taxes. No taxation is legal without parliamentary consent. But if the government has other sources of income it can free itself from this control.

If war becomes unavoidable, a genuinely democratic government is forced to tell the country the truth. It must say: "We are compelled to fight for our independence. You citizens must carry the burden. You must pay higher taxes and therefore restrict your

---

* Such is the essence of the monetary teachings of Lord Keynes. The Keynesian school passionately advocates instability of foreign exchange rates.

† Lord Keynes did not coin this phrase in order to recommend short-run policies but in order to criticize some inadequate methods and statements of monetary theory (Keynes, *Monetary Reform*, New York, 1924, p. 88). However, the phrase best characterizes the economic policies recommended by Lord Keynes and his school.

consumption." But if the ruling party does not want to imperil its popularity by heavy taxation, it takes recourse to inflation.

The days are gone in which most persons in authority considered stability of foreign exchange rates to be an advantage. Devaluation of a country's currency has now become a regular means of restricting imports and expropriating foreign capital. It is one of the methods of economic nationalism. Few people now wish stable foreign exchange rates for their own countries. Their own country, as they see it, is fighting the trade barriers of other nations and the progressive devaluation of other nations' currency systems. Why should they venture to demolish their own trade walls?

Some of the advocates of a new international currency believe that gold is not fit for this service precisely because it does put a check on credit expansion. Their idea is a universal paper money issued by an international world authority or an international bank of issue. The individual nations would be obliged to keep their local currencies at par with the world currency. The world authority alone would have the right to issue additional paper money or to authorize the expansion of credit by the world bank. Thus there would be stability of exchange rates between the various local currency systems, while the alleged blessings of inflation and credit expansion would be preserved.

These plans fail, however, to take account of the crucial point. In every instance of inflation or credit expansion there are two groups, that of the gainers and that of the losers. The creditors are the losers; it is their loss that is the profit of the debtors. But this is not all. The more fateful results of inflation derive from the fact that the rise in prices and wages which it causes occurs at different times and in different measure for various kinds of commodities and labor. Some classes of prices and wages rise more quickly and to a higher level than others. While inflation is under way, some people enjoy the benefit of higher prices on the goods and services they sell, while the prices of goods and services they buy have not yet risen at all or not to the same extent. These people profiteer by virtue of their fortunate position. For them inflation is good business. Their gains are derived from the losses of other sections of the population. The losers are those in the unhappy situation of selling services and commodities whose prices have not yet risen at all or not in the same degree as the prices of things they buy for their own consumption. Two of the world's greatest philosophers, David Hume and John Stuart Mill, took pains to construct a scheme of inflationary changes in which the rise of prices and wages occurs at the same time and to the same extent for all commodities and services. They both failed in the endeavor. Modern monetary theory has provided us with the irrefutable demonstration that this disproportion and nonsimultaneousness are inevitable features of every change in the quantity of money and credit.*

Under a system of world inflation or world credit expansion every nation will be eager to belong to the class of gainers and not to that of the losers. It will ask for as much as possible of the additional quantity of paper money or credit for its own country. As no method could eliminate the inequalities mentioned above, and as no just principle for the distribution could be found, antagonisms would originate for which there would be no satisfactory solution. The populous poor nations of Asia would, for instance, advocate a per capita allotment, a procedure which would result in raising the prices of the raw materials they produce more quickly than those of the manufactured goods they buy. The richer nations would ask for a distribution according to national incomes or according to the total amount of business turnover or other similar standards. There is no hope that an agreement could be reached.

7. *Planning International Capital Transactions*

The most amazing suggestions for international planning concern foreign loans or investments. They aim at a fair distribution of the capital available.

Let us assume that American capitalists are prepared to grant a loan to the government of Venezuela or to invest money in a mine in Chile. What can an international body do in this case? Certainly it will not have the power to force the American capitalists to lend the money to China rather than Venezuela, or to make the investment in Persian railroads instead of in Chilean mining.

Or the American Government might want for various reasons to subsidize the construction of motor roads in Mexico. Would the international authority order it to subsidize Greek textile plants instead?

The international capital market has been disintegrated by economic nationalism, as has every other branch of economic internationalism. As investments and loans mean business and not charity, capitalists have lost the incentive to invest abroad. It will be hard work, and it will take a good while, to rebuild the international money and capital market. The interference of international authorities would not further these endeavors; it would be more likely to hinder them.

Labor unions are likely to be hostile to capital export because

---

* See Mises, *Theory of Money and Credit* (New York, 1934), pp. 137–145, and *Nationalökonomie* (Geneva, 1940), pp. 375–378.

they are eager to raise as far as possible the domestic marginal productivity of labor. Many governments put a general embargo on capital export; foreign loans and investments are not permitted without a special government license. It is not probable that a change will occur immediately after the war.

The poorer countries have done all that they could to promote the disintegration of the international capital market. Having inflicted as much harm as possible upon foreign capitalists and entrepreneurs, they are now anxious to get new foreign capital. However, today they meet only with reluctance. Capitalists shun unreliable debtors, and labor is unwilling to let capital emigrate.

XII. PEACE SCHEMES

1. Armament Control

IT would be an illusion to assume that any nation today is
prepared to abandon protectionism. As the ruling parties
favor government interference with business and national
planning, they cannot demolish the trade barriers erected
by their own countries. Thus the incentives for war and conquest
will not disappear. Every nation will have to be ready to repel
aggression. War preparedness will be the only means of avoiding
war. The old saying *Si vis pacem para bellum* will be true again.

But even the abolition of trade barriers would not safeguard
peace if migration barriers were not abolished too. The comparatively overpopulated nations will hardly acquiesce in a state of affairs which results in a lower standard of living for them. On the
other hand, it is obvious that no nation could, without imperiling
its independence, open its frontiers to the citizens of totalitarian
states aiming at conquest. Thus, we are forced to recognize that under present conditions no scheme can eliminate the root causes of
war. Prospects are not bright for more friendly international relations in the coming postwar period.

It is even very doubtful whether it would be of any value at all
to conclude a formal peace treaty with Germany after its defeat.
Things have changed considerably in these last thirty years. International treaties in general, and especially peace treaties, are not
what they used to be. This is not only the fault of those Germans
who boast that treaties are but scraps of paper. The Allies too are
not free from guilt.

One of the worst blunders committed by the Allied Powers in
1919 was the awkward arrangement of the peace negotiations. For
centuries it had been the custom to conduct peace negotiations in
accordance with the usages of gentlemen. The delegates of both
parties, the victorious and the defeated, would meet as civilized
people meet to conduct business. The victors neither humiliated
nor insulted the vanquished; they treated them as gentlemen and
equals. They discussed their mutual problems in quiet and polite
language. Such were the age-old rules and observances of diplomacy.

The Allied Powers broke this usage. They took delight in treat-
ing the German delegates with contempt and insults. The delegates
were confined in the houses assigned to them; guards were posted
at the doors; no delegate had the right to leave the house. They

were taken like prisoners from the railway station to their lodgings, and from the lodgings to the meeting hall, and back again in the same manner. When they entered the assembly room, the delegates of the victors answered their greetings with manifest disdain. No conversation between the German delegates and those of the victors was permitted. The Germans were handed a draft of the treaty and asked to return a written answer at a fixed date.

This conduct was inexcusable. If the Allies did not wish to comply with the old-established rule of international law requiring oral discussion between the delegates, they should have so informed the German Government in advance. The Germans could have been spared the sending of a delegation of eminent men. For the procedure chosen by the Allies a letter carrier would have sufficed as German delegate. But the successors of Talleyrand and Disraeli wished to enjoy their triumph to the full.

Even if the Allies had behaved in a less offensive way, of course the Treaty of Versailles would not have been essentially different. If a war results not in a stalemate but in one party's victory, the peace treaty is always dictated. The vanquished agree to terms which they would not accept under other circumstances. The essence of a peace treaty is compulsion. The defeated yield because they are not in a position to continue the fight. A contract between citizens can be annulled by the courts if one of the parties can prove that it was forced to sign under duress. But these notions of civil law do not apply to treaties between sovereign nations. Here the law of the strongest still prevails.

German propaganda has confused these obvious matters. The German nationalists maintained the thesis that the Treaty of Versailles was null because it was dictated and not spontaneously accepted by Germany. The cession of Alsace-Lorraine, of the Polish provinces, and of northern Schleswig is invalid, they said, because Germany surrendered to coercion. But they were inconsistent enough not to apply the same argument to the treaties by which Prussia had acquired, since 1740, its provinces of Silesia, West Prussia, Posen, Saxony, Rhineland, Westphalia, and Schleswig-Holstein. They neglected to mention the fact that Prussia had conquered and annexed, without any treaty, the kingdom of Hanover, the electorate of Hessen, the duchy of Nassau, and the republic of Frankfort. Out of the twelve provinces which in 1914 formed the kingdom of Prussia, nine were the spoils of successful wars between 1740 and 1866. Nor did the French, in 1871, surrender Alsace-Lorraine to the Reich of their own free will.

But you simply cannot argue with nationalists. The Germans are fully convinced that compulsion applied by them to other nations is fair and just, while compulsion applied to themselves is criminal. They will never acquiesce in a peace treaty that does not satisfy their appetite for more space. Whether they wage a new war of aggression will not depend on whether or not they have duly signed a peace treaty. It is vain to expect German nationalists to abide by the clauses of any treaty if conditions for a new assault seem propitious.

A new war is unavoidable if the United Nations do not succeed in establishing a world order preventing the Germans and their allies from rearming. As long as there is economic nationalism, the United Nations will have to watch their ramparts day and night.

The alliance of the victorious nations must be made lasting. Germany, Italy, and Japan must be totally disarmed. They must be deprived of the right to maintain armies, navies, or air fleets. A small police force, armed with rifles only, can be permitted to them. No kind of armament production should be tolerated. The guns and the ammunition for their policemen should be given to them by the United Nations. They should not be permitted to fly or build any planes. Commercial aviation in their countries should be operated by foreign companies using foreign planes and employing foreign pilots. But the main means to hinder their rearmament should be a strict control of imports on the part of the United Nations. No imports should be permitted to the aggressor nations if they dedicate a part of their production to armaments or if they try to pile up stocks of imported raw materials. Such a control could easily be established. Should any country, under the pretext of neutrality, not be prepared to coöperate unconditionally in this scheme, it would be necessary to apply the same methods against this country as well.

No Ersatz production could frustrate the efficacy of this scheme. But if a change in technological possibilities imperils the working of the control system, it will be easy to force the country concerned to surrender. The prohibition of all food imports is a very effective weapon.

This is not a very pleasant solution of the problem, but it is the only one that could work satisfactorily, provided the victorious nations maintain their alliance after the war.

It is wrong to regard unilateral disarmament as unfair to the vanquished. If they do not plan new aggressions, they are not in need of arms. If they dream of new wars and are stopped by lack of arms, unilateral disarmament will favor them no less than the victorious nations. Even if they were to be deprived of the instruments to assault other peoples, their independence and their right to rule themselves would remain untouched.

We must see conditions as they really are, not as we want them to be. If this war does not result in making it forever impossible for the Germans to wage a new war, they will try, sooner or later, to kindle a new conflict. As the victorious nations will not concede them what they want, world hegemony, they will not renounce their aggressive plans so long as the two strategical advantages of high population figures and interior lines remain unchanged. Nazism would be resurrected in a new form and under a new name.

The peace settlement will further have to make special provisions for the punishment of those Nazis responsible for murdering and torturing innocent people. It will have to force the German nation to pay indemnities for the robberies committed by their rulers and mobs. This will not revive those murdered. It will be impossible, after the passage of years, to allot to every individual injured the fair amount of compensation. But it is of the greatest importance to hold the Germans answerable for all their acts. It would be absurd to allow all their atrocities to go unpunished. The Nazis would consider it both a success and a justification of their conduct. They would think: "After all, we have attained at least a partial success; we have reduced the population and the wealth of the 'inferior' races; the main burden of this war falls on them, not on us." It would be scandalous indeed if the Germans suffer less from the consequences of their aggression than those assaulted.

The Kellogg Pact outlawed war. Germany, Italy, Japan, Hungary, and Rumania signed this document. If there was any meaning at all in this compact, then it was that aggressors are guilty of an illegal act and must bear the responsibility for it. Those citizens of these nations who did not openly oppose the dictators cannot plead their innocence.

Every endeavor to make peace last will be futile unless people abandon spurious hero worship and cease to pity the defeated aggressor more than his victims. The cult of Napoleon I, almost universal in nineteenth-century Europe, was an insult to common sense. He certainly had no excuse for the invasions of Spain and Russia; he was not a martyr; he enjoyed infinitely more comfort in his exile in St. Helena than the many thousands he had caused to be maimed and mutilated. It was an outrage that those responsible for the violation of Belgian neutrality in 1914 escaped punishment. It gave a belated justification to their contemptuous description of treaties as scraps of waste paper. The attitude of public opinion—outside of France and Belgium—with regard to German

reparations was a serious mistake. It encouraged German nationalism. These blunders must be avoided in the future.

2. A Critique of Some Other Schemes Proposed

It is vain to expect that defeat will change the mentality of the
defeated and make them peace loving. They will cling to peace
only if conditions are such that they cannot hope to conquer. Any
schemes based on the assumption that any German party will immediately after the defeat renounce aggression and voluntarily embark upon a policy of sincere coöperation are futile. A German politician opposing war, if there were any real chance of success of a
new aggression, would meet the fate of Erzberger and Rathenau.

The Germans will one day recover their reason. They will remember that modern civilization was to some extent an achievement of their own. They will find the way back to the ideals of
Schiller and Goethe. But this process of recovery must come from
within. It cannot be forced upon Germany—nor upon Italy or
Japan—by a victorious army or by compulsory education on the
part of foreign teachers. The Germans must learn that their aggressive nationalism is suicidal, and that it has already inflicted
irreparable evils upon themselves. They will have spontaneously
to reject their present tenets and to adopt again all those ideas
which they dismiss today as Christian, Western, and Jewish. Out
of the midst of their own people men will have to emerge who address them with the words once used by Saint Remigius at the bap-
tism of King Clovis: "Adore what you used to burn, and burn what
you used to adore."

Some groups have hatched out a plan for the political dismemberment of Germany. They recall that Germany in the days of
the *Deutscher Bund* (1815–66) was divided into about forty sovereign states and that at that time the Germans did not venture upon
aggression. In those years the nation was prosperous. If all the German princes had fulfilled the obligation, imposed on them by the
settlement of Vienna, to grant their citizens parliamentary institutions, the Germans would have had no reason to change their
political organization. The German Confederation safeguarded
them against foreign aggression while preventing them from waging wars of conquest. Thus the system proved beneficial both to
Germany and to the whole of Europe.

These belated eulogists of Prince Metternich ignore the most
important facts of German history. They do not realize that the
Germans of those days were liberal, and that their ideas of national greatness differed radically from those of modern national-

ism. They cherished the values which Schiller had praised. "The German Empire and the German nation," said Schiller in the draft of his unfinished poem "German Greatness," are "two different things. The glory of Germany was never vested in the persons of its leaders. The German has established his own values quite apart from political values. Even if the Empire goes astray, German dignity would remain untouched. It is a moral eminence, vested in the nation's civilization and character, which do not depend on political vicissitudes." * Such were the ideas of the Germans of the early nineteenth century. In the midst of a world marching toward genuine liberalism the Germans also were enthusiastically liberal. They would have viewed the Deutscher Bund as a satisfactory solution of the political problem if it had not been the realm of despotic princes. Today, in this age of nationalism, the Germans also are nationalists. They have to face a very serious economic problem, and their etatistic prejudices prevent them from seeing any solution other than the conquest of Lebensraum. They worship the "brute force" whose elimination Schiller had hoped for. Under such conditions nationalism could not be overthrown by a partition of the Reich into a score of independent states. In each of these states the heat of nationalist passions would flare up; the bellicose spirit would virtually coördinate and unify their political and military activities, even if formally the independence of each section were to be preserved up to the day of the new mobilization.

The history of Central Europe could have taken a different course. A part of those people who today get their education in classical German, taught in school or learned at home, and used in conversation with people whom they do not address in their local dialect, might be using another of the present-day languages or a language of their own. One group of the people using the Low German dialect (*Platt*) has created the Dutch language; another, more numerous group of the Low Germans has joined the linguistic community of the High Germans. The political and economic process which made the Dutch people into a nation with a language of its own could have resulted in a more important diminishing of the German linguistic group. If the Counter-Reformation and Jesuitism had not crippled all spiritual, intellectual, and literary freedom in Bavaria and in Austria, the idiom of the Saxon chancellery, which owes its supremacy to Luther's version of the Bible and to the Protestant writings of the first two centuries of the Reformation, might have found a serious rival in a literary language developed out of the Bavarian dialect. One could indulge even

* Cassirer, *Freiheit und Form, Studien zur deutschen Geistesgeschichte* (Berlin, 1916), pp. 475 ff.

further in such reveries, whether with regard to the Swabian dialect or to the Slavonic and Baltic idioms of the northeast. But such dreams cannot change historical facts and political reality. The Germans are today the most numerous linguistic group in Europe. The age of etatism and nationalism must recognize the importance of this fact. The greater part of the German-speaking group affirm the principle of nationality; they want a unified German state including all German-speaking men. France and Great Britain deserve no credit for the fact that the Austrians and the Swiss reject these plans and are anxious to stay outside the Reich. On the contrary. In suicidal infatuation the French, and later the English, have done much to weaken Austria and to strengthen Prussian aspirations. The Bourbon kings associated in their fight against Austria not only with Prussia but even with the Turks. Great Britain was Prussia's ally in the Seven Years' War. What business had Napoleon III to attack Austria? It should be noted that the present-day Axis constellation was but a revival of the league of 1866, when Prussia and Italy assailed Austria, Hungarian nationalists prepared an upheaval with Bismarck's aid, and the Hohenzollern Prince of Rumania tried to arm for the purpose of giving the finishing stroke. At that time governments and public opinion both in Paris and in London sympathized with the aggressors. The French and the English learned only later that they had been working *pour le roi de Prusse.*

Our problem would be simpler if all men spoke the same language or if the various linguistic groups were at least more equal in size. But the presence of seventy million German nationalists in the Reich is a datum, a necessary point of beginning, of present-day politics. It cannot be brushed aside by the dismemberment of the Reich. It would be a fatal delusion to assume that the problem could be solved in this way. To safeguard the independence of Austria and Switzerland must, it is true, be the foremost aim of all future plans for a reconstruction of Europe. But the dismemberment of the old Reich (the *Altreich,* as the Germans say, in order to distinguish it from *Gross-Deutschland* including Austria and the Sudetenland) would be a futile measure.

Clemenceau has been credited with the dictum that there are twenty million Germans too many. Some fanatics have suggested as the panacea the wholesale extermination of all Nazis. This would solve the problem in a way which from the Nazi point of view would be the logical result of total war. The Nazi concept of total victory implies the radical extermination of the French, Czechs, Poles, Jews, and other groups; and they have already started to execute this plan. They therefore could not logically call it unfair or bar-

barous if the United Nations profited from their victory to exterminate the "Aryan" citizens of the Reich. Neither could the Italians, the Japanese, the Magyars, and the Rumanians. But the United Nations are not brutes like the Nazis and Fascists.

Some authors believe that the problem of linguistically mixed populations could be solved by forcible transplantation and exchange of minorities. They refer to the allegedly favorable results of this procedure as applied in the case of Turkey and Greece. It seems indeed to be a very obvious method of dealing with the unpleasant consequences of linguistic promiscuity. Segregate the quarreling groups and you will prevent further struggles.

These plans, however, are untenable. They disregard the fundamental problem of present-day antagonisms—the inequality of the various parts of the earth's surface. Linguistic promiscuity is the result of migrations on the part of men eager to improve their standard of living. Workers move from places where the marginal productivity of labor is low to where it is higher—in other words, from comparatively overpopulated areas to those comparatively underpopulated. To prevent such migrations or to try to undo them by forcible expulsion and repatriation of the immigrants does not solve the problem but only aggravates the conflicts.

The same holds true for peasants. There are, for instance, the German farmers in the Banat, one of the most fertile districts of Europe. These people immigrated in the eighteenth century. At that time the region was at a very low stage of civilization, thinly populated, devastated by Turkish misrule and continuous wars. Today the Banat is a bone of contention between the Serbs, Rumanians, and Hungarians. The German minority is a thorn in the side of all three claimants. They would all be glad to get rid of the Germans. But what kind of compensation could they offer them in exchange for their farms? There are no farms in the countries inhabited by German majorities that are owned by Serbs or Rumanians, and no equivalent farms owned by Hungarians on the borders of Germany. The expropriation and expulsion of the German peasants would not be a step toward pacification; it would only create new grievances. Similar conditions prevail all over Eastern Europe.

Those who are under the illusion that segregation could solve the international problems of our day are blind to reality. The very fact that the Australians succeeded in maintaining linguistic and racial homogeneity in their country helped to push the Japanese into aggression. The closed-door policy is one of the root causes of our wars.

In Great Britain and America many people are frightened by

the prospect of a communist Germany. They are afraid of contagion. But these anxieties are unfounded. Communism is not a disease and it does not spread through germs. No country will catch communism because it has moved nearer to its frontiers. For whatever chance there is of a communist regime coming to power in America or Great Britain the mentalities of the citizens of these countries are responsible. Pro-communist sympathies within a country have nothing to do with whether its neighbors are communist or not.

If Germany turns toward communism it cannot be the task of foreign nations to interfere. The numerous friends of communism in the Anglo-Saxon countries will oppose preventing a country from adopting a system which they themselves consider the only beneficial one and advocate for their own countries. The intelligent opponents of communism, on the other hand, will not understand why their nation should essay to prevent the Germans from inflicting harm upon themselves. The shortcomings of communism would paralyze and disintegrate Germany's industrial apparatus and thereby weaken its military power more effectively than any foreign intervention could ever do.

Russia's military strength lies in the remoteness and the vastness of its land. It is impregnable because it is so spacious and impassable. Invaders have defeated the Russian armies; but no one has succeeded in overcoming the geographical obstacles. Charles XII, Napoleon, Hindenburg, and Hitler penetrated deep into Russia; their victorious advance itself spelled the doom of their armies. The British and the French in the Crimean War and the Japanese forty years ago only excoriated the edge of the Czar's Empire. The present war has proved anew the thesis of old Prussia's military doctrine that it is futile to beat the Russian forces. After having easily conquered hundreds of thousands of square miles, the Nazi armies were broken by the vastness of the country. The main problem that an invading general has to face in Russia is how to withdraw his forces safely. Neither Napoleon nor Hitler has solved this problem.

Communist economic management did not weaken Russia's ability to repel aggression; it did not interfere with geographical factors. Communism in Germany, i.e., the wholesale liquidation of the bourgeoisie and the substitution of bureaucratic socialism of the Soviet pattern for Zwangswirtschaft, would seriously impair or even destroy Germany's capacity to export manufactures. Those who believe that a communist Germany could rearm as easily as Russia fail to recognize the fundamental difference between the two countries. While Russia is not forced to import foreign raw materials, Germany must. But for the export of manufactured goods Germany would not have been in a position to import all the raw materials needed for its rearmament. The reason why the Nazis preferred the Zwangswirtschaft system to the Soviet system was that they fully recognized the fact that plants directly managed by government clerks cannot compete on the world market. It was German export trade that provided the materials required for the building of the formidable *Blitz* machine. Bolshevism did not impair Russia's potential of defense. It would annihilate Germany's potential of aggression.

The real danger of communism in Germany lies in the probability that its inevitable economic failure may restore the prestige of Nazism lost by the defeat in this war. Just as the unsatisfactory results of the Nazi regime are now making communism popular with the German masses, the bad consequences of communism could possibly contribute to a rehabilitation of Nazism. The German problem is precisely this, that Germany has no party ready to support liberalism, democracy, and capitalism and that it sees only the two alternatives: Nazism, i.e., socialism of the German pattern of all-round planning (Zwangswirtschaft), on the one hand, or Bolshevism, i.e., socialism of the Russian pattern of immediate state management, on the other. Neither of these two systems could solve Germany's economic problem. Both of them will push Germany toward a policy of conquering more Lebensraum.

3. The Union of the Western Democracies

The main need is a lasting coöperation among the nations today united in their efforts to smash the totalitarian aggression. No plan can work if the nations concerned do not transform their present alliance into a permanent and lasting union. If they resume their prewar policies after the victory, if they return to political rivalries and to economic warfare, the result will be a repetition of the developments of 1919–39. There can be neither effective political coöperation nor solidarity and collective security among nations fighting each other in the economic sphere.

If the Western democracies do not succeed in establishing a permanent union, the fruits of victory will be lost again. Their disunity will provide the defeated aggressors with the opportunity to enter anew the scene of political intrigues and plots, to rearm and to form a new and stronger coalition for another assault. Unless they choose effective solidarity, the democracies are doomed.

They cannot safeguard their way of life if they seek to preserve what the terminology of diplomacy calls "national sovereignty." * They must choose between vesting all power in a new supranational authority or being enslaved by nations not prepared to treat them on an equal footing. The alternative to incorporation into a new democratic supernational system is not unrestricted sovereignty but ultimate subjugation by the totalitarian powers.

This is obvious in the case of small nations like the Dutch, the Danes, the Norwegians. They could live in peace only as long as the much abused system of the European balance of power protected them. Their independence was safeguarded by the mutual rivalry and jealousy of the big powers. The countries of Latin America enjoyed their autonomy because the Monroe Doctrine and the British Navy prevented any attempts at invasion. Those days are gone. Today these small nations must themselves guard their independence. They will have to renounce their proud isolationism and their intransigent pretensions in any case. The only real question is whether they will become slaves in a totalitarian system or free men in a supernational democracy.

As for Great Britain and France, there can be no doubt at all that they will spell their own doom if they are not prepared to abandon their traditional aspirations for unrestricted national sovereignty. This may be still more true for Australia and New Zealand.

Then there are the United States and Canada. In the course of the nineteenth century they were in the happy position of islanders. Thousands of miles of ocean separated them from potential invaders. They were safe because technical conditions made aggression impossible. But in this age of air power they have become close neighbors of dangerous foes. It is not impossible that in ten or twenty years more an invasion of the North American continent will be technically as easy for Germany or Japan as was the occupation of the Netherlands in 1940 and that of the Philippines in 1941 and 1942. The citizens of the United States and of Canada will have to realize that there is no other way for them to live in peace than to coöperate with all other democratic peoples.

It is therefore obvious that the Western democracies must desist from all further measures of economic warfare in their mutual relations. True, it is still the firm public conviction that it is absurd to hope for a general return to free trade all over the world. But if trade barriers are not removed between the individual countries forming the suggested democratic union, there will be no union at

---

* Of course, the preservation of every nation's full sovereignty would not hinder peaceful coöperation if the nations were to return to a free market economy without any trade or migration barriers.

all. In this respect all plans proposed for a postwar settlement agree. All are based on the expectation that the democracies will stop warring upon one another with the methods of economic nationalism. But they fail to realize what such a solution requires and what its consequences must be.

It must be emphasized again and again that economic nationalism is the corollary of etatism, whether interventionism or socialism. Only countries clinging to a policy of unhampered capitalism, today generally derided as reactionary, can do without trade barriers. If a country does not want to abandon government interference with business, and nevertheless renounces protectionism in its relations with the other member nations of the new union to be formed, it must vest all power in the authority ruling this union and *completely* surrender its own sovereignty to the supernational authority. But our contemporaries are not at all likely to accept this.

The core of the matter has been neglected because the belief prevails that the establishment of a federal union would solve the problem. Some powers, people assert, should be given to the supernational union government, the rest should remain with the governments of the member nations. Federal government has succeeded very well in many countries, especially in the United States and Switzerland. There is no reason, people say, to suspect that it would not prove very satisfactory in the great federal union of the Western democracies suggested by Clarence Streit.*

Unfortunately neither Mr. Streit nor the advocates of similar projects take into account the changes that have occurred in the structure of these two federal governments (as in that of all other federations) with the spread of economic interventionism and socialism. The federative systems both in America and in Switzerland were founded in an age which did not consider it the task of civil government to interfere with the business of the citizens. There were in the United States federal customs duties, a federal postal service, and a national currency system. But in almost every other respect civil government was not concerned with the control of business. The citizens were free to run their own affairs. The government's only task was to safeguard domestic and external peace. Under such conditions it was simple to divide powers between the federal government and the governments of the various member states. To the federal government those matters were assigned which went beyond the boundaries of the states: foreign affairs, defense against foreign aggression, the safeguarding of trade between the states, the management of the postal service and of

---

* *Union Now* (London, 1939); *Union Now with Great Britain* (London, 1941).

customs. Moreover the federal government did not interfere with the local affairs of the states, and the states did not interfere with what were considered the private affairs of the citizen.

This equilibrium in the distribution of jurisdictional powers was entirely upset by the policy of interventionism. New powers accrued not to the member states but to the federal government. Every step toward more government interference and toward more planning means at the same time an expansion of the jurisdiction of the central government. Washington and Berne were once the seats of the federal governments; today they are capitals in the true sense of the word, and the states and the cantons are virtually reduced to the status of provinces. It is a very significant fact that the adversaries of the trend toward more government control describe their opposition as a fight against Washington and against Berne, i.e., against centralization. It is conceived as a contest of state's rights versus the central power.

This evolution is not accidental. It is the inevitable outcome of policies of interference and planning. Such measures must be put on a national basis when there are no trade barriers among the member states. There can be no question of adopting these measures for only one state. It is impossible to raise production costs within a territory not sheltered by trade walls. Within a system of interventionism the absence of interstate trade barriers shifts the political center of gravity to the federal government. Seen from the formalistic viewpoint of constitutional law, the United States and the Swiss Confederation may doubtless still be classified as federations, but in actual fact they are moving more and more toward centralization.

This is still more the case within a socialist system. The various republics which nominally form the Soviet Union have only a spurious existence. The Soviet Union is a wholly centralized government.* The same is true for Germany. The Nazis have replaced the federal constitution with a unitary government.

It would be a mistake to believe that resistance to an international unification of government would arise only out of considerations of national pride and vanity. Such obstacles would not be unsurmountable. The main source of opposition would be more

---

* The decree of the Supreme Soviet of February 1, 1944 (see *New York Times*, February 3, 1944), does not interfere in any way with the perfect centralization of the Soviet economic management and domestic administration. The conduct of all economic and administrative affairs of the whole territory subject to the Soviets remains in the hands of the central offices of Moscow. They alone have the power and the right to direct all economic and political activities. And now, as before, the central committee of Moscow appoints and removes all officials of all the sixteen nominally independent republics.

deeply rooted. The shift of sovereignty from the national authorities to a supernational authority implies a total change in the structure of political forces. Pressure groups which were very powerful in the national frame and were in a position to shape policies may become impotent in the supernational frame, and vice versa. Even if we are prepared to set aside the ticklish question of migration barriers, the fact is evident. The American cotton producers are eager for higher prices of cotton and, although they are only a minority in the United States, are in a position to force a policy of high cotton prices upon their nation. It is doubtful whether within a union including many countries importing cotton their influence would be the same. On the other hand, British motor-car producers are sheltered against American competition through very effective protectionist measures. They would not like to lose this advantage. Examples could be multiplied indefinitely.

The most serious and dangerous opposition to the supernational unification of government would come from the most powerful of all modern pressure groups, labor. The workers of those countries in which wage rates are higher would feel injured by the competition of countries with lower wages. They would find this competition unfair; they would denounce it as dumping. But they would not agree to the only measure which could raise wage rates in the countries with less favorable conditions of production: freedom of migration.

Modern government interference with business is a policy of protecting influential pressure groups from the effects of free competition in an unhampered market economy. The pressure groups concerned have taken it as a more or less unalterable fact that in the absence of trade barriers between the various parts of a nation they cannot be protected against the competition within their own country. The New York dairy farmer does not ask for import duties on Wisconsin cheese and butter, and the workers of Massachusetts do not ask for immigration laws against the intrusion of cheap labor from the South. They submit more or less to the fact that there are neither trade barriers nor migration barriers within the United States. The attempts to erect interstate trade barriers have succeeded only to a small degree; public opinion is opposed to such endeavors.*

On the other hand, people are so much under the influence of the generally accepted tenets of economic nationalism that they acquiesce in the disadvantages inflicted upon them by protectionism. The consumer makes little protest against an import duty

* See Buell, *Death by Tariff* (Chicago, 1938); Melder, *State Trade Walls* (New York, 1939).

which forces him to pay more than the world market price for the benefit of the producers of some commodity within his own country. But it is very doubtful whether he would put up in the same way with an import duty levied for the benefit of producers in other parts of a supernational union. Would the American consumer be ready to pay higher prices for a commodity in order to further the interests of English manufacturing? Would he not find that the discrimination thus applied against cheaper products of German, Italian, or Japanese origin was prejudicial to his interests? We may wonder whether a supernational policy of protectionism would not lack the ideological foundations which render national protectionism feasible.

The main obstacle to the establishment of a supernational customs union with internal free trade among the member nations is the fact that such a customs union requires unlimited supremacy of the supernational authorities and an almost complete annihilation of the national governments if etatism is to be retained. Under present conditions it makes little difference whether the constitution of the suggested union of the Western democracies is shaped according to the legal pattern of unitary or of federal government. There are only two alternatives open: trade barriers among the member states, with all their sinister consequences, economic nationalism, rivalries and discord; or free trade among the member states and (whatever the constitutional term adopted for it) strictly centralized government. In the first case there would be not union but disunion. In the second case the President of the United States and the Prime Minister of Great Britain would be virtually reduced to the status of provincial governors, and Congress and Parliament to provincial assemblies. It is unlikely that the Americans or the British will easily agree to such a solution of the problem.*

The policies of government interference with business and of national planning beget economic nationalism. The abandonment of economic nationalism, an indispensable condition for the establishment of lasting peace, can only be achieved through a unification of government, if people do not want to return to the system of unhampered market economy. This is the crux of the matter.

The weakness of Mr. Streit's plan lies in the fact that he is not aware of this fundamental problem. It is impossible to avoid this

---

* It is futile to ask people whether they are in favor of a renunciation of their own nation's sovereignty. Most laymen do not understand the meaning of the term "sovereignty." The correct formulation for the question would be: Do you advocate a system under which your nation could be forced to submit to a measure which the majority of your fellow citizens oppose? Are you ready to see essential laws of your country (for example, immigration laws) altered by a Union Parliament in which the members returned by your country are a minority only?

difficulty by a mere legalistic solution. The precariousness of the union project is not of a constitutional character. It lies in the essence of interventionist and socialist policies; it stems from present-day social and economic doctrines; and it cannot be disposed of by some special constitutional scheme.

But let us not forget that such a union must be established if any peace scheme is to work. The alternative to the realization of a union of the Western democracies is a return to the ominous conditions prevailing from 1918 to 1939, and consequently to new and still more dreadful wars.

4. Peace in Eastern Europe

The attempts to settle the political problems of Eastern Europe by the application of the principle of nationality have met with complete failure. In that corner of the world it is impossible to draw boundaries which would clearly and neatly separate the various linguistic groups. A great part of this territory is linguistically mixed, that is, inhabited by people of different languages. The rivalries and the mutual hatreds of these nations make them an easy prey for the "dynamism" of the three big adjacent powers, Germany, Russia, and Italy. If left alone they will sooner or later lose their independence unless they cease from discord.

Both world wars originated in this area. Twice the Western democracies have drawn the sword to defend the threatened independence of these nations. Yet the West has no real material interest in preserving the integrity of these peoples. If the Western democracies succeed in establishing an order that safeguards them against new aggressions, it will make no difference to them whether Warsaw is the capital of an independent Polish state or a provincial town of Russia or Germany, or whether Athens is a Greek or an Italian city. Neither the military nor the economic power of the Western democracies would be seriously imperiled if Russia, Germany, and Italy were to partition these lands among them. Nor will it matter for them whether a Lithuanian language and literature persist or whether they disappear.

The interest of the Western democracies in East European affairs is altruistic and unselfish. It is the outcome of a disinterested sympathy, of an enthusiasm for freedom, and of a sense of justice. These feelings have been grossly exploited by all these Eastern nations. Their friends in the West did not want to help them oppress minorities or make inroads upon their weaker neighbors. When the Western democrats hailed Kossuth, it did not occur to them that they favored ruthless oppression of Slovaks, Croats, Serbs,

Ukrainians, and Rumanians. When they expressed their sympathies for Poland, they did not mean to approve the methods applied by the Poles against Ukrainians, Lithuanians, and Germans. They sought to promote liberalism and democracy, not nationalistic tyranny.

It is probable that the political leaders of the East European linguistic groups have not yet become aware of the change going on in the attitudes of the Western nations. They are right in expecting that their nations will be restored to political independence after the victorious end of the war. But they are badly mistaken if they assume that the Western nations will fight a third world war for them. They themselves will have to establish a political order which enables them to live in peace with their immediate neighbors, and to defend their independence against future aggression on the part of the great powers Russia, Germany, and Italy.

All the plans suggested in the past, for the formation of an East European or Danubian customs union or federation, or for a simple restoration of the Austro-Hungarian Empire, were doomed to fail because they were based on erroneous assumptions. Their authors did not recognize that a customs union, in this age of government interference with business, is incompatible with maintaining the sovereignty of the member nations. They did not grasp the fact that under present conditions a federation means that virtually all power is vested in the supernational federal government, and the national governments are reduced to the status of provinces. The only way to substitute peace and coöperation for the existing disunion in Eastern Europe, or in any other part of the world, is the establishment of a unitary government—unless the nations will return to laissez faire.

Unitary government is the more adequate and indispensable in Eastern Europe in that it also provides the only solution for the peculiar problem of boundaries and linguistic minorities. A federation could never succeed in this respect. Under a federative system the constitution assigns some governmental powers to the federal government and others to the local governments of the member states. As long as the constitution remains unchanged the federal government does not have the power to interfere in questions which are under the jurisdiction of the member states. Such a system can work and has worked only with homogeneous peoples, where there exists a strong feeling of national unity and where no linguistic, religious, or racial differences divide the population.

Let us assume that the constitution of a supposed East European federation grants to every linguistic minority group the right to establish schools where its own language is taught. Then it would be illegal for a member state to hinder the establishment of such schools directly or openly. But if the building code or the administration of public health and fire fighting are in the exclusive jurisdiction of the member states, a local government could use its powers to close the school on the ground that the building did not comply with the requirements fixed by these regulations. The federal authorities would be helpless. They would not have the right to interfere even if the grounds given proved to be only a subterfuge. Every kind of constitutional prerogative granted to the member states could be abused by a local government.

If we want to abolish all discrimination against minority groups, if we want to give to all citizens actual and not merely formal freedom and equality, we must vest all powers in the central government alone. This would not cripple the rights of a loyal local government eager to use its powers in a fair way. But it would hinder the return to methods whereby the whole administrative apparatus of the government is used to harm minorities.

A federation in Eastern Europe could never abolish the political implications of the frontiers. In every member state there would remain the problem of minorities. There would be oppression of minorities, hatred, and Irredentism. The government of every member state would continue to consider its neighbors as adversaries. The diplomatic and consular agents of the three great neighboring powers would try to profit from these quarrels and rivalries, and might succeed in disrupting the whole system.

The main objectives of the new political order which has to be established in Eastern Europe must be:

1. To grant every citizen full opportunity to live and to work freely without being molested by any linguistic group within the boundaries of Eastern Europe. Nobody should be persecuted or disqualified on account of his mother tongue or his creed. Every linguistic group should have the right to use its own language. No discrimination should be tolerated against minority groups or their members. Every citizen should be treated in such a way that he will call the country without any reservation "my country" and the government "our government."

2. Not to lead any linguistic group to expect improvement in its political status by a change in territorial organization. The difference between a ruling linguistic group and oppressed linguistic minorities must disappear. There must be no "Irredenta."

3. To develop a system strong enough to defend its independence against aggression on the part of its neighbors. Its armed forces must be able to repel, without foreign assistance, an isolated

act of aggression on the part of Germany or Italy or Russia. It should rely on the help of the Western democracies only against a common aggression by at least two of these neighbors.

The whole territory of Eastern Europe must therefore be organized as a political unit under a strictly unitary democratic government. Within this area every individual should have the right to choose where he wishes to live and to work. The laws and the authorities should treat all natives—i.e., all citizens of East Europe—alike, without privileges or discrimination for or against individuals or groups.

Let us call this new political structure the "Eastern Democratic Union" (EDU). Within its framework the old political units may continue to function. A dislocation of the historically developed entities is not required. Once the problem of borders has been deprived of its disastrous political implications, most of the existing national bodies can remain intact. Having lost their power to inflict harm upon their neighbors and upon their minorities, they may prove very useful for the progress of civilization and human welfare. Of course, these former independent sovereign states will in the framework of the EDU be nothing more than provinces. Retaining all their honorary forms, their kings or presidents, their flags, anthems, state holidays, and parades, they will have to comply strictly with the laws and administrative provisions of the EDU. But so long as they do not try to violate these laws and regulations, they will be free. The loyal and law-abiding government of each state will not be hindered but strongly supported by the central government.

Special commissioners of the EDU will have to oversee the functioning of the local governments. Against all administrative acts of the local authorities injured parties will have the right to appeal to this commissioner and to the central government, provided that such acts do not come under the jurisdiction of a law court. All disagreements between local governments or between the commissioner and the local government will be ultimately adjudicated by the central government, which is responsible only to the central parliament. The supremacy of the central government should not be limited by any constitutional prerogatives of local authorities. Disagreements should be settled by the central government and by the central parliament, which should judge and decide every problem in the light of its implications for the smooth working of the total system. If, for instance, a dispute arises concerning the City of Wilno—one of the innumerable neuralgic points of the East—the solution will be sought not only between the Polish and Lithuanian local governments, or between the Polish and Lithuanian members of the central parliament; the central government and the central parliament will try to find a solution which may also be applied with justice to similar cases arising in Budweis, in Temesvár, or in Salonika.

In this way it may be possible to have a unitary government with a practically satisfactory degree of administrative decentralization.

The EDU would have to include all the territories between the eastern borders of Germany, Switzerland, and Italy and the western borders of Russia, including all Balkan countries. It would have to take in the area which in 1933 formed the sovereign states of Albania, Austria, Bulgaria, Czechoslovakia, Danzig, Estonia, Greece, Hungary, Latvia, Lithuania, Poland, Rumania, and Yugoslavia. It would have to include the territory that in 1913 comprised the Prussian provinces of East Prussia, West Prussia, Posen, and Silesia. The first three of these provinces belonged neither to the Holy Empire nor to the German Confederation. Silesia was a part of the Holy Empire only as an adjunct of the Kingdom of Bohemia. In the sixteenth and seventeenth centuries it was ruled by dukes who belonged to a branch of the Piasts, the old royal family of Poland. When Frederick the Great in 1740 embarked on the conquest of Silesia, he tried to justify his claims by pointing out that he was the legitimate heir of the Piast family. All four of these provinces are inhabited by a linguistically mixed population.

Italy must cede to the EDU all the European countries which it has occupied since 1913, including the Dodecanese Islands, and furthermore the eastern part of the province of Venice, Friuli, a district inhabited by people speaking a Rhaeto-Romanic idiom.

Thus the EDU will include about 700,000 square miles with some 120,000,000 people using 17 different languages. Such a country when united will be strong enough to defend its independence against one of the three mighty neighbors, Russia, Germany, and Italy.

The most delicate problem of the EDU will be the linguistic problem.

All seventeen languages need, of course, to be treated equally. In every district, county, or community the tribunals, government agencies, and municipalities would have to use every language which in that district, county, or community was spoken by more than 20 per cent of the population.

English ought to be used as an international subsidiary language for dealings among members of the different linguistic groups. All laws would be published in English and in all seventeen national idioms. This system may seem strange and complicated. But we have to remember that it worked rather satisfactorily in old Austria with its eight languages. Contrary to a widespread and erroneous notion, the German language had no constitutional preëminence in imperial Austria.

The governments of Eastern Europe abused the system of compulsory education in order to force minorities to give up their own languages and to adopt the language of the majority. The EDU would have to be strictly neutral in this respect. There would be private schools only. Any citizen or group of citizens would have the right to run an educational institution. If these schools complied with standards fixed by the central government, they would be subsidized by a lump sum for every pupil. The local governments would have the right to take over the administration of some schools, but even in these cases the school budgets would be kept independent of the general budget of the local government; no public funds but those allocated by the central government as subsidies for these schools should be used.

The politicians and statesmen of these Eastern nations are united today on only one point: the rejection of such a proposal. They do not see that the only alternative is permanent unrest and war among them, and perhaps partition of their territories among Germany, Russia, and Italy. They do not see it because they rely on the invincibility of the British and American forces. They cannot imagine the Americans and British having any task in this world but to fight an endless sequence of world wars for their benefit.

It would be merely an evasion of reality for the refugee representatives of these nations to try to convince us that they intend to dispose peacefully of their mutual claims in the future. It is true that Polish and Czech refugees, before Germany invaded Russia, made an agreement concerning the delimitation of their boundaries and future political coöperation. But this scheme will not work when actually put into practice. We have ample experience that all agreements of this type fail because the radical nationalists never accept them. All endeavors at an understanding between Germans and Czechs in old Austria met with disaster because the fanatical youth rejected what the more realistic older leaders had proposed. Refugees are, of course, more ready to compromise than men in power. During the first World War the Czechs and Slovaks, as well as the Serbs, Croats, and Slovenes, came to an understanding in exile. Later events proved the futility of their agreements.

In addition, we must remember that the area which is claimed by both the Czechs and the Poles is comparatively small and of minor importance for each group. There is no hope that a similar agreement ever could be effected between the Poles on the one hand and the Germans, Lithuanians, Russians, or Ukrainians on the other hand; or between the Czechs on the one hand and the Germans or Hungarians or Slovaks on the other. What is needed is not delimitation of specific border lines between two groups but a system where the drawing of border lines no longer creates disaffection, unrest, and irredentism among minorities. Democracy can be maintained in the East only by an impartial government. Within the proposed EDU no single linguistic group would be sufficiently numerous to dominate the rest. The most numerous would be the Poles and they would comprise about 20 per cent of its whole population.

One could object that the territory assigned to the EDU is too large, and that the different linguistic groups involved have nothing in common. It may indeed seem strange that the Lithuanians should coöperate with the Greeks, although they never before have had any other mutual relations than the ordinary diplomatic ones. But we have to realize that the very function of the EDU would be to create peace in a part of the world ridden by age-old struggles among linguistic groups. Within the whole area assigned to the EDU it is impossible to discover a single undisputed border line. If the EDU has to include both Lithuanians and Poles, because there is a large area in which Poles and Lithuanians live inextricably mixed and to which both nations vigorously lay claim, it must include the Czechs too because the same conditions prevail between the Poles and the Czechs as subsist between the Poles and Lithuanians. The Hungarians, again, must be included for the same reasons, and so must the Serbs, and consequently the other nations which claim parts of the territory known as Macedonia, i.e., the Bulgarians, Albanians, and Greeks.

For the smooth functioning of the EDU it is not necessary that the Greeks should consider the Lithuanians as friends and brothers (although it seems probable that they would have more friendly feelings for them than for their immediate neighbors). What is needed is nothing else than the conviction of the politicians of all these peoples that it is no longer possible to oppress men who happen to speak another language. They do not have to love one another. They merely have to stop inflicting harm upon one another.

The EDU would include many millions of German-speaking citizens, and more than a hundred thousand Italian-speaking citizens. It cannot be denied that the hatred engendered by the methods used by the Nazis and the Fascists during the present war will not disappear at once. It will be difficult for Poles and Czechs to meet for collaboration with Germans, and for Serbs and Slovenes to coöperate with Italians.

But none of these objections can be considered valid. There is no other solution of the East European problem. There is no other solution that could give these nations a life of peace and political independence.

5. The Problems of Asia

When the age of liberalism dawned, the Western nations began to have scruples about their colonial enterprises. They felt ashamed of their treatment of backward peoples. They became aware of the contrast between the principles of their domestic policies and the methods applied in colonial conquest and administration. What business did they, liberals and democrats as they were, have to govern foreign nations without the consent of those ruled?

But then they had an inspiration. It was the white man's burden to bring the blessings of modern civilization to backward peoples. It would be unjust to say that this exculpation was mere cant and hypocrisy. Great Britain had reshaped its colonial system radically in order to adjust it to the best possible promotion of the welfare of the natives. In the last fifty years British administration of Indian and colonial affairs has been by and large government *for* the people.

However, it has not been government *by* the people. It has been government by an alien master race. Its justification lay in the assumption that the natives are not qualified for self-government and that, left alone, they would fall victim to ruthless oppression by conquerors less civilized and less benevolent than the English. It further implied that Western civilization, with which the British wanted to make the subdued natives happy, was welcome to them. We may take it for granted that this was really the case. The proof is that all these colored races were and are anxious not only to adopt the technical methods of Western civilization but also to learn Western political doctrines and ideologies. It was precisely this acceptance of Western thought that finally led them to cry out against the absolute rule of the invaders.

The demands for liberty and self-determination on the part of the Asiatic peoples are a result of their Westernization. The natives are fighting the Europeans with ideologies borrowed from them. It is the greatest achievement of Europe's nineteenth-century Asiatic policies that the Arabs, the Hindus, and the Chinese have at length grasped the meaning of Western political doctrines.

The Asiatic peoples are not justified in blaming the invaders for atrocities committed in previous years. Indefensible as these excesses were from the point of view of liberal tenets and principles, they were nothing extraordinary when measured by the standards of oriental customs and habits. But for the infiltration of Western ideas the East might never have questioned the propriety of slaughtering and torturing foes. Their autochthonous methods were much more brutal and abominable. It is paradoxical to bring up these bygone grievances in the very hour when the most numerous Asiatic nations can preserve their civilizations only with the military aid of the Anglo-Saxons.

A defeat of the United Nations would spell the doom of the Chinese, of the Hindus, of the Moslems of Western Asia, and of all the smaller nations of Asia and of Africa. The victory of the United Nations will bring them political autonomy. They will get the opportunity to demonstrate whether they have absorbed more from the West than the modern methods of total war and total destruction.

The problem of the relations between East and West is obscured by the shortcomings and deficiencies of current ways of dealing with political issues. The Marxians purposely ignore the inequality of natural conditions of production in different parts of the world. Thus they eliminate from their reasoning the essential point. They bar their own way to either a satisfactory interpretation of the past or an understanding of the tasks of the future.

In the face of the inequality of natural resources there are today no such things as internal affairs of a country which do not concern the rest of mankind. It is to the vital interests of every nation that all over the earth the most efficient methods of production should be applied. It hurts the well-being of everybody if, for instance, those countries which have the most favorable conditions for the production of rubber do not make the most efficient use of their resources. One country's economic backwardness may injure everybody else. Autarky in one country may lower the standard of living in every other country. If a nation says: "Let us alone; we do not want to interfere with your affairs, and we will not permit you to mind our business," it may wrong every other people.

It was these considerations that led the Western nations to force China and Japan to abandon their age-old isolation and to open their ports to foreign trade. The blessings of this policy were mutual. The drop of mortality figures in the East proves it clearly. East and West would both suffer if the political autonomy of the Asiatic nations were to result in a fall in their production, or in their partial or complete withdrawal from international trade.

We may wonder whether the champions of Asiatic home rule have fully grasped the importance of this fact. In their minds modern ideas are in a curious way blended with atavistic ones. They are proud of their old civilizations. They are apt to despise the West. They have a far sharper recognition of the shortcomings of

Europe and America, their militarism and nationalism, than of their great achievements. Marxian totalitarianism appeals more to them than "the bourgeois prejudices" of liberty, capitalism, and democracy. Do they realize that there is but one way to prosperity open for their nations, namely, the unconditional adoption of Western industrialism?

Most of the leaders of the oriental nations are convinced that the West will turn toward socialism. But this could not change the main issue. Backwardness in the East would offer the same problems for a socialist West as for a capitalist West.

The age of national isolation of individual countries is gone with the progress of division of labor. No nation can now look with indifference at the internal conditions of other countries.

6. The Role of the League of Nations

The League of Nations which the Covenant of 1919 established in Geneva was not an international world government. It was mainly an organization for periodical conferences of the delegates of those national governments that were prepared to attend them. There were no international executive offices. There was only a staff whose duty consisted mostly in writing reports and in collecting statistical materials. Further, many of the staff considered themselves not officers of the international body but unofficial representatives of the governments of their own nations. They got their appointments on the recommendation of their own governments. They were eager to serve their own governments well in order some day to get better positions in the civil service of their own countries. Some of these officials were not only not internationally minded but imbued with the spirit of nationalism. There were some strange figures among them. Vidkun Quisling, for example, served for some time as an officer of the League. Rost van Tonningen was for many years a member of the Secretariat and in 1931 became the League's delegate in Vienna; he left this important position after some years in order to become deputy chief of the Dutch Nazi party, and is today one of the outstanding figures in the puppet administration of the Netherlands. There were in the League also, it is true, some of our most brilliant and high-minded contemporaries. But unfortunately conditions paralyzed their efforts and most of them left disappointed.

It is of little concern whether the League of Nations is restored after the war or not. It contributed very little to the promotion of peace and international coöperation. It will not be any more successful in the future. Nationalism will frustrate its work as it did in the years before 1939.

Many distinguished Americans indict their own country for the failure of the League. If America had joined the League, they say, it would have cloaked this institution with the prestige needed for the fulfillment of its tasks. This is an error. Although formally not a member of the League, the United States gave valuable support to its efforts. It mattered little that America did not contribute to its revenues or send official delegates to its meetings. The world knew very well that the American nation backed the endeavors to maintain peace. American official coöperation in Geneva would not have stopped the aggressor nations.

As all nations today indulge in nationalism, the governments are necessarily supporters of nationalism. Little for the cause of peace can be expected from the activities of such governments. A change of economic doctrines and ideologies is needed, not special institutions, offices, or conferences.

The chief shortcoming of many plans suggested for a durable peace is that they do not recognize this fact. Eminent champions of the League of Nations, such as Professor J. B. Condliffe and Professor J. E. Meade, are confident that the governments will be wise enough to eradicate by common efforts and mutual agreements the most objectionable excrescences of economic nationalism and to mitigate conflicts by granting some concessions to the complainants.* They recommend moderation and restraint in the use of national sovereignty. But at the same time they advocate more government control, without suspecting that this must necessarily push every government toward intransigent nationalism. It is vain to hope that a government committed to the principles of etatism could renounce striving for more insulation. We may assume that there are in every country men ready to endorse the proposals of Messrs. Condliffe and Meade; but they are minorities whose opinions do not find a wide response. The further a nation goes on the road toward public control of business, the more it is forced to withdraw from the international division of labor. Well-intentioned exhortations on the part of internationally minded economists cannot dissuade an interventionist government from measures of economic nationalism.

The League of Nations may continue to combat contagious disease, the drug traffic, and prostitution. It may continue to act in the future as an international bureau of statistics. It may develop its work in the field of intellectual coöperation. But it is an illusion to hope that it could render more than minor services for the promotion of peace.

* J. E. Meade, *The Economic Basis of a Durable Peace* (New York, 1940); J. B. Condliffe, *Agenda for a Postwar World* (New York, 1942).

CONCLUSION

I

THE eighteenth-century liberals had full confidence in man's perfectibility. All men, they held, are equal and endowed with the faculty of grasping the meaning of complicated inferences. They will therefore grasp the teachings of economics and social philosophy; they will realize that only within a free market economy can the rightly understood (i.e., the long-run) interests of all individuals and all groups of individuals be in complete harmony. They will carry into effect the liberal utopia. Mankind is on the eve of an age of lasting prosperity and eternal peace, because reason will henceforth be supreme.

This optimism was entirely founded on the assumption that all people of all races, nations, and countries are keen enough to comprehend the problems of social coöperation. It never occurred to the old liberals to doubt this assumption. They were convinced that nothing could stop the progress of enlightenment and the spread of sound thinking. This optimism was behind the confidence of Abraham Lincoln that "You can't fool all of the people all of the time."

The economic theories on which the liberal doctrine is based are irrefutable. For more than a hundred and fifty years all the desperate endeavors to disprove the teachings of what one of the greatest precursors of totalitarianism and Nazism, Carlyle, described as the "dismal science," failed pitifully. All these would-be economists could not shake the Ricardian theory of foreign trade, or the teachings concerning the effects of government meddling with a market economy. Nobody succeeded in the attempts to reject the demonstration that no economic calculation is possible in a socialist system. The demonstration that within a market economy there is no conflict between rightly understood interests could not be refuted.

But will all men rightly understand their own interests? What if they do not? This is the weak point in the liberal plea for a free world of peaceful coöperation. The realization of the liberal plan is impossible because—at least for our time—people lack the mental ability to absorb the principles of sound economics. Most men are too dull to follow complicated chains of reasoning. Liberalism failed because the intellectual capacities of the immense majority were insufficient for the task of comprehension.

It is hopeless to expect a change in the near future. Men are sometimes not even able to see the simplest and most obvious facts. Nothing ought to be easier to understand than victory or defeat on the battlefield. And yet scores of millions of Germans are firmly convinced that it was not the Allies but Germany that was victorious in the first World War. No German nationalist ever admitted that the German Army was defeated at the Marne both in 1914 and 1918. If such things are possible with the Germans, how can we expect that the Hindus, the worshipers of the cow, should grasp the theories of Ricardo and of Bentham?

Within a democratic world the realization even of the socialist plans would depend upon the acknowledgment of their expediency on the part of the majority. Let us for an instant put aside all qualms concerning the economic feasibility of socialism. Let us, for the sake of argument, assume that the socialists are right in their own appraisal of socialist planning. Marx, imbued with Hegelian *Weltgeist* mysticism, was convinced that there are some dialectic factors working in the evolution of human affairs that push the proletarians, the immense majority, toward the realization of socialism—of course his own brand of socialism. He tacitly assumed both that socialism best suits the interests of the proletariat and that the proletarians will comprehend it. Said Franz Oppenheimer, once a professor of the Marxian-dominated University of Frankfort: "The individual errs often in looking after his interests; a class never errs in the long run." *

Recent Marxians have abandoned these metaphysical illusions. They had to face the fact that although socialism is in many countries the political creed of the vast majority, there is no unanimity with regard to the kind of socialism that should be adopted. They have learned that there are many different brands of socialism and many socialist parties fighting one another bitterly. They no longer hope that a single pattern of socialism can meet with the approval of the majority, and that their own ideal will be supported by the whole proletariat. Only an elite, these Marxians are now convinced, has the intellectual power to understand the blessings of genuine socialism. This elite—the self-styled vanguard of the proletariat, not its bulk—has the sacred duty, they conclude, to seize power by violent action, to exterminate all adversaries, and to establish the socialist millennium. In this matter of procedure there is perfect agreement between Lenin and Werner Sombart, between Stalin and Hitler. They differ only in respect to the question of who the elite is.

The liberals cannot accept this solution. They do not believe

* F. Oppenheimer, *System der Soziologie* (Jena, 1926), II, 559.

that a minority, even if it were the true elite of mankind, can lastingly silence the majority. They do not believe that humanity can be saved by coercion and oppression. They foresee that dictatorships must result in endless conflicts, wars, and revolutions. Stable government requires the free consent of those ruled. Tyranny, even the tyranny of benevolent despots, cannot bring lasting peace and prosperity.

There is no remedy available if men are not able to realize what best suits their own welfare. Liberalism is impracticable because most people are still too unenlightened to grasp its meaning. There was a psychological error in the reasoning of the old liberals. They overrated both the intellectual capacity of the average man and the ability of the elite to convert their less judicious fellow citizens to sound ideas.

II

The essential issues of present-day international problems can be condensed as follows:

1. Durable peace is only possible under perfect capitalism, hitherto never and nowhere completely tried or achieved. In such a Jeffersonian world of unhampered market economy the scope of government activities is limited to the protection of the lives, health, and property of individuals against violent or fraudulent aggression. The laws, the administration, and the courts treat natives and foreigners alike. No international conflicts can arise: there are no economic causes of war.

2. The free mobility of labor tends toward an equalization of the productivity of labor and thereby of wage rates all over the world. If the workers of the comparatively underpopulated countries seek to preserve their higher standard of living by immigration barriers, they cannot avoid hurting the interests of the workers of the comparatively overpopulated areas. (In the long run, moreover, they hurt their own interests also.)

3. Government interference with business and trade-union policies combine to raise domestic costs of production and thus lower the competitive power of domestic industries. They therefore would fail to attain their ends even in the short run if they were not complemented by migration barriers, protection for domestic production, and—in the case of export industries—by monopoly. As any dependence on foreign trade must restrict a government's power to control domestic business, interventionism necessarily aims at autarky.

4. Socialism, when not operated on a world scale, is imperfect if the socialist country depends on imports from abroad and therefore

must still produce commodities for sale on the market. It does not matter whether the foreign countries to which it must sell and from which it must buy are socialist or not. Socialism too must aim at autarky.

5. Protectionism and autarky mean discrimination against foreign labor and capital. They not only lower the productivity of human effort and thereby the standard of living for all nations, but they create international conflicts.

6. There are nations which, for lack of adequate natural resources, cannot feed and clothe their population out of domestic resources. These nations can seek autarky only by embarking upon a policy of conquest. With them bellicosity and lust of aggression are the outcome of their adherence to the principles of etatism.

7. If a national government hinders the most productive use of its country's resources, it hurts the interests of all other nations. The economic backwardness of a country with rich natural resources injures all those whose conditions could be improved by a more efficient exploitation of this natural wealth.

8. Etatism aims at equality of income within the country. But, on the other hand, it results in a perpetuation of the historically developed inequalities between poorer nations and richer nations. The same considerations which push the masses within a country toward a policy of income equality drive the peoples of the comparatively overpopulated countries into an aggressive policy toward the comparatively underpopulated countries. They are not prepared to bear their relative poverty for all time to come simply because their ancestors were not keen enough to appropriate areas better endowed by nature. What the "progressives" assert with regard to domestic affairs—that traditional ideas of liberty are only a fraud as far as the poor are concerned, and that true liberty means equality of income—the spokesmen of the "have-not" nations declare with regard to international relations. In the eyes of the German nationalists there is only one freedom that counts: *Nahrungsfreiheit* (freedom from importing food), i.e., a state of affairs in which their nation could produce within its own borders all the food and raw materials it needs in order to enjoy the same standard of living as the most favored of the other nations. That is their notion of liberty and equality. They style themselves revolutionaries fighting for their imprescriptible rights against the vested interests of a host of reactionary nations.

9. A socialist world government could also abolish the historically developed inequalities between the citizens of comparatively overpopulated areas and those of underpopulated areas. However, the same forces which frustrated the attempts of the old

liberals to sweep away all barriers hindering the free mobility of labor, commodities, and capital will violently oppose that kind of socialist world management. Labor in the comparatively under-populated countries is unlikely to relinquish its inherited privileges. The workers are unlikely to accept policies which for a long period of transition would lower their own standard of living and improve only the material conditions of the underprivileged nations. The workers of the West expect from socialism an immediate rise in their own well-being. They would vigorously reject any plan to establish a democratic system of world government in which their votes would be outnumbered by those of the immense majority of underprivileged peoples.

10. Federal government can work only under a free market economy. Etatism requires a strictly centralized government if there are no trade barriers insulating the member states from one another. The present plans for a world federation, or even only for a federation of the Western democracies, are therefore illusory. If people refuse to abandon etatism, they cannot escape the curse of economic nationalism except by vesting all power in a unified supernational government of the world or of a union of democratic nations. But unfortunately the vested interests of powerful pressure groups are opposed to such a renunciation of national sovereignty.

It is useless to indulge in reveries. Government control of business engenders conflicts for which no peaceful solution can be found. It was easy to prevent unarmed men and commodities from crossing the borders; it is much more difficult to prevent armies from trying it. The socialists and other etatists were able to disregard or to silence the warning voices of the economists. They could not disregard or silence the roar of cannon and the detonation of bombs.

All the oratory of the advocates of government omnipotence cannot annul the fact that there is but one system that makes for durable peace: a free market economy. Government control leads to economic nationalism and thus results in conflict.

III

Many people console themselves by saying: "There have always been wars. There will be wars and revolutions in the future too. The dreams of liberalism are illusory. But there is no cause for alarm. Mankind got along very well in the past in spite of almost continuous fighting. Civilization will not perish if conflicts continue in the future. It can flourish fairly well under conditions less perfect than those depicted by the liberal utopians. Many were happy under the rule of Nero or of Robespierre, in the days of the barbarian invasions, or of the Thirty Years' War. Life will go on; people will marry and beget children, work and celebrate festivals. Great thinkers and poets spent their lives in deplorable circumstances, but that did not prevent them from doing their work. Neither will present or future political troubles hinder coming generations from performing great things."

There is, however, a fallacy in such thinking. Mankind is not free to return from a higher stage of division of labor and economic prosperity to a lower stage. As a result of the age of capitalism the population of the earth is now vastly greater than on the eve of the capitalist era and standards of living are much higher. Our civilization is based on the international division of labor. It cannot survive under autarky. The United States and Canada would suffer less than other countries but even with them economic insulation would result in a tremendous drop in prosperity. Europe, whether itself united or divided, would be doomed in a world where each country was economically self-sufficient.

We have to consider, further, the burden of continuous war preparedness which such an economic system requires. For instance, in order to be in a position to repel onslaughts from Asia, Australia and New Zealand would have to be transformed into military camps. Their entire population—less than ten millions—could hardly be a force strong enough for the defense of their coasts until help arrived from other Anglo-Saxon countries. They would have to adopt a system modeled upon that of the old Austrian *Militärgrenze* or of the old American frontier but adapted to the much more complex conditions of modern industrialism. But those gallant Croats and Serbs who defended the Habsburg Empire and thereby Europe against the Turks were peasants living in economic self-sufficiency on their family homesteads. So were the American frontiersmen. It was a minor calamity for them when they had to watch the borders rather than till the soil; their wives and children in their absence took care of the farms. An industrial community cannot be operated on such terms.

Conditions will be somewhat better in other areas. But for all nations the necessity of being ready for defense will mean a heavy burden. Not only economic but moral and political conditions will be affected. Militarism will supplant democracy; civil liberties will vanish wherever military discipline must be supreme.

The prosperity of the last centuries was conditioned by the steady and rapid progress of capital accumulation. Many countries of Europe are already on the way back to capital consumption and capital erosion. Other countries will follow. Disintegration and pauperization will result.

Since the decline of the Roman Empire the West has not experienced the consequences of a regression in the division of labor or of a reduction of capital available. All our imagination is unequal to the task of picturing things to come.

IV

This catastrophe affects Europe primarily. If the international division of labor is to disintegrate, Europe can only feed a fraction of its present-day population, and those only at a much lower standard. Daily experience, rightly understood, will teach the Europeans what the consequences of their policies are. But will they learn the lesson?

INDEX

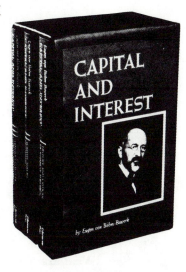

Shorter Classics of Böhm-Bawerk

Five Essays   Cloth, 392pp.

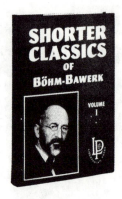

These essays pertain to that "revolution" in economics, known principally under the name of Austrian Neoclassical Economics.

I The Austrian Economists
II Whether Legal Rights and Relationships Are Economic Goods
III Control or Economic Law?
IV Unresolved Contradiction in the Marxian Economic System
V The Ultimate Standard of Value

What are key facets of that "revolution"?

1. Do you believe that the *total cost* of something determines its *price?* If so, you are still confused by the reasoning of the *classical* economists. Graduate to being a *neo-classical* economist. See Essay V: **The Ultimate Standard of Value.**

2. Or do you believe that *one element in cost* (that *one* element only, namely, *labor*—the activity of a workman) determines prices? (As in the case of No. 1, many businessmen will say "yes," but they may add a hesitant "but . . ." It is Karl Marx who is the leading exponent of this theory, that *one* form of cost *determines* prices, namely, that form which consists in labor. But Marx was wrong on this. See Essay IV: **Unresolved Contradiction in the Marxian Economic System.** Substitute reading this for Marx's *Das Kapital;* and save yourself much time.

3. Do you think any government can control, in a price controversy? For the answer to that question, see Essay III: **Control or Economic Law?**

4. Economics has been afflicted, as other sciences, with ideas which have no substance. Böhm-Bawerk probes the depths in regard to what is and what is not an economic good. See Essay II: **Whether Legal Rights and Relationships Are Economic Goods.**

5. What are the key ideas of the Austrian *Neo-classicists?* For the answer, see Essay I: **The Austrian Economists.**

Ludwig von Mises

The Anti-Capitalistic Mentality

Paper, 140pp.

This is one of the more easily read books by this famous economist.

Capitalism is the most beneficent economic system possible; it contributes marvelously (a) to social cooperation and (b) to prosperity; nothing else can equal it.

But *psychologically* the case for capitalism is very bad. The psychology of people disappointed with their own performance will tend to be *anti*-capitalistic. Unless you understand that, you will under-estimate the popular hostility to capitalism and possibly ineffectually support it.

Planning for Freedom

Fourth Edition, enlarged   Paper, 296pp.

This book has grown, from thirteen essays to seventeen essays. It is now the largest ever. There are now four *new* (additional) essays of special merit.

Also, for the first time, an analytical and descriptive essay has been added, *The Essential Von Mises,* by a former student, Murray N. Rothbard, which is extraordinarily helpful.

How introduce Mises into your thinking? Read these essays, and Rothbard's superior analysis, and you will be a better-informed person.

Socrates considered ethics to be the queen of all the sciences; if so, economics is the bridegroom.

Nobody can afford to be ignorant of economics, unless he is indifferent about having knowledge in the second-most important of the social sciences.

Bureaucracy

Ludwig von Mises Paper, 128pp.

Beware the rise of bureaucratism! It is the avant-garde of a political command system and the socialist state. Mises discussed the rightful role of bureaucracy, and the maleffects inherent in operating businesses by bureaucratic methods. Find out why youth is the primary victim in bureaucratization, and why the spread of bureaucratic means spells ruin for both our economic and political way of life.

Omnipotent Government

Ludwig von Mises Paper, 291pp.

An excellent sequel to *Bureaucracy*, *Omnipotent Government* shows how economic nationalism and the trend toward economic self-sufficiency stem from government intervention in private enterprise. These social and economic doctrines, now internationally prevalent, were the cause of both World Wars, and now threaten freedom everywhere. Find out what damage trade barriers and "special interest" privileges do to world peace and productivity.

Death and Taxes

Hans F. Sennholz Paper, 105pp.

Now in its second revised edition, *Death and Taxes* confronts the issue of death duties. What is their stated purpose? What do they really do? What can I do to avoid having my estate ravaged by taxes? See how you can let inflation work for you to transfer your wealth tax free.

Age of Inflation

Hans F. Sennholz Paper, 207pp.

Deficit spending and expansion of money and credit have ushered in the age of inflation. In this era comes the economic upheaval and social disorder that politicians try to legislate away. See why inflatable currency and liberty are incompatible in the long run. Discover how you can protect yourself and your loved ones.